the girl with three legs

the girl with three legs

a memoir

soraya miré

Lawrence Hill Books
Chicago

Library of Congress Cataloging-in-Publication Data
Mire, Soraya.
The girl with three legs : a memoir / Soraya Miré.
   p. cm.
Includes index.
ISBN 978-1-56976-713-9 (cloth)
1. Mire, Soraya. 2. Women—Somalia—Biography. 3. Women—Somalia—
Rites and ceremonies. 4. Female circumcision—Social aspects. 5. Female
circumcision—Psychological aspects. 6. Female circumcision—Prevention.
I. Title.
HQ1795.Z75M576 2011
392.1'4—dc22
[B]

                                                    2011019348

Interior design: Jonathan Hahn
All interior images are from the author's collection unless otherwise noted.

Published by Lawrence Hill Books
An imprint of Chicago Review Press, Incorporated
814 North Franklin Street
Chicago, Illinois 60610
ISBN: 978-1-56976-713-9
Printed in the United States of America
5 4 3 2 1

To Anderson Cooper for exposing the plight of Lucienne M'Maroyhi and so many others in his story "War Against Women in Congo," and to my brothers Adaax and Asis for keeping their hearts open, no matter what.

In memory of those who passed away: my father, "Farole"; Laurance Rockefeller, who made everything possible; Lloyd Bridges and Michael Jackson for their giving hearts; and my mentor Teshome Gabriel.

Out of the huts of history's shame
I rise.
Up from a past that's rooted in pain
I rise.
—MAYA ANGELOU, "Still I Rise"

contents

preface

My first death threat came in 1995, at the premiere of my film on female genital mutilation (FGM), *Fire Eyes*. I have had to live in hiding at times, and I recognize that the publication of this book may elicit more threats to my safety, because I dare to speak out against child abuse—a form of child abuse that is handed down from mother to daughter like a treasured heirloom, child abuse that is protected by the word *culture*, as if culture provides absolution.

After being forced to live in hiding for years, I understood that the closer we activists get to our goal—which for me is protecting children from harmful traditional practices—the more frantically those obsessed with maintaining the status quo will fight us. They protest like rats cornered by a dozen cats. The situation can become very dangerous; they don't want to find a common ground.

In the case of my cause, they do not want to end the useless ritual that chops off young girls' healthy organs and often, as happened with my body parts, feeds them to the street dogs. Wanting to end abuse of girls and women is seen as a threat to manhood and a man's psyche, and many become reactive and violent.

In 2003 I received a call from the authorities in Gwinnett County, Georgia, asking me for consultation. A two-year-old had had her genitals mutilated by her father. After talking with the child's mother, Fortunate, and the social worker, and asking them to seal her medical records until we could find a lawyer, I decided to move to Atlanta to help with the case.

With the assistance of Nadin Thomas and others who brought in powerful lawyers, the case was won, and the judge sentenced the father, Khalid Adem, to ten years in prison. State representative Mary Margaret Oliver and mother Fortunate Adem worked to get a law passed outlawing female genital mutilation. The law was enacted in May 2005. Georgia's governor, Sonny Perdue, invited the activists, the child's mother, the family, and the lawyers to stand behind him while he signed the bill making female genital mutilation a felony in the state of Georgia. That day, in city hall, standing beside those who were survivors or spokespersons for survivors or both, I spoke. The Somali women in the crowd rose and wrapped their arms around me, thanking me for speaking against the harm done to children. They, too, felt the father did not have the right to touch or cut off his daughter's healthy organs.

Each one of us decided to continue with our work to end the practice of female genital mutilation. I thought the storm had passed, and I focused on other things.

Then CNN called for an interview. I was accused of being among the Americans who put an African man in jail for ten years. My words were closely scrutinized, and some went so far as to analyze these simple lines: "When I saw that child, I saw myself. I could see the pain in her eyes."

The Somalis did what they know best, numb themselves with fanaticism, using Islam like an anesthetic from the pain within, calling anyone who raises a dissenting voice *shaitan*, or devil. My response to those who wished I would vanish from the planet was to say Khalid Adem deserved life in prison for violating his daughter's human rights.

Many do not want to hear or understand why our mothers and grandmothers put our bodies through the mutilating ritual and watched us become nothing more than the pleasurable commodity of men. By the grace of God, we, the survivors of female genital mutilation, know how to use our pain to bring this human rights violation to an end.

Today, we are the generations that recognize the deep wound, the private pain, because we live with the anguish of what has been done to us and our loved ones. Together, we certainly can make a difference. We will continue to transform our pain and suffering by bringing this horrendous act of cultural violence, which I call the ultimate child abuse, to an end.

My activism on this issue has not only brought about threats to my safety, but it has been the cause of estrangement with many of my family members, especially with my mother. Before writing this memoir, I hadn't spoken to Mother since March 2007, when the Somalis told my sister Amal I was going to be gunned down while walking the streets of Boston. I was on my way to give a lecture at Lesley College in Cambridge.

But to write my story, I had to speak with her. I needed to ask Mother questions about my ex-husband, cousin Yusuf, and I called her.

"*Salaama*, Mother," I greeted her when she came to the phone.

"I can't speak to you," she replied.

"Why not?"

"I heard you're putting people in jail. . . . I don't want to say anything."

"Who did I put in jail?"

"That Ethiopian father—ten years!"

"Mother, did Yusuf lose his mind when I ran away from him?"

"He became an alcoholic, but I remember rescuing you before you escaped."

"No. . . ."

"What was that woman's name at the Geneva embassy who was helping you?"

"Mother, you didn't rescue me. You came too late."

"All the abuse happened before I got to Geneva!"

"No, Mother, you were sitting in the guest room, listening to my anguish. Didn't you hear me that first night?"

"What do you want?"

"I want to tell the truth. . . . I have been writing a book. And it will not smell like a cleanup."

"A cleanup?"

"Yes. It will not be filled with pretty pictures retelling the same story. Do you want to hear?"

I have known two kinds of pain. The first, a stabbing between my legs; the second, reliving it to tell my story. The latter is for the highest good, but it is painful and challenging. The other one is destructive. If I were writing this book to wage war and to hurt those people I care about, it would be entirely different. I'm doing it to free myself and to heal a deep and private wound. I choose to speak the truth as I know it. Anything I can do to shed light on my life is going to shed light on the global issue of female genital mutilation. I know I must bring more healing and understanding to this crucial human rights issue.

As for my mother, she has the choice and the right to further alienate me. She has decided never to make atonement. She has refused to hear anything I have to say on this harmful issue or my arranged marriage to cousin Yusuf. But she can no longer stop me from having my catharsis by releasing my experience into the world so that I can have a life.

The burden of shame will no longer have a grip on my heart. I have to tell my story, and if it gets in the way of Mother's reality, that will be something she needs to work on for herself.

"I'm ashamed of you. Why don't you marry a wealthy Arab?"

"Can I ask about Grandmother's shrouding?"

She ignored my question. "I saw the picture!"

"What picture?"

"The one in which you're holding the white girl's hand—the lesbians—what kind of people are they?"

"At least they don't practice arranged marriages."

"I'm your mother. Don't speak to me that way."

"Mother, it's genetic, and people are born that way—"

"I'll pray for you."

the girl with three legs

prologue

When I was born, I became footprints in water. In my darkened world, I came in with cursed body parts where my ancestors waged wars with womanly sensation. This curse burns the blood and rots the flesh.

The year was 1961 in Beledweyne when I took my first breath and passed through Mother's gate. Beledweyne was the capital city of Hiraan and one of the oldest cities of Somalia, through which the Shabelle River runs. I was the sixth surviving child, and three siblings followed after me. But my conception brought Mother face-to-face with her past pain, and I knew trouble from the moment she laid eyes on me. The tip of my tongue and the back of my neck were dark, and I couldn't drink her breast milk. There is an African saying, "The baby that refuses its mother's breast will never be full." The doctors told Mother that I was born with birthmarks and that I was allergic to her breast milk because she loved to eat too much lamb meat. These were signs to Mother that shaping my destiny, unlike that of my siblings, would be very difficult.

With the help of my beloved grandmother, Mother and I stayed indoors for forty days after my birth as our culture required, but no one remembered if I wore the special bracelet that would protect me from the evil eye. Everyone agreed that a lamb must be slaughtered and incense burned in all corners of the house.

Father, a man with silent power, an army officer, tried to participate in the baby-naming ceremony, but Mother, the one wearing his uniform "invisibly" in the house, canceled my special event. She wasn't mad at Father or me but at Grandmother, who suggested my face resembled the shining star and therefore I should be named after one. The matter was settled, and I was named Soraya.

The family moved to Mogadishu, and Father became a general. Our house expanded as part of a quiet row of huge homes surrounded by beauty, the homes of the wealthy army families. Respecting one another was one of the daily lessons we learned as children. As the oldest, sister Sakiya was responsible for transmitting Mother's marching orders to us and the house workers. When angry, she would bark one of those famous proverbs, such as "One refusing a sibling's advice breaks his arm."

But suppressing our emotions and silencing our voices were the honor code, especially for girls. Like a Somali cat with big ears and curious eyes, I chased rumors around the neighborhood, climbed over the walls, and hid under other people's beds to find the truth. Others would taunt or even scold me for my adventures and my mischief, calling me the Girl with Three Legs.

One day, Aunt Ubax told us a story about lively nomad girls who were caught by an old blind woman when they were out in the woods fetching food. The old woman's duty was to cut off the evil flesh that dangled between girls' legs. If she didn't, the girls would have three legs, and no one would want to touch or marry them. This piece of flesh was so strong that the girls who still had it did not know right from wrong. God had not blessed them with minds like the nomad boys, whose warrior intelligence allowed them to trick or even fight with lions to save the herds. A mother's duty was to order the blind woman to secure the chastity of their girls, cutting off the evil flesh and preparing each girl-child for her destiny. The old blind woman forced the captive girls to sit on hot sand full of thorns. In unbearable pain, the girls wailed and wailed, like the desert trees crying because they were forsaken by God's rain. And the old blind woman roared, *It is time! Time to become a woman!*

After the blind woman removed the evil between the girls' legs, they could become honorable wives.

When Aunt Ubax finished the tale, I argued with her, telling her that she was changing last week's story about Caraweelo, a feared woman who cut off the penises of men. I did not understand that when Aunt Ubax and others created these captivating stories, there were hidden messages. I listened, then laughed like everyone else and went to my warm bed without fear. In my world, no one had a wicked heart like the old blind woman or Caraweelo.

They are too evil, I would say to myself as I fell asleep.

PART ONE

a daughter of africa
1960–1979

I cried and wailed until I could cry no more.
My voice grew hoarse, and the cries could not come out,
I wriggled as the excruciating pain ate into my tender flesh.
Hold her down! cried the cursed cutter,
and the biggest female jumbo sat on my chest.
I could not breathe, but there was nobody
to listen to me.
Then my cries died down, and everything was dark.
As I drifted, I could hear the women laughing,
joking at my cowardice.

It was over.
All over my thighs were marks from the ropes,
dotted with patches from the lice wounds.
Now I was to look after myself,
to ensure that everything remained intact
until the day I married.

      —MARYAM SHEIKH ABDI, "THE CUT"

When the violin can forgive
Every wound caused by
Others
The heart starts singing.

          —HAFIZ

new beginning

I was nine years old when my family life changed abruptly. Just six days after the assassination of Somalia's president, Abdirashid Ali Shermarke, by his own bodyguard, the army staged a coup and seized power. Somalia had gained its independence in 1960, and Shermarke was our country's second elected president, but factionalism and pending reconciliation with Ethiopia, traditionally an enemy of Somalia, had led to unrest.

General Mohamed Siad Barre led the coup d'etat, and he was now the head of state as president of the Supreme Revolutionary Council. He suspended the constitution, demolished the National Assembly, and nationalized all industries and businesses. As a general in the Somali army, my father was responsible for securing the northern regions during the coup, and under Siad Barre, Father eventually became head of the Somali National Army Forces in Hargeisa. The country would be renamed the Somali Democratic Republic. Much about the Somali people is said by the flag of Somalia, which shows a five-pointed star, each point representing an area where the most Somali people live: Somali North (colonized by Britain), Somali South (colonized by Italy), Djibouti (colonized by France), Ogaden (colonized by Ethiopia), and northern Kenya.

Both the Somali North and South united after independence, and the idea of Greater Somalia was born. The goal was to free the other three regions and unite all the Somalis.

I was not aware of all the political maneuverings and implications at the time. All I knew was that, suddenly, men with machine guns guarded our polished gate. Our pink brick wall was painted white, and the wooden windows got uglier, painted green. The army elites decided to act bourgeois, living inside painted houses, many—unlike my father—forgetting about the poor. President Siad Barre became a regular guest in our house along with his army entourage. Father's blood pressure would rise as he tried to rotate the living room's availability between them and Mother's "interior designers"—Xaawo, the head cook, and Abdulqaadir, Father's personal chef and assistant.

It was not clear why Mother would ask Xaawo to decide on which wall to hang the family pictures or how to arrange a room. She was as stubborn as Mother. Sometimes after pushing her over the edge, Xaawo would let her vent, then say, "I'm sorry for upsetting you."

Friday is the day God ordered the Muslims to rest, to pray, and, in my case, to take a walk in the hot sand on the Jasira Beach, only minutes from our house and one of the most beautiful beaches in Mogadishu, famous for its gorgeous water and warm sand. Families went to Jasira to eat at the restaurants, play soccer, or just swim for hours. I would go there with friends or family members whenever I could get away without Mother catching me. Even on Fridays, Mother's marching orders kept coming in, and I would picture her as if she were wearing Father's general uniform as she barked out her instructions.

At the crack of dawn, I would wake up to the sound of a metal stick slamming against my window. It was one of the army guards who, following Mother's instructions, used his gun-cleaning stick to rouse me out of bed to join my siblings in moving the furniture out of the living room. Mother obsessed about cleaning and loved to rearrange furniture. If I didn't get up and follow Mother's orders, I would face punishment, often being denied my quiet reading time, listening to the BBC news with brother Malik, or seeing friends.

So I would join my brothers and sisters on Mother's work crew, and the commotion would begin. I'd watch as army trucks would speed into the courtyard and workers rushed to unload rice, olive oil, sugar, and flour. They would stack the supplies in the storage room, in which we were not allowed. In case Mogadishu was attacked, we were safe with a storage room full of supplies that would last a long time. Soon my family also built a place to hold a clean water supply.

Despite our good fortune, my siblings and I wanted the wonderful, forbidden Friday siesta. Father, however, would not ask Mother to let us rest on Friday; he saw how my siblings and I took comfort in living the abundant life and worried that we might take everything for granted. We had always lived well, but after the coup our standard improved; the house got bigger, and suddenly guards and more workers showed up. Father was a man who always felt the need to speak for those less fortunate, a man of great thoughtfulness, and a humble soul who believed in the equality of all. He rarely showed anger, except when Mother threw her extravagant parties and made us wear the elegant dresses. Father wanted us to remain humble about ourselves and grateful for the privileges.

But we lived a sheltered life in a fantasy world surrounded by white brick walls. Most of us expressed the joy of attending Mother's parties and loved the clothes cousin Khalifa—the adult daughter of Mother's sister—sent us from Belgium.

Every day, Father rang the bell and my nine brothers and sisters and I would run into the living room to listen to a life lesson. He talked to us about his values and ideals, hoping to instill compassion and offset the materialistic aspects of our lives. He wanted my siblings and me to recognize how lucky we were.

One day, he felt it was time for us to witness how most of the people lived and to interact with those less fortunate. He packed us into two cars, and we drove to the nearest town. We passed through a neighborhood where people suffered in poverty. For the first time in my life, I saw children my age running around naked. With bright eyes, they wore beautiful smiles and, like all children at play, appeared happy as they ran around in the dirt. I was ashamed and embarrassed by my own outfit—a white short dress and matching underwear from cousin Khalifa.

All I could do was rest my forehead on the car window and sob. Brother Asis squeezed my hand and leaned over, placing his head on my shoulder.

The drivers stopped the cars, and Father encouraged us to get out and talk with the people. We looked at one another; as usual, Mother had groomed us as if we were celebrating the end of the sacred month of Ramadan or going to perform the *Salatu'l eid*, the traditional times to wear your best outfit.

But today was not the time to focus on Ibrahim wanting to sacrifice his son and how quickly God responded and gave a lamb as the sacrifice. This was the first time my siblings and I had visited the town where Bantu people lived. We had heard a lot about them being the minority ethnics who come from Mozambique, Malawi, and Tanzania. They speak Somali but love their ancestral language of Zigua. Bantu people appreciate nature and work in the fields.

My siblings and I watched as women stopped cleaning and looked at us from a distance as Father got out of the car and walked toward them. Slowly, people gathered around Father as he talked to them. We came forward and listened as people complained about the missing rain and why God was not hearing their prayers. Father talked with them about their concerns as he walked around greeting everyone. After he had heard their stories, taken notes, and said his good-byes, my siblings and I followed him back to the cars, and we silently drove on.

That day was most dramatic, a life-altering experience that I will never forget. Change began to show up in my family home. Instead of each of us ordering whatever meal struck our fancy each day, my siblings settled for *canjeera* (pancakes) for breakfast and pasta with lamb for lunch. I couldn't change my diet, since I ate only vegetables and fruits, and those only once a day. But none of us wanted to compromise when it came to those delicious afternoon English teas and snacks.

Soon after our trip to town, Father agreed to my idea to open our gate and share the rice, flour, sugar, oil, and water with the needy people.

⁂

During this time, Mother grew increasingly irritable, seeming annoyed just to see the warmth in Father's face. She complained about our house becoming like an army camp. But we had always lived this way; the difference was that we now had more house workers who wore uniforms, like white hats, shirts, and gray pants with black dots, like chefs in the United States. Xaawo wore traditional outfits.

It was the habit of my six-year-old sister, Shams, twelve-year-old brother, Asis, three-year-old sister, Raha, and me to hide behind Mother's door to watch her secretly and listen to her complaints.

Knowing how to melt Father's heart when she wanted something, Mother would make her grand gesture by dropping her shining long dark hair on her back and slowly reaching for her brush. Father would gasp for air. My mother, who sometimes kept her hair covered with one of her many short wigs, which sat on a rack in the far corner, was aware of the power of her beautiful hair.

"I'm not going to put up with your political gangs taking over my living room," Mother said, shaking out her hair.

Adaax, who had been asleep in the crib, began crying. Father walked over and picked him up. Mother brushed her hair as she described how her Persian rug was suffering under the heavy boots of the army men marching into the living room. In our culture, shoes were not allowed inside the home.

"I'm not going to post a sign on the wall telling them what they should already know and ruin the paint," Mother said.

"Shoes will be removed—I promise," Father said.

Mother tied her hair back, making a big bun, and turned to Father. "Does he think I'm going to poison him?" Mother asked.

"Who?" Father said.

"The president," Mother replied.

Father shot her a look that we did not understand, but we noticed a change in the expression on Mother's face.

"Then why is he bringing the food tester?" Mother asked.

"Because he can," Father said. "He is the president!"

President Siad Barre and the constant guests feasted on Xaawo's delicious cooking. But before each meal, a slender man headed for the kitchen and tasted the food before Abdulqaadir served it to President Siad Barre. If the man did not drop dead, then everything was deemed good, and Abdulqaadir took the tray to the living room, where they ate.

As if not hearing Father promising that his guests would remove their shoes, Mother got up, opened the closet door, and removed the black shawl. "I don't want those boots ruining my rugs. . . ."

Without saying a word, Father walked out. Mother wrapped the shawl around her and stared into the mirror, admiring her smooth, honey-toned, glowing skin. Soon after, Mother began keeping herself busy by plunging deeply into the family affairs.

⁜

Mother's focus on my baby brother and household issues often allowed me personal time with my father, a time that I cherished. Brother Adaax had just turned one, and Mother didn't allow us to crowd around him or breathe on his face. He was constantly drinking milk from her breast and then falling asleep on her chest. One night, quietly, I opened the door and walked into Mother's bedroom. She was reading a book in bed while Adaax slept next to her. Seeing she was occupied, I glanced at Father's open bedroom door and noticed the lights were still on. As in most Somali households, our parents had separate rooms.

"Go massage Father's legs," she said absentmindedly, not even looking up at me.

"OK." I smiled to myself. This was a family ritual for which each child hoped to be chosen.

Mother continued reading as I slowly walked into Father's bedroom. He had fallen asleep wearing his reading glasses, and I saw a red file resting on his chest. I removed his glasses and noticed the Italian word *urgente* written on the file. I was not supposed to read anything without permission, but as usual, my curiosity got the better of me. I glanced at the doorway to Mother's room; all was quiet.

With shaking hands, I picked up the file and ran my eyes down the pages. The message to my father had something to do with the Supreme Revolutionary Council's leader, the army commander. It talked about the changes the new regime was making and asked all military generals to comment on the constitution *sospeso*, the suspended constitution. I put the file and the glasses on the nightstand and watched Father sleep. I got up and walked out of the room.

Later that night we heard shouting coming from our parents' quarters. I jumped up and rushed toward their bedrooms, followed by Asis, Shams, and Raha.

We stopped at the door to Mother's room just as Father said, "I'm being transferred to Hargeisa."

Shocked, Mother stared at Father for a long moment. Mogadishu was our home; it was all we knew. Hargeisa was the second-largest city in Somalia, more than eight hundred kilometers from Mogadishu, known for its cool tropical weather, rainy seasons, beautiful mountains, and wild animals.

"I'm going to be the commanding officer at the base—"

"And you expect us to be living in planes?" Mother screamed.

Frightened, we burst into the room and shouted in unison, "No plane rides!"

Mother shouted over our wailing, "I will not relocate!"

Adaax began to cry like never before. Mother rushed to pick him up. She cuddled him until he relaxed.

"Do we have to go into the plane?" Shams asked.

I had never flown before but was claustrophobic and terribly afraid of being locked inside the plane for hours. None of us wanted to fly. But Father assured us that everything would be smooth and we'd come to enjoy it. I refused and reminded him about my fear of tight spaces.

"You'll have air on your face," Father said. "The plane is not small." He paused and smiled at me. "Do you remember telling me about your dream of becoming a pilot like Uncle Hussein?"

He was right; despite my claustrophobia, my wildest dream was to become a fighter pilot. I had once visited my uncle Hussein at the base, startling him when I ran in shouting, "I want to go up in the clouds!"

But Uncle Hussein had walked out of the room, and, surprised, I chased after him repeating, "I want to go up to the clouds!"

"Never!" he shouted and didn't look back.

2

whispering voices

But, of course, Father had to go where he was sent. We visited him in Hargeisa whenever school was out, but our main family home remained in Mogadishu, and Father returned often to visit us as well.

In the early seventies, Mogadishu was a place where fresh flowers bloomed and people listened to local music and ate late-night desserts at the city's fancy restaurants. There was still much hope, although anxiety was beginning to spread over the government's implementation of scientific socialism. Muslims feared that they would have no control over their lives, that the new regime would control everything. People were afraid to speak openly about clanship because the leaders of a northern clan had been imprisoned. Tribalism was denounced, and the focus was on community rather than family lineage. Some gossiped about the National Security Courts, where armed forces members became head prosecutors. With the military taking over the court, people were fearful that justice would be lost.

My family and others who were wealthy were eager to build villas at the never-ending beauty of Jasira Beach, but Aunt Ubax stopped the nonsense in our family. She argued with Father about politics, not understanding why the government needed to set up the peacekeepers, who replaced traditional leaders and represented the government. Aunt Ubax was floored when she heard about people losing their hard-earned money; she could not understand why everything was becoming nationalized government property.

Then we all heard the doors slamming shut, the euphemism for imprisonment in Qansax Dheere, where former leaders, poets, and civilians were being herded. Aunt Ubax was not the only one opposed to my father and government officials calling themselves the nation's saviors.

During that time, I would hear the president's voice blasting from Radio Mogadishu, calling himself the Aabaha Aqoonta, the Father of Knowledge. My siblings and I listened to the BBC Somali service with our ears glued to the radio. The president was becoming larger than life—a godlike figure. Father would voice his anger with Barre when the president came to our house, and they found ways to calm each other down. But army officials who spoke out publicly or agreed with those who opposed Barre's regime went to prison, and Father did not want to bring harm to our family.

Eventually, our house near the army base in Mogadishu expanded. Rooms were added and improvements made. It became part of a quiet row of huge brick houses surrounded by beautiful flowers, vegetation, and fruit trees—the homes of the wealthy army families.

Beyond our home and the serenity of our street, distraught Somalis flocked into the Cabdulcasis Mosque to pray for the ten *wadaad*, religious leaders who had been convicted of violating state law in their quest to maintain Islamic law. Their execution was imminent. The regime feared a foreign Islamic country was providing funds to religious fanatics, hoping to create a religious state where, among other things, a woman's head covering—a *hijab*—was mandatory.

The execution was public, and I went with my cousin Fadwa and neighborhood friends. The firing squad stopped only to adjust the hoods covering the imans' heads before unleashing the hot bullets.

That was when Mother's dark *hijab* appeared in her closet. Mother never liked to talk about her heritage, but she had worn a *hijab* until she married Father. He felt she didn't need to cover her long hair. Now, however, Mother wanted to show support for those who felt betrayed by the government and the killings of the ten *wadaad*. Father warned her that the Red Berets, the trained and dreaded Presidential Security Forces, were on high alert, with orders to arrest any woman caught wearing a *hijab*. Father was in favor of secularizing the country and opposed to foreign countries empowering the *wadaad*, but in Mother's case, he simply wanted to protect her.

Despite his opposition to Mother's wearing of the *hijab* because of the political climate, Father was a devoted Sunni, as was the rest of my family. Everyone, that was, except me. I was devoted to and followed the third element in Hindu Trinity, Lord Shiva. As a child, I would follow Grandmother and watch the Hindu family perform *puja* (worship) to their God and offer flowers, fruits, incense, and water.

My father had missed the chance to burn the *hijab*; he did not know she had kept it. As tension in the country rose, he continued to warn her.

One day I overheard him say, "You must consider your safety—"

"How did it feel when the bullet pierced your hand?" Mother interrupted. During World War II, Father had lost two fingers on his left hand and was nicknamed "Farole," or "Fingerless." Mother hoped to distract him from her *hijab* with a feigned interest in his war stories.

"Throw away that *hijab* before the walls develop eyes and ears," Father insisted.

"Then I'm hiring my own tailor!" Mother shouted. This meant she would be able to have more of the fancy clothes and Western-style gowns that she loved.

Father closed his eyes, took a deep breath, and left the room. Mother contacted Odey, her tailor, and the *hijab* disappeared.

3

smoke rising from
her ears

While the struggle continued between the president and the religious men, so did my struggle to understand our cultural behavior, knowing that my family honor depended on my reputation. President Siad Barre had reversed sharia law and introduced family law, whereby Somali women had equal inheritance rights. Although the status of women was elevated in eyes of the state, the *wadaad* continued to protest against the country's move away from Islam. And the cultural thinking never changed.

I heard rumors that, on the wedding night, the bride feels pain instead of pleasure, that the groom's touch makes "smoke rise from the bride's ears." I was determined to understand this and perhaps even witness it.

One day my older sisters, Sakiya and Amal, were in sister Asra's bedroom; I could hear them talking and laughing. I quietly entered the room and stood listening until Sakiya noticed me.

"What do you want?" she asked.

I hesitated, then blurted out, "What does it mean when the groom makes smoke rise from the bride's ears?"

Suddenly, hands were flying in my face accompanied by loud yelling. Sakiya, my oldest sister, pushed me out the door. That unbearable shouting made my head spin and my spine ache with fear. I rushed to the cotton tree and sat down.

But soon enough the fear passed, and not getting an answer just made me more curious. I could not stop wondering about it. I looked up at the sunlight filtering through the leaves, thinking. In the distance I could hear the sound of the employees preparing for the dinner party that night.

An idea rushed through my head, and I sat up and said aloud, "I must get close to the workers—they know all the secrets!"

Our employees had friends working in the other houses surrounded by white brick walls. I often saw them talking animatedly and overheard bits and pieces of conversations.

I went to our head cook, Xaawo, to work out a deal. With my allowance, I began to pay her to pass on the current rumors. She told me that my distant cousin's wedding was fast approaching. If I followed her instructions, I might get lucky and find the answer to my question and maybe even witness the "smoke rising from the bride's ears." Xaawo encouraged me to make myself useful and help the workers decorate my distant cousin's new home. I offered my help to my cousin, and she accepted.

When I told my playmates at Jasira Beach about my quest to find the answer to why the groom's touch would make smoke rise from the bride's ears, they looked at me, horrified, and shouted, "You're *shaitan*—the devil!" Most of them were very content talking about mothers flying to Rome for shopping or the cousins they might one day marry. Traditionally, young Somali girls expect to have an arranged marriage to a cousin from their mother's side. This practice is believed to keep the family alliance strong, but in fact the tradition makes it difficult for the young to express their feelings and objections. Family means everything, and for a daughter to become a wife is the mother's ultimate joy in life.

I joined the workers preparing my cousin's new home for the couple, decorating the beautiful garden while keeping alert to gossip and to my surroundings to become familiar with the house. I would walk around the garden, thinking about my plan and how much wiser I was than my playmates at Jasira Beach.

When I left that lovely garden I smiled graciously at my coworkers, all the while observing and memorizing every door and window in the house, just in case I might need to revisit the place. I took one last stroll through the interior.

I noticed two female workers standing in front of a closed bedroom door. I walked over and smiled.

"Hello," I greeted them in my most charming voice. "Whose room is this?"

The younger worker giggled, while the other told me we were in front of the bedroom of the soon-to-be bride and groom. "You are forbidden to enter," she said sternly.

I didn't get upset or yell out my signature word, *Why?* Instead, I continued to smile at them and made myself useful by picking up a couple of the pillows they were delivering and moving next to the door, where I stood holding them.

Knowing something was up, the elder girl frowned and took the pillows from me. "Why are you so cheerful?" she barked at me.

"I'm thinking about my red dress!"

They looked skeptical.

I was cheerful, of course, because I had discovered which room the bride and groom would sleep in that night. They stood there, watching me as I left to go home to get ready for the reception.

❖

At my house, as the reception hour approached, all of my brothers and sisters crowded into Mother's dressing room. She had a very strict dress code and rules about hygiene, and we had to submit to it. If we didn't, we would be miserable for a very long time.

I got in line behind my sisters Shams and Raha. Both wore identical white satin-neckline gowns, golden belts at the waist, white shoes, and large octopus crystal clips in their hair. Mother was pleased with them and sent them off to the car.

I cast my eyes downward and held my breath as I awaited Mother's appraisal. She always decided what we would wear, but I always changed at the last minute, usually after plotting with my cousin Fadwa, whose mother was not as strict about her appearance.

When Mother's eyes landed on my sleeveless V-neck red satin gown, she gasped. Just seeing her face twist in frustration weakened my knees. She knocked me out of the line and shouted, "Change to your black velvet dress!" This was cruel, and Mother knew it. Even on a cool night, wearing black velvet in Mogadishu was like a death sentence.

I watched as my eighteen-year-old brother, Malik, stepped in front of Mother. He wore a white shirt, black pants, and black shoes with a black jacket draped over his arm. Mother loved everything, except the huge space between his front teeth. She put a hand over his mouth, covering it. "Why don't you let me correct them?"

"I was born with these teeth, Mother." He pushed her hand away.

"But your smile frightens us!"

Asis burst out laughing, which made Amal, Sakiya, and me slap our hands over our mouths to keep from laughing. Asis, who was twelve, shoved his body between Mother and Malik. When Mother saw his sandals and *macawiis*—a sarong—shock waves flew through her system. He cringed as she twisted his ear.

"Who are you trying to be?" Mother asked. "You are not a grown man!"

"It's hot, Mother, and I'm not going to wear black *surwaal!*" Asis said with conviction, referring to his trousers.

"Are you a nomad without a *waran*, no spear, going to visit camel herds?"

Infectious laughter erupted, which made even Asis break a smile. Mother's fingers ran through his soft, curly black hair. "Stay home and have dinner with Father."

I stood at the door and watched how much Mother loved Sakiya's sparkling embroidered long black dress, with the silk scarf on her shoulders. At twenty-four, Sakiya felt she should be the one wearing the wedding dress. Mother wanted to find her the perfect match, but it was taking too long. It was almost time for Mother to send her to Saudi Arabia, where many Somali women go to find husbands.

Sister Amal wore a long tangerine silk dress, and Mother completed dressing her by clipping two crystal hair forks in her hair. Amal had just turned fifteen and struggled with sleep-walking. Asra's light blue gown still hung by Mother's closet. At twenty-one, she had come down with a strange sickness. Everyone told Mother to let her marry the man who had her heart, but Mother thought he was not good enough. She was still looking for the perfect match for Asra, too.

Mother and I arrived late at the wedding reception. I ended up wearing a short white satin gown, with a gold belt and gold butterfly hair clip. Some guests gathered around tables, while others stood in groups exchanging gossip. I saw my cousin Fadwa eating hungrily. Statuesque at fourteen, Fadwa had silk-dark skin and white teeth. We were not only cousins but also partners in crime, which didn't sit well with our mothers.

Fadwa was a troublemaker who made her mother wonder—as mine did about me—if she had been switched at birth. Tonight, as usual, Fadwa had gotten away with wearing the sleeveless V-neck red satin dress we wanted to wear to match.

Two workers carried in a smoked lamb and placed it in front of the bride and groom, and a crowd gathered around the couple. Curious about the smoked lamb, I pushed through the crowd of women in their long, beautiful gowns and saris, inhaling their intoxicating Somali rose oil. The women broke into a loud ululating chant, like those you hear at large Indian weddings. I clapped my hands over my ears, fearing that I might lose my hearing.

I kept pressing my body through the crowd and finally found myself standing in front of the bride and groom. The groom's thin, long fingers picked up the shiny silver knife and cut the lamb's stomach. Colorful vegetables and rice spilled onto his hand. Slowly, he cut a piece of flesh and offered it to the bride. She put the lamb's flesh into her mouth and chewed. Flashing a shy smile, she looked at him, then bent her head down, and stared at her folded hands. She clenched and unclenched her hands, as if to prevent him from seeing her hands shake. I covered my ears as the women rang out another loud chant. My body moved forward when someone pushed me from behind, and I turned and saw Fadwa. Angry, she threw her hands on her hips as her eyes scanned my dress.

"Why aren't you wearing the red dress?" she asked.

"You know Mother doesn't like it when we wear matching outfits."

I whispered my plan into her ear. Intrigued, Fadwa shot a wide-eyed look at me. She grabbed my hand and pulled me closer to her.

"What if someone sees us sneaking in?

"No one will. I promise," I said, feeling my feet bouncing, ready to run off into the darkness to find the smoke rising from the bride's ears.

Fadwa, eyes wild with excitement, scanned the tables, looking for her mother, Xadiyo. I looked over and saw Xadiyo sitting with Mother and their other women friends.

Like two little bandits, Fadwa and I clutched hands and found our escape route toward the house. It wasn't long before Fadwa and I were in the bride and groom's bedroom, hiding under the bed.

Chills of excitement ran through our bodies; potential punishment was far from our minds. We just wanted to giggle nervously under the bed and witness this mysterious smoke rising from the bride's ears.

Before long, the door slammed open, and the bride and groom entered. They closed the door behind them and, without warning, the wedding dress fell to the Persian rug. In shock, I turned to Fadwa and saw her big, blinding white teeth smiling back at me. I heard the window shutting and felt all the air escape from my lungs. I suddenly felt suffocated and couldn't breathe. I wanted to come out from under the bed and open the window, but Fadwa squeezed my hand. We heard the groom softly repeating, "Relax, relax . . ."

Struggling, I tried to poke my head out from under the bed to find air, but I couldn't move. Fadwa slid her body closer to mine, cupped my face in her hands, and blew air into my nostrils. Her curry breath made me want to vomit, but I was grateful to have air on my face. She pointed toward the door, as more garments and shoes fell to the floor.

To help me forget my search for air, I began chatting to myself in my head. As long as my mind was busy, I felt better. I thought about Asis's orphan cats, birds, and my pet baboon. I thought about how I played hide-and-seek with the snake that liked to appear at my window.

I saw the couple's feet move forward. They dropped their bodies on the edge of the bed, making the mattress hit the top of our heads. I can't say how many beats my heart missed.

My claustrophobia had just been cured. Like a magnet, Fadwa's body drew mine closer, and slowly we pushed our heads down on the Persian rug. We heard strange noises coming from over of our heads. They went on and on, and occasionally the bride would shout, "No!"

Nothing I had ever heard before matched the foreign noises made by the bride and groom. Then I remembered sitting in Malik's bedroom and hearing his friends talk about the wailing sinners. Italian men would lure innocent Somali women into their cars and make them wail, while the men released foreign noises. Those confused and polluted women would later find themselves standing on street corners, like nomads without shields.

The bride shouted, "Stop!" and Fadwa leaped out from under the bed.

Quickly, I too rushed out from under the bed and found myself standing next to Fadwa in front of two naked bodies. I had never seen naked bodies that looked like bread and Somali jelly smashed into one. The couple didn't even notice us.

The groom's body moved like he was being carried away by ocean waves. He kept releasing foreign noises and was not paying attention to the bride at all.

I fixed my eyes on the bride's ears, looking for any sign of smoke, but I saw no flames growing near them. In shock, I saw her left hand tightly holding on to the bedpost while her teeth pushed down into her lip. Her face twisted in pain, and her right arm tightly grabbed the white sheet. A sob was rising in me just from witnessing her pain.

"Stop!" the bride yelled out.

Like watching a movie in a slow motion, I saw Fadwa remove one of her new shoes, climb onto the bed, on top of groom's naked back, and angrily yell as she hit him with her shoe.

"Stop hurting her!"

Everything froze as the bride's dark olive eyes spilled tears like a monsoon rain pouring down from the ceiling. In terror, the bride and groom scrambled to grab sheets to cover their naked bodies. A thundering sound erupted as their bodies fell off the other side of the bed and hit the blue painted wall. I was certain that the couple's heads were split open and blood was washing onto the Persian rug. I began to tremble as I felt my feet sticking to the rug. I cried and cried until Fadwa slapped me so hard that my head was spinning, and I saw the blue wall circling and dancing around me.

"Open the door!" Fadwa shouted.

I'm not sure how I did it, but I found myself running behind Fadwa toward home. At one point, she stopped suddenly, and I crashed into her, making us fall down in the hot sand.

Before any pain registered, Fadwa glared at me. "Did you see the smoke rising from her ears?"

"No. But I did see something hanging between his legs."

"That was Gus," she said, getting up from the ground and wiping off the sand.

"Gus?" I asked.

"That's what a man forces into woman's *siil* to make babies with." She laughed.

"Have you seen one before?" I asked.

She said that in her backyard, she caught her guard holding it and peeing. Then, from the second floor window, she heard her mother shouting at him in Italian. "Zip your *belino* [penis] and get out of my yard!"

By the time we got to Fadwa's house, even God couldn't have saved us from punishment.

The call had already come, and we found Xadiyo standing in the courtyard, mixing hot green pepper and lemon in a bowl. Fadwa disappeared into the house. I stood five feet from Xadiyo, sobbing and begging, "It was me. It was my idea to get under the bed!" I pleaded with her, but she didn't look at me. Mother hurried into the courtyard and made that horrible gesture of thumbs-up, which clearly said that I had done something obscene.

"You have become a reign of terror!" she shouted.

Mother snapped her two fingers on her right hand and ordered me to sit on the cement. Doing this would be the end of me, and I wasn't yet ready to leave the earth.

"I won't. I'm sorry, Mother."

"Stop talking or I'll cut out your *carabkaaga*!" Mother threatened, referring to my tongue.

"It's her third leg that needs cutting, not the tongue," Xadiyo said, as she mixed the spices. "That will calm her down."

"What do you mean?" I asked, frightened.

Their attention turned to Fadwa as she was brought into the courtyard by the workers. Her mother pushed her to the woman on the stool. Mother walked away, and I didn't understand why.

Fadwa was crying and begging the whole time as the woman's thick hands reached up and held Fadwa's waist, dropping her flat butt to the ground. This brought back the image of uniformed men, with stripes on their arms, raiding people's homes and holding guns on trembling men in front of their children, wives, and neighbors. Fadwa's body was locked between the woman's thick thighs while two females held each of her legs.

No one was trying to help Fadwa, and I was drowning in tears and begging for forgiveness. Xadiyo knelt in front of Fadwa and pushed her trembling legs open.

"Shameful one," she said, "I'm going to burn your vagina and tongue."

Without hesitation, Xadiyo lifted up a spoonful of the hot and spicy liquid and dropped a spoonful into Fadwa's vagina. Her body jerked upward. In pain, Fadwa screamed and shook, waking up the ancestors from their long sleep. Xadiyo dropped another spoonful of the liquid into Fadwa's mouth. It was hard to watch Fadwa wail as she felt the burning pain cooking her organs.

I stood there in a panic, my mind racing, thinking, *Just like God's hot sun, I have no power to melt the frozen cry from Fadwa's face.* But, somehow, God's sky lifted me up as I found myself running and feeling the hot sand on my feet. I don't know how I ran through the iron gate without being caught.

I'm very lucky to have escaped from the ordeal of the hot green pepper and lemon in my vagina and on my tongue. I stopped and I looked back at the gate.

A female worker was galloping toward me. Was she really heartless, or was she, too, fleeing from the predators? I ran toward the sandy hill near the house and didn't look back.

4

white turban man

Escaping the burning punishment of Fadwa's mother seemed miraculous. But still I felt the anxiety and the emotional wound of her words about cutting my third leg. I did not really understand, but I knew I had been an embarrassment to Mother.

For my punishment, every day Mother handed me a wooden slate that seemed to be nearly as big as me and ordered me to sit under the hot sun and study the Quran with the imam. Usually, she sent me out right after lunch, when the Mogadishu sun is merciless and while my siblings relaxed.

I would sit there and wait for the White Turban Man to show up. Looking at the sun and the hot light reflecting off the ground, I knew by now my brothers and sisters were taking their wonderful afternoon naps. The White Turban Man would arrive, and as the lesson dragged on, my mind wandered. Eventually my well-rested siblings would stroll out of their rooms and sit under the shady tree to have their afternoon snacks. Great snacks, like *sambuus*, or samosas, and hot tea with milk, sugar, cinnamon, and cloves. No, it was not Ramadan. In our house, this feast took place at four every afternoon, and it was my favorite time of the day. Xaawo would supply dates and other nonanimal ingredients to the cookie maker, who would make a special batch of vegetarian sweets just for me. Later, I discovered that Mother almost fired Xaawo for this kindness to me.

One day as the sun beat down and the White Turban Man droned on, I watched as Amal and Asis looked for their *doolshe* cake, then realized that Mother had taken it off the snack list. Instead, they would have the *jalaato*, made with milk—*caano*—and spiced up with lots of sugar. I was sure Xaawo had not forgotten to pick up my eggless snacks from the neighborhood cookie maker. I closed my eyes, imagining the treats to come. When I opened my eyes, I looked at the White Turban Man.

"I'm thirsty," I said.

Frustrated, he closed the Quran and stared down at his feet. I turned again to watch my brothers and sisters under the tree enjoying their afternoon snacks. The White Turban Man lifted up his wooden stick and aimed at my legs, smacking the hell out of me.

In pain, I threw my wooden slate toward him and knocked the turban off his head. Like I'd stuck a knife into his heart, he gasped and glared at me. I realized that knocking his turban off was a great insult.

"It was your fault!" I shouted.

I watched as he grabbed the long scarf and wound it around his head. His hands did not seem to be moving as quickly as he would have liked. He struggled and twisted the cloth, which became a mountain on his head. He got very upset when he saw my curious eyes following his marching fingers as they tucked the tail of the white cloth underneath the edge. Now the turban sat on his head, but it was loose and could fall at any moment. It looked like the sandy hill near our house, waiting to invade well-groomed doorsteps.

Then the turban fell, landing on his feet. He grabbed it, jumped up, and started the winding process all over again.

Wanting to be kicked out of the lesson, I told the White Turban Man that Grandmother knew God better than he did. She would read the Quran aloud, then ask God to answer what she couldn't understand.

"You mean she talks to herself?" he asked. I could see him trying to control his anger. To him, this was blasphemy.

"She talks to God," I said.

To make matters worse, I told him that Grandmother had a very complicated relationship with God. Even though my parents were one hundred percent devoted Muslims, Grandmother did not understand why she was forbidden to see her friends who saw God differently. I would later discover that some family members feared that, because of her openness, Grandmother might be tempted away from her own faith. Muslim Somalis lived alongside non-Muslims, but it was not acceptable to go to their places of worship.

As if he were confronting the devil, the White Turban Man shouted a chapter from the Quran, then stormed out. Father, who was visiting from Hargeisa, arrived, and I watched him heading toward me.

"What happened?" Father asked.

"He hit me with a stick." I moved to stand facing him.

"Who told you to get under other people's beds?"

I looked up at his tired eyes. His left hand with the missing fingers rose to his face, and he removed his uniform hat. I noticed that Father had gotten a new haircut; his salt-and-pepper hair was cut close to the scalp.

"Who tells you these things—things like smoke rising from a woman's ears?" Father asked.

"It's going around the neighborhood," I said.

His tired body dropped into the green beach chair, and he looked up at me.

"Do you believe you're my favorite child?" Father asked.

"Yes, the others seem to think so," I replied, thinking how they resented me because of it.

Father glanced at his watch, then stared off as the guards replaced one another for the post. He locked his lips on my forehead and walked away.

Xaawo found me sitting in the green beach chair and wrinkled up her face.

"The information you gave me was wrong," I said.

"Did you see any part of the bride's body?" Xaawo asked.

"I didn't see any smoke passing out her ears."

Xaawo explained that the bride's private part has been sealed. The wedding night, the husband lies next to her, wanting to make babies, but his touch pains her.

I sat up and whispered in her ear, "You mean, he forces his Gus into her!"

She frowned.

"Fadwa told me," I said.

"Well, then—the snake moves around her, searching for the tiny dark hole," Xaawo said.

"Dark hole?" I asked, surprised.

Xaawo told me that the groom's job is to find it, and when he does, then the bride would feel unbearable pain. The pain is like fire burning inside, and then she releases smoke through her ears. Suddenly, we saw my shirtless father walk out of the house toward the courtyard in sight of everyone, his large protruding stomach leading the way. Malik rushed to him and said something. Xaawo hurried back to the kitchen.

I watched as Father walked toward the back of the house, where Mother was doing a secret decorating project. I started after him, but he was too fast. I rushed to the back and peeked through the window into Mother's sanctuary, the sitting room where she met her guests.

Mother was surrounded by colorful fabrics and pillows.

"Who are you making them for?" Father asked.

"For my *asilo*, my shelter," Mother said.

She got up and grabbed curtain material and walked to the window, and I moved back so I wouldn't be seen. She placed each piece of material over the window, deciding which color to pick.

"And what have you done to my room?" Father asked,

"I put a firm mattress and expensive bedsheets on the floor," Mother said.

"What for?" Father asked.

"Your bed will not support my weight and your pregnant stomach!" Mother said.

Mother went on and on about how some of us were sneaking into those nasty Italian movies, and she thought Sakiya and Asra might elope soon if they didn't do something about it.

"Do you know what your wall-climbing daughter did?" She looked up from the fabric, a challenge in her eyes. "You know that she is forbidden to leave the house but somehow gets over the wall to go around spying."

"I had a talk with her."

"She goes around the neighborhood acting like the secret police."

Father got closer and wrapped his arms around her. I stepped away from the window and went to feed Asis's long-haired orphan cats. Not long afterward, my brothers' and sisters' movement out of the house was restricted as well.

⚜

I was counting the days when I could be free from the White Turban Man and plotted a way to get rid of him, this time for good. At our next lesson, I told the White Turban Man about visiting Grandmother's friends and that the moon is where God's big head rests. I continued my story by talking about the day I ran down to the shore and saw a group of Indians wearing black, throwing flowers and praying to the sun.

He pushed his long finger toward my face. "Worshiping anything or anyone other than Allah is the worst sin, ever!"

I watched him get up and speed into the house as Mother's friend Raqiya pulled up in her Mercedes. She got out of the car, wearing a blinding yellow *guuntiino*—a cloth that ties over the shoulder and drapes around the waist. In one hand, she carried a box of cigarettes, and in the other she held a huge bag. Everyone admired Mother's friends, and some envied their lavish beauty and lifestyle.

But lately they had decided to help the less fortunate ones. They were assisting Mother in raising money for the orphanage.

Most of these women were married to uniformed men with gold stars on their shoulders, just like Father. Like their privileged husbands, these women acted like they cared about the community, which meant showing up at one or two meetings. I remember Raqiya's daughter, Basra, telling me that it is the girl who keeps the family honor. All we have to do is keep our legs together until we're allowed to become wives to honorable husbands, just like our mothers.

Basra also insisted her mother was more religious than mine because she prayed five times a day, unlike my mother. Well, Mother was known to perform the *fajr* prayer around dawn but skip *dhuhr*, the noon prayer, along with *asr* and *maghrib*, but pick it up at *isha*, evening prayer. Facing Mecca, Mother would kneel on the embroidered prayer rug, bow, and prostrate herself for hours. Later, lighting a cigarette, she would get ready to go out with Father. Asis and I would scramble around the room, trying to defuse the smell before Father returned.

Raqiya could pray all she wanted, but there was something about her that I didn't trust. Maybe it was her roving eyes as she often chatted with Malik's young male friends. Mother defended her and told us that we should treat her like Aunt Ubax. But Raqiya was nothing like Aunt Ubax, except they both had soft, honey skin. Like those famous Egyptian singers, Raqiya floated as she walked, pushing her chin up and her shoulders back. She flashed a smile as she stood in front of me. I inhaled her cloud of perfume as she stood before me, but her big leather bag was distracting. I could see the plastic bag and cigarette cartons.

"Where is your mother?" she asked.

Suddenly, Mother and the White Turban Man rushed out and charged toward me.

"You just committed the greatest sin!" Mother yelled.

"What did I miss?" Raqiya asked. She had a bad habit of interfering and making a problem worse.

"What is *iblis*?" Mother asked.

"I don't know," I replied. I knew what Mother was asking but didn't want to respond. *Iblis* is a sort of fallen angel; he disobeyed God and became a devil. Some see him as jinn or, in my case, *kaafir*, or nonbeliever.

Frustrated, the White Turban Man threw his hands in the air and stormed away, and that was the last time I sat in front of him. Mother grabbed my neck and pushed me inside the house, all the way into Father's bedroom.

But I smiled. My plot to get rid of the White Turban Man had worked.

5

grandmother's shrouding

Early one morning, when I was twelve years old, I woke up feeling the earth shake and the sky cry softly above me. I looked up at the ceiling as the sky threw its heavy tears over the roof. Only a prayer would bring this heavy rain, but this one carried sorrow. In my mind's eye, I saw Grandmother's face. Feeling the knot in my stomach, I grabbed my pillow and put it over my face. I knew Grandmother had left me. I was crying underneath the pillow, and it was difficult to breathe. I wished the rain would lift me up to the clouds and place me on the moon, next to Grandmother.

There was a knock at the door, but there was no way I was going to get out from under the pillow and let others see my tears. The door opened, and I felt Mother get into bed and lie next to me.

"Grandmother saw the dazzling sight of Azreal," Mother said, talking about the Islamic Angel of Death.

"She shook the tree?" I asked.

"He shook the tree and took Grandmother's soul," Mother said.

"Did she look pretty when the angel took her?" I asked.

"Allah is pleased with her."

"I'm not crying," I said, choking back the tears.

"Don't—they will burn only her body," Mother said.

Mother's hand slipped under the pillow, and her fingers ran through my hair. Her other hand slipped under my chin and, quickly, I pushed it away, not wanting her to feel my tears.

"Would you help me wash her body?" Mother asked.

I threw the pillow out of my face and stared at Mother. She took a piece of her sari and wiped the tears from my eyes.

Later that day, I entered a room where Grandmother's body was lying on top of the washing table. She was covered with a white sheet, and cotton pads were inserted into her ears and nostrils. Cotton pads rested on top of her eyelids, and her arms were straightened at her sides. Her thick white hair reached almost to the ground, and her toes and ankles were bound. Mother picked up a jug and threw water on her body. She repeated this three times. I noticed stacks of white towels, soap, shampoo, more cotton pads, a box of white gloves, and three white sheets sitting on the top of a table covered with a fourth white sheet.

Mother picked up a bucket of water with dissolved camphor and washed Grandmother's body. Amal and Aunt Ubax held a white sheet above Grandmother while Mother removed the wet one. She replaced it with the dry white sheet, then slid her hands beneath, rubbing the camphor into Grandmother's body. Mother took a white towel and began drying Grandmother, gently tilting her body from side to side.

Mother slid another towel underneath the body, and she, Aunt Ubax, and Amal kept tilting Grandmother's body from side to side to dry it. All the wet sheets and towels were removed, and a dry, white sheet was again placed on Grandmother's body.

I picked up the fragrant attar and rubbed it on my palms. I walked over to Grandmother and gently rubbed the attar on her forehead. She seemed to be at peace, sleeping beautifully, like a baby. It was hard to hold back the tears.

Then suddenly I felt a breath of joy rush inside me as I heard Grandmother's voice echoing in my head: *When I fly away, I will be watching you from the full moon.*

In my mind's eye, I saw Grandmother's luminescent eyes smiling back at me. *All is well*—that is what I heard in my heart. Slowly, I walked out of the room as Mother and Aunt Ubax began shrouding Grandmother's body like a mummy.

For the next months after Grandmother's death, I would dream of her and console myself knowing that her spirit would always be with me. As if I were empowered with night vision, Grandmother's aroma of Somali rose continued to lead my steps.

6

the girl with three legs

At school, I could hear my schoolmates whispering behind me, and many of them started to look at me differently. On one particular day, I didn't notice the burning heat showering me with sweat, but I felt the sharp pain, due to stress, stabbing at my organs. I stood by the courtyard and watched the other students exchange hugs and laughter as they celebrated the last day of school. Books were thrown and became soccer balls, feet danced about, and cheers erupted from the wild crowd. I should have been happy and joyous like them, but I wasn't. I had heard enough laughter earlier, when they called me "the Girl with Three Legs." Their laughter brought chills to my body. I remembered when Fadwa's mother said that my third leg needed cutting, not my tongue. I wanted to know the meaning of it, but I was frightened.

In the far corner sat three of my friends. I walked over to them.

"Why stab me with words I can't understand?" I asked.

One of them rolled her eyes and turned her back on me.

"How old are you now?" another asked with a frown.

"Thirteen," I said, closely watching their facial expressions.

"You can't play with us."

"Not as long as you walk with three legs!"

They giggled and acted silly, but this was not a joke for me.

"What does that mean?" I asked.

"It means you're not like us."

"Of course not!" I exclaimed. All girls were different, unique.

"You think you're better. . . ."

"The Girl with Three Legs!"

I looked back at the crowd and saw hands up in the air, followed by loud applause. The girls got up and faced me.

"You are not clean, like us."

I gathered my books as fast as I could and headed outside to wait for my ride to arrive. I climbed into the backseat of the car, next to Asis and Shams. The driver stopped in front of the gate to our house and honked. A guard, with mosquito netting over his head, opened the side door and approached us. He struggled to ease the itch on his back while balancing the rifle on his shoulder.

"No one got stung?" the driver asked.

"The soldiers are removing the last of them," the guard said. He looked at us and said, "The last of the killer bees, that is."

When she heard the word *bees*, Shams screamed and jumped up, hitting her head on the roof of the car. She became frantic, as books flew all over the inside of the car. Asis grabbed her arm and forced her back into the seat.

"Stop!" Asis shouted.

"Put up the windows and stay in the car!" the guard said.

The guard's hand tapped the hood of the car as he walked back and opened the gate. The driver turned the air conditioner on and watched as Asis and I rolled up the windows. The car moved toward the house.

The courtyard looked like an army camp. A group of army men, mosquito nets and handkerchiefs over their heads, were carefully removing a killer bee nest from the rock wall. We watched in amazement. The driver kept the car running, and the cool air from the air conditioner calmed our nerves.

On the other side of the courtyard, near the coconut trees, the workers were moving chairs, and I could see cut grass and flowers scattered all around the ground. Tables and chairs were stacked by the white wall, where Mother was planning to open a home theater. The workers were in full swing, obviously getting ready for something special. Mother loved to race ahead of destiny, and I figured out that she must be throwing another big party for the scanners. At the scanning event some would get lucky and find wives, while others rushed to the next home, the next living room, looking for a woman more to their liking.

I noticed Xaawo exiting the kitchen holding a large pot. I watched how fast she put the pot on the ground, looked up at the meat line, and counted all the clips on the wire that was stretched between trees. She dipped her henna-decorated hands into the pot, lifted up a long, trimmed piece of meat, blood dripping from her hands, and clipped it to the meat line. One by one, Xaawo hung the meat strips on the line, clipping each piece firmly to the wire, like hanging towels on a clothesline to dry. The sight of the dripping meat made my stomach turn.

In the far corner, behind the coconut tree, two of Asis's orphaned cats watched Xaawo, waiting for the perfect time to pounce. "Your orphans are hungry and ready to attack," I said.

Asis and Shams scooted over and leaned over me, looking out the window.

"Good for them!" Asis said.

Horror in her eyes, Shams clapped her hand over her mouth and pointed her finger toward the cotton tree, where two scared lambs were tied. Struggling, they jerked their heads upward, trying to uproot the tree and escape with their lives. Blood dripped from their necks onto the white rope tying them to the tree.

Forgetting about the killer bees, I opened the door, jumped out of the car, and rushed toward the lambs. Frantically, I untied the rope from their necks. Like bullets, the lambs ran straight into the courtyard, aiming for the army men removing the bees from the wall. Chaos erupted, but these were good, trained soldiers, not to be outwitted by animals, and the lambs were caught, dragged back, and again tied to the cotton tree.

Just as the lambs were brought under control, out of the corner of my eye I saw Asis's orphan cats flying, like large albatrosses expanding their wings, swooping to the first meat line. Stunned, Xaawo watched the orphan cats fly off with her lamb meat. She fixed her eyes on the hot cement and followed the blood trails up the coconut tree, where the cats were feasting on the fresh lamb.

One of the army men was so impressed and unaware that he clapped his hands, as if cheering his favorite soccer team scoring the perfect goal. Like a furious wind, Xaawo charged toward him, and when he saw the infuriated lines on her forehead, he escaped into the mass of workers and soldiers. With the perfect view, the orphan cats watched the maddened crowd as they licked the fresh blood from their mouth.

"You are useless!" Xaawo said angrily to the army man.

A car honked. The guard opened the gate and saluted toward the car with its waving Somali flag. Father, wearing his uniform, sat in the backseat, watching as the army men completed their killer bee mission. One of the army men rushed toward him and saluted.

He opened the door, and Father hurried into the house. Then Asis and Shams got out of the other car and chased after Father.

I stepped up to the kitchen door and saw a dead lamb, surrounded by cut vegetables, lying on the stainless metal table. Xaawo dropped rice cooked with raisins and onions on top of the vegetables. The lamb's skin was already removed, with Xaawo stuffing the rice and vegetables inside the stomach; her short fingers pushed them down into the opening. It was a sickening sight.

"You're hurting her!" I cried out.

"The lamb?"

Xaawo lifted up a needle and thread and began tightly stitching the lamb's stomach together.

"The sweeping search is on!" she said. When something was up, Xaawo always talked over my head.

"You're stitching—I don't need to know."

"Men with soft mustaches and shining shoes are coming for dinner," she said.

"You mean the scanners?"

Xaawo looked up and nodded.

"Do my sisters know about Mother's plan?"

"Sakiya knows."

"What about Asra?"

"She will elope soon."

Suddenly, I heard a strange sound behind me. I turned and saw a flying sandal coming straight at me. It hit me on the forehead, and, before any pain registered, Mother yelled, "Stay out of the kitchen!"

I stood there, trying to regain my poise.

"Was that a curse, Mother?" I asked, holding my hand over my bruised forehead.

She inspected my wound.

"What does it mean to have three legs, Mother?" I asked.

"Did someone call you that?"

"My playmates said something evil is hanging between my legs."

"Then it's time for you to receive your gift."

"What kind of gift?"

Ignoring my question, Mother went into the kitchen and inspected the dead lamb.

7

the secret house and the ghost house

One evening just after dark, Halgaan, a hot-tempered army officer who worked for Father but did not get along with him, said he had something important to tell me. The only way I could sneak out of the house was by bribing Xaawo. I rolled my eyes, handed over the money, and crept out the back door.

Halgaan was waiting for me in the stable behind our house. I looked both ways to make sure none of my siblings was watching, then slid through the door. Halgaan handed me an Italian magazine, called *Fotoromanzo*. I had heard that these magazines polluted young girls' minds. I was curious to know what they were all about.

"I got what you asked me for. *Fotoromanzo* will tell you everything about *caasi*, the sinners."

"The wailing sinners?" I asked.

Quickly, I opened up the magazine, hoping to find all the secrets. Instead, I found faces in boxes, with stories of love and the pain of separation. The last page ended with the man's lips locking with a woman's lips.

"What is qat?" I asked, looking straight into Halgaan's dark eyes. He had a long face and held his head erect, as if wearing peacock feathers on his head. He was a tall and elegant man but a troublemaker, and that was why we got along just fine.

Halgaan said that qat was nothing but leaves and twigs that excite and stimulate the mind and put a person who chews it into a state of ecstasy.

"I know a secret house where people gather to chew qat for hours." He paused and looked me up and down. "Would you like to see it?" he asked.

Halgaan got inside his jeep, which was parked in front of the stable, and started the engine. Hesitantly, I climbed in. I stared straight ahead, trying to figure out why we were circling through my neighborhood, passing by the community orientation center. Finally we stopped near a Western-style house with a huge black gate.

The house was completely dark; no one lived there. Halgaan lit a cigarette and stared at the closed gate. In silence, we just sat in the car and waited.

A black Mercedes drove up and stopped in front of the gate. Because of our distance from the car, I could not see any faces inside it. The car flashed its lights twice. The gate opened, and the car drove through. Minutes later, two jeeps pulled up and stopped in front of the gate. One flashed its lights, the gate opened, and both cars sped inside.

Everything was quiet again, and the house was still dark. I saw a few women, wearing *toob*—African dresses—and scarves, walking into the alley. Halgaan scanned the area, threw his cigarette out the window, and opened the car door.

"Come with me."

I was very curious to know about the Secret House, but fear choked my throat. Still, I do well when I'm fearful, so I got out of the car and ran after Halgaan. In darkness, Halgaan and I stood at the back of the house, where construction was being done. Half a brick wall stood, hiding the back windows. I moved forward and stepped on broken ceramic tiles. My heart raced. Halgaan took my hand and pointed to the windows with bright lights. I got so excited that I leaped forward and fell into a hole. I yelled into the darkness, almost blowing our cover.

"*Shhh!*"

Halgaan's hand reached mine, and he pulled me out. Immediately, I rushed toward the window, but Halgaan took my hand and led me to a small wooden side door. He tried to open it but couldn't. I walked back to the window and peeked in. A curtain hid everything from my view. Halgaan lit another cigarette.

I sensed his frustration and moved closer to him and waited. A light came on in the last window. Halgaan threw his cigarette on the ground and told me to peek through that window. The curtains were pulled to the side, and I could see five barefooted men, wearing *macawiis*, being ushered into a beautiful room, decorated with colorful rugs and Indian cushions. In the middle of the room, incense burned in a plaster container with a handle, releasing *unsi* smoke.

The men formed a circle on the rug, grabbing soft pillows to put behind their backs, adjusting them to rest against the walls. The door opened, and I saw Uncle Hussein, leading in Raqiya, who was carrying the big leather bag I had seen her carrying in the past. Xadiyo, Fadwa's mother, followed them in with two other women I didn't know.

In shock, I shot a look of alarm to Halgaan as the image of Fadwa and me, hiding under the bed of the groom and bride, came to mind. And this was my uncle, who was a well-respected officer in the army and who was married to a very beautiful woman.

I was distracted by hearing Halgaan peeing in the corner; he finished by shaking his body, then zipping his *surwaal*. He walked over to me and peeked through the window.

"You need to wash your hands," I said.

"My hands are perfectly clean."

I knew why Xadiyo shouted "Zip your *belino*" to the guard when she found him peeing. She threw him out of the house.

But it was only now that I understood why women were not allowed to shake men's hands.

I peeked through the window again and saw Xadiyo snapping each leaf with her delicate forefingers and popping them into her mouth. She chewed and chewed, then took a sip of hot tea.

The conversation and laughter all around brought delight, which made hands collide and land in others' laps. They removed the incense burner and soft drinks, and naked legs started to snake around each other. Uncle Hussein lifted his long arm and let it rest in a young woman's lap. She picked up a cigarette and put it between his lips, grabbed a lighter, and lit it for him. His hands ran across her face, his blind mind lost in fantasy. I was dumbfounded by this shocking behavior.

Halgaan startled me when he put his hand on my shoulder.

Without saying a word, Halgaan walked away. I chased after Halgaan and found him in the car, smoking. A taxi drove by us and stopped in front of a two-story house, not far from the Secret House. I stood outside the jeep and watched as the taxi driver honked and a light illuminated the door. An elderly woman stepped to the door and waved.

A woman came out of the taxi, went around the back of the car to open the other door, and removed a suitcase. A young, slender girl stepped out as the elderly woman rushed from the house and took her hand. The girl's walk made me think that she was sick. The elderly woman led her inside the house, while the other woman put the suitcase down at the open door and hurried back into the taxi. I got in the jeep, and we drove in silence. I looked back at the house and saw the suitcase still sitting at the open door, as if the sick girl's belongings were rubbish.

As we passed the stable behind my house, my head was spinning with thoughts, and I was coming to my own conclusions. But nothing made sense. I thought about the Secret House and the naked legs. I had so many questions to ask Halgaan, but I was scared. I did not understand the meaning of what I had just witnessed. If Uncle Hussein went there, maybe Mother or

Father did, too. Xadiyo was married to a powerful man who oversaw the well-being of the nation. Raqiya's husband was one of the peacekeepers, and he was independently wealthy.

Halgaan drove us into a dark alley near my house, where we noticed cars flashing their lights and figures rushing toward them. I heard doors slamming shut and car engines starting. I got out of the car and walked toward my house. Looking back, I saw another car enter the alley. Halgaan was still sitting in his car with the lights off. All was quiet, and it was hard to see anything, but then the door of the other car opened, and light illuminated the interior.

Sister Sakiya stepped out of the car and, without skipping a beat, hurried toward home. The car flashed its lights a few times as Sakiya disappeared from the alley. Without turning on the car lights, the driver exited the alley, but I could not see his face. I was not worried because I was certain Xaawo, who knew everything about everybody, would be able to tell me the man's identity. I moved away and walked toward the back door. I could see that Sakiya was struggling with the doorknob. The door was locked.

Angrily, Sakiya kicked the door and walked away. She went to the main iron gate and rang the bell. The guard peeked through the gate and saw her. The side door opened, and Sakiya went into the house. I waited for the door to close, then hurried back to the dark alley and climbed up the wall. I ran to the guesthouse, where I had resided ever since my pet baboon became my roommate.

In the living room, I found Asra lying on the couch and throwing up into the bowl full of sand that Mother held. Sakiya had come into the guesthouse as well, and she stood by the window frowning as Asra continued to vomit. Xaawo knelt by Mother. She raised her head and smiled at me. Amal handed a medicine bottle to Asra. She wiped her mouth and took the pills. Asra suffered monthly from painful menstrual cramps. When drinking the hot tea did not help, she threw up.

Mother looked up at Sakiya and stared for a moment.

"Where were you?" Mother asked.

"I was around, Mother," Sakiya said.

Without saying a word, Mother got up and walked out of the room.

"Mahad came searching for you," Xaawo said to me. Mahad was a friend of mine, a kind but misunderstood person.

"Is he still letting boys slap him on the butt?" Sakiya asked.

"Just because his mother is a fortune-teller doesn't make him weird!" I barked at her.

In tears, I ran out of the guesthouse searching for a dark place to hide. I noticed white chairs stashed against the big white wall that separated us from the home of our neighbor Kulmie, a general commander in the army. I dropped my aching body into one of the chairs and thought about everything.

My younger sisters Shams and Raha exited from our parents' quarters into the courtyard. They looked freshly bathed and wore matching black-and-white-striped pajamas. Raha seemed to be upset. They came to where I was sitting, and Raha pushed her tiny finger into my cheek.

"Asis's cat ate the bird!" she exclaimed, her voice quavering.

"Animals do that. They eat each other," I said.

"But the cat ate her brother!" she sobbed.

I explained to her that just because the cats liked to play with each other and with birds around the coconut tree, it did not make them brothers and sisters. Frustrated, Shams grabbed Raha and took her away.

Just after they left the courtyard, Xaawo came out. She stared at me for a moment.

I was confused about what I had heard and all that I had seen that night. My head was reeling, and I blurted out one of the many questions whirling in my mind: "Why would a boy let another boy slap him on the butt?"

"What makes a mother raise her daughter's bastards?" she asked, then said softly, "I ask myself that question often."

Xaawo caught me off guard. I did not know that her grandchildren were illegitimate. Xaawo sat beside me and looked up at the star-glowing sky.

"Why do people marry?" I asked her.

Xaawo stood again, started folding up the chairs, and placed them by the wall.

"We marry because we want to be off the shelf. . . ." She hesitated for a moment, then continued, "We want to smell and look good to our master."

"Master?" I asked.

"God created women for men. After the wedding, the man's head becomes swollen with empty air. Soon after he becomes her master."

"My father is kind to Mother," I said.

"Wealthy men have many options."

Xaawo talked about the men who didn't possess shillings, circling around Casa d'Italia, the country club, with big eyes, like *un capriolo prigioniero illuminazione*, like a deer caught in headlights. She sighed, shook her head slightly, and turned to go back inside.

I watched her walk away. I felt her sadness, but I also saw her amazing strength.

For the next few weeks, I would wander past the Secret House, still pondering what I had seen. Often I would pause in front of the house where I saw the sick girl taken in by the elderly woman. Confusion, worry, and my imagination had taken over. In my mind, I began to call it the Ghost House.

One day, about a month after my nighttime adventure with Halgaan, I decided to stop at the Ghost House on my circuit past the Secret House. As usual, I paused in front of the Ghost House, trying to envision what might go on inside. Taking a deep breath, I stepped forward and knocked on the wooden door.

No answer. I hesitated only a moment before my curiosity won out. I turned the doorknob, and the door opened.

The overwhelming stench of urine knocked me back when I entered the wet hallway. I gagged, feeling as if the smell of rotten flesh was sinking into my skin.

At the end of the hallway I saw a well. Slowly moving closer, I heard a loud commotion coming from behind a closed door. I rushed to the door and leaned my ear against it. I didn't hear anything more. Without even thinking of the consequences, I inched the door open and peeked in.

It looked like a hospital ward, with five iron beds crammed into the small room. Four crying women lay under white sheets, and a frail young girl stood by her bed. Like a sudden stream, water gushed between her legs. She stood sobbing as her skinny shoulders shook.

In the hallway, a loud object hit the concrete floor. Quickly, I moved to the center of the hallway and saw a large metal bucket sitting by the well. A young woman leaned forward and tied a plastic bucket to a thick rope, then dropped it into the well. There came the sound of the bucket crashing into the water. Slowly, she pulled the rope toward her, harder and harder. She grabbed the plastic bucket and dumped the water into the big metal bucket.

Quietly, I left the house. No one had seen me. But what was this Ghost House? Why were the girls suffering so?

I felt a rising panic and raced home to my only reliable source of information. I rushed through the door, ran to Xaawo, and breathlessly described what I had seen.

Xaawo set down her bean soup and focused her dark eyes on mine.

"The girls have a fistula," she said, "because they had childbirth difficulties." Oftentimes, she explained, when a young girl pushed out a baby, the baby's head got stuck in her vagina because her pelvis was too small. This put pressure on the rectum and bladder, which led to perforation of the tissue that separated them. "The girls can no longer hold their bodily fluids," she said. "Their husbands and families abandon them. They are thrown into dark homes to die."

"Where are the doctors?" I asked. I thought of the young girl standing by her bed.

Xaawo just shook her head.

My heart ached for these girls. Although the health care system was free, some doctors charged their patients. And even as a child I knew that those with the means received the most and the quickest care.

⁂

My allowance money paid for lots of information, but when I needed to find out why I was called the Girl with Three Legs, no one would answer. Even Xaawo's response always was "Ask your mother."

Almost in tears, I would go and ask Father, "Why am I called the Girl with Three Legs?"

And he would answer, "It's like asking me to describe to you how Mother brought you to this earth!"

I asked my brother, Asis, the same question.

He said, "Listen, I have two long legs and one short one. That short one is reserved for my future wife."

"So why am I called the Girl with Three Legs?" I asked.

"Because you snoop around and jump off the walls, like a baboon on fire!" Asis shouted.

Suddenly, like being hit by blazing hot dust, I realized what the "short leg" was. The *belino*. But that made no sense for a girl.

"I've seen enough *belinos* to know I can't be a boy and have three legs."

"You don't have to worry, because Mother will make sure to cut yours off." Asis laughed.

Fear rose inside me at the sound of his laugh. I covered my ears and ran from the house.

8

the sound of the scissors

Early one morning during the school break when I was thirteen, Mother came to me and said she was going to buy me a gift and that I should come with her. Getting into the car, I couldn't help but to feel happy and proud.

"*Ahlan.*" The driver smiled and greeted me with a hello.

I smiled back and wished him a good morning, "*Subax wanaagsan.*"

Mother, carrying a silver bowl and small towel, got into the backseat of the car and sat next to me. We left the house and drove to Hamar Jajab, the shopping district in Mogadishu.

Smiling faces greeted us as we passed through shops. Finally, Mother and I walked into a shop where the owners were kneeling for prayer and customers were browsing through the merchandise. I saw beautiful summer dresses and sandals, and I pointed to a dress on display.

"That is the one I want for my gift, Mother!" I smiled as I imagined what Fadwa would say when she saw my new outfit.

But Mother took my hand, and we walked out of the shop.

"What about my gift, Mother?" I asked.

"You will get one."

Mother and I walked into the shop of Odey, our tailor. I was overwhelmed by the nonstop whirring roar of the sewing machines. Usually, Odey came to our house, taking measurements for our amazing dresses. One of the workers came over to talk with Mother.

As I watched Mother in conversation, I looked around at the people transforming brightly colored cloth into dresses. I remembered how, after I had gotten my first period, Father suggested my style of dress should change. Unlike Fadwa, I was to wear long dresses with long sleeves. When the dresses arrived, I would put them on, one by one, and show them to Father. After he approved, I would call Fadwa, and together we would sneak back to Odey's shop to have him redesign them to my liking. Fadwa and I would watch Odey's old hands pick up the red scissors, cut off the long sleeves, and put each sleeve on the sewing machine perfectly, right under the needle. He would adjust his thick glasses and, with his foot, push the pedal to the floor. The sewing machine would roar, the sound reminding me of the car engines of the Somali Armed Forces that blasted into people's homes and dragged men, like bedsheets, onto the hot concrete to their execution. The loud noise hurt my head and pained my skin, as did just seeing the wild needle biting through my dress. Later, Father would notice the changes to my dresses and throw his hands up, sigh in annoyance, and tell Mother that I was causing his high blood pressure. "I give up," he finally said.

On this day, the day of my gift, Mother smiled and handed the worker money, making him smile, just like a proud Somali Arab.

"*Ma assalama*," he said good-bye, still smiling.

Mother nodded, and I followed her out of the shop and back into the waiting car. She loved to give money to people and watch them smile until their faces hurt. I thought I wasn't going to get my gift that day, but it felt good that Mother and I were having time alone. I was glad that Mother chose me instead of my siblings. I couldn't wait to see the looks on their faces when we returned home.

Our car entered a residential area, with Arab-style white-washed houses made of stone, covered with plaster and cement. Some had bar-covered windows. I looked up and saw an open window where a young girl poked her head between the bars, her hands grabbing them firmly. Like a prisoner, she watched a group of young men talking below her window. I pointed her out to Mother.

"Why is that girl locked up in there?" I asked.

"It's her destiny," Mother said.

"Destiny?"

"She will be locked in her room until her parents find her a match."

"She's in prison!"

"It could have been you!"

I looked out the back window of the car and noticed that we had passed every store in town. We had even passed the Baraka Market in the middle of the city. We stopped in front of the outside market where groups of lambs and goats were kept within a silver fence.

A few people gathered around the animals, inspected their teeth and ears, and checked their weight. Suddenly, a jeep sped by us, throwing hot sand in the air. The jeep stopped in front of the fence. A man wearing a flowing plaid *macawiis*, white shirt, and embroidered cap leaped from the jeep and hurried toward the animals. The man acted like one of the government's secret police on his day off as he ignored his fellow Somalis. He pushed toward the fence, making others step to the side as they trembled with fear.

They watched him walk inside the fence and scan the animals, like a lion choosing his victim. Reading the man's clouded mind, the animals sensed the danger and began bleating wildly as they tried to jump over the fence.

The man ordered the owner to chase one of the lambs. The owner grabbed the neck of a lamb, looked back at the man, and put a thumb under the lamb's chin, indicating the lamb was in good health. The man nodded his head in agreement, and the owner dragged the frightened and bleating lamb toward the man.

"What are you waiting for?" Mother asked.

"The jeep is blocking us." Frustration rose in the driver's voice.

"Get me out of here!" Mother shouted.

Our driver moved the car backward and went through an alley. We entered a busy street and stopped at the light by the gas station. Mother was sad to see three young homeless boys holding T-shirts up to their noses and inhaling gas fumes, a cheap way of getting high. She bent her head down and stared at the silver bowl on her lap. I wanted to ask about my gift but thought it might not be the right time.

We entered a middle-class residential neighborhood. A few people were walking around, and I could see a woman passing a spice bottle from her second-floor window to the neighbor's house. The woman smiled and waved as the other woman closed her window.

Finally, our car stopped in front of a two-story yellow house with a flat roof and white windows. Bars covered the lower windows, and glass covered the upper ones. Two old Mercedes were parked in front of the house.

Mother opened her door and turned to me. "Come with me."

I got out of the car and followed her toward the thick wooden door. She pushed the door open and took my hand as we stepped into the house. I was hit by an offensive odor. Quickly, I covered my mouth with my other hand as we walked down the long, dark hallway, but the smell was so strong I could feel it entering my body.

The house smelled nothing like our house: no incense burning in every corner, no fleeting scents of lavender air freshener to cover Mother's cigarette smoking. The odor of this house was shocking. It smelled like a hospital but also like burning blood and rotting flesh. I felt sick. My stomach was turning fast. I looked over, and Mother didn't seem to mind it at all.

"Mother!" I shouted.

"Walk with me!" she said, grabbing me and forcing me to continue walking.

I felt cold and afraid as I looked back at the door. Suddenly, the last door of the hallway opened. A woman, wearing a white mask and white coat over a colorful *dirac*—a long billowing dress worn over petticoats—led another woman carrying a young girl of around seven.

The girl's mouth was open, but there was no sound. All the air was stuck inside her. Her frozen cry was like unexploded shells. It was only a matter of moments before her wailing exploded, shattering the walls. To me, her shrieks sounded like they could demolish the city of Mogadishu, but no one else heard her screams or noticed the earth shaking. My hope was that they would at least feel cold chills, like the ones running down my own spine, and do something.

In terror, I lost the feeling in my feet and could not take another step. I felt like I was caught in tripwires, walking down the enemy line. The women rushed the girl into a room and shut the door. I looked up at Mother and met her dark olive eyes.

She touched my forehead and smiled down at me. "It's time. Time to become a woman," she said.

I opened my mouth, but the words were stuck inside of me, and I could feel the tingling nerves tightening my backside. This was always my first signal when something horrible was going to happen. I was five years old when I developed this signal, when one of the guards forced his fingers through my underwear. Since that painful experience, I had become very protective of my body and had begun to question everything.

"After today, no one will ever call you the Girl with Three Legs," Mother said.

Now I understood! I had been too afraid, too naive—why didn't I understand when Aunt Ubax and others created captivating stories with hidden messages? Who was I to think that this day would never arrive for me? I realized that I was now one of the nomad girls in Aunt Ubax's tale, one of the girls who had been caught by the old blind woman, forced to sit on hot sand and thorns. But the hands clutching my body were not those of a blind woman. They were the hands of my own mother. "You're going to cut off my third leg!" I cried.

"This is my gift to you," Mother said, without blinking.

I wanted to run but couldn't. I had no strength to move my limbs. Fear hit me as I watched the white-coated woman rush toward me. I don't know how it happened, but I found myself blinded by the hot sun and my hands clinging to the outside door. I saw the driver leaning back on the car, smoking.

"Help me!" I shouted.

The driver gave me a blank stare as smoke rose from his mouth. He looked like a camel choking from the wooden *koray*, the halter around his neck.

"I want my father!"

Suddenly, I felt a hand around my neck, and, at that moment, I saw the image of the two scared lambs tied to our cotton tree. Now I understood why Grandmother used to argue with God. I just wanted to see his big head in the full moon and shout, *I don't want to become a woman!*

I regained consciousness as the nurse tied my wrists and legs down to the surgical table. Lying under the ghastly bright clinical lights, I could feel the top of my head opening as I tried to give birth to safe thoughts, like sitting in the backseat of the black Fiat with Mother, joyously thinking about how proud I made her in my new ivory short dress, matching underwear, and sandals. After today, I would never again wear a short dress. With Somali rose oil in my washed hair, I imagined I smelled like Grandmother. I had tied my thick, long black hair with white satin bows and let it bounce freely on my back. I looked pretty and felt very, very clean. But Mother had not noticed my effort; she didn't say anything.

Suddenly, I saw a man with glasses, wearing a white coat, holding up a syringe. For a moment, he looked like our tailor, Odey. I saw his old hand pushing upward on the syringe, like Odey's old hand pushing my dress through the sewing machine.

The white-coated man disappeared into the white sheet. I felt a sharp pain between my legs as Mother put a cold, wet towel on my forehead. The man hovered over me, looking down at me.

"Be brave," he said.

I screamed with pain and fought to get free. I felt strange feelings, like the lower part of my body was becoming paralyzed. Everything down there felt numb, but like it was expanding. Mother took the small towel and dipped it into the silver bowl. Gently, she placed the wet towel on my forehead again. For a moment, the towel soothed my spinning head.

But the numbness of my vulva only lasted for a moment because I felt thick, rough fingers running all around my genitals. Firmly, the rough fingers grabbed something. Sharp pain rose from a place that I never would have imagined. Hot air passed through my organs, and I could have sworn that thick smoke was escaping from my ears. Was this the smoke that I'd been chasing, trying to see, for the past four years?

I struggled, kicking my feet to stop the pain. But instead, I felt those rough fingers pulling at parts of me; I felt a knife digging deep into my organs.

"*Stop!*"

I shouted, but no one listened to me, not even Mother. My cry wasn't frozen like that on the face of the girl I had seen earlier. It was burning, like bullets shattering the walls that kept me captive. My cries were like waves, rising from depths inside me. I saw an image of a young mother, living not far from our home, screaming because her baby's head was stuck in her vagina. She died from pushing and bleeding around her dead baby's head. I wished I could be that lucky and just escape to the other side.

The pain was unbearable; I had become a tortured prisoner for trusting my own mother. A rubber-gloved hand grabbed my leg and, suddenly, my body was not my own anymore. My body felt like ripped cloth. It belonged to someone I didn't even know.

I felt the prick of the sharp needle, then hands plucked at my lips—my labia minora and majora—like a giraffe feasting on thorny branches. Frightening images flashed through my mind; hearing the sound of the scissors cutting away my flesh, I saw a vision of my body lying on the same sewing machine I had seen earlier. Father and God had abandoned me. I was cursed for being born into a female body. How could I cope with this pain? Mother's hand passed across my forehead, and I panicked, imagining I was swallowing my own flesh and blood.

The smell coming from my own body was the very one that had hit me as I walked down the hallway. The odor circulated in the air, persistent like a fly. Mother breathed into my mouth and gently said, "Feel the air rushing through the open window."

I could feel wetness on my back and fire burning between my legs. The white-coated man came out from under the white sheet and looked not at me but at Mother.

"Would you like to look at it?" the white-coated man asked Mother.

Mother pulled her hand away from my chest and rushed beside him to look.

"Perfect. Just perfect," she said, flashing a smile at him.

His glasses came off as he wiped the sweat from his dark, glowing face. He watched as Mother helped the white-coated woman untie my legs from the table, just as had been done with the dead lamb on our stainless-steel table in the kitchen.

Mother rubbed my ankles and looked at me. I stared at the white-coated man, lifting his shoulders like a proud nomad squatting under a shady tree to relieve himself. Images and thoughts exploded in my head, ignited by the unbearable pain.

I will make him swallow what he took from me! I screamed the words silently to myself.

As the white-coated woman grabbed the tray full of my flesh, my feet kicked, the way Asis would kick his soccer ball.

The tray flew up to the ceiling, hit the clean wall, and, like blood rain falling madly, my flesh splashed on their heads. Even Mother could not escape the bloody drops falling onto her face. I was not blessing them; my wish was they would choke deeply on my own flesh and blood.

I did not hear the surgical tools crashing to the floor, but the white-coated man shouted, "Get the rope and hold her!"

That was the last thing I remembered. I entered a darkened world and unthinkable lifelong pain.

9

betrayal

Lying in the backseat of the car, I saw the iron gate opening. *I am home*, I thought. *I am forever mutilated. I will never be the same.*

I heard thundering ululating chants from a joyous crowd. Mother hurried from the car and disappeared into the house. My pain was excruciating, but through the fog I managed to look up and see the faces of my five sisters, Amal, Sakiya, Asra, Shams, and Raha. I didn't see my three brothers, Asis, Malik, and Adaax, but I saw my aunt Ubax, neighbors, and classmates. The very same classmates who would not touch or play with me, the girls who called me the Girl with Three Legs and said I was not clean. On this day they smiled down on me because my body had passed through the sewing machine and now I was made perfect, infibulated, just like them. This state of "perfection" had been achieved by cutting off my clitoris, labia minora, and most of my labia majora and sewing the raw edges together, leaving a small hole no bigger than my little finger to be forced open by a future husband on our wedding night. Yet the women and girls around me acted joyous, welcoming me into the sacred circle of womanhood. I must take a place on the shelf.

My limbs were weak from too long on the sewing machine. A voice inside my head said, *Your body is not flesh; it is a cloth.* *Who are you?* I asked.

The voice said, *I'm you at five, when your body was still flesh.*

I ached everywhere. I could not move my legs. I could not feel them, because a tight rope was tied around them. I didn't know where Mother was. Everything outside was bright, in colorful celebration. My heart was heavy with pain and betrayal. I felt my body falling straight into a black world.

My aunt Ubax came in to see me in the car, her shining, thick, dark hair falling on my face as she kissed my forehead. I smelled the scent of her Somali rose oil, which soothed me for a moment. She wrapped her arms around me and carried me to my room at the back of the house. Incense filled the room, where a mattress had been placed on the floor. There were colorful pillows on it. With the help of Amal, they laid me flat on my back on the stiff mattress.

"Today you have become a woman!" Aunt Ubax said.

I stared at her and wondered how she could tell me this when pain wouldn't let me feel my waist. I saw the image of the white-coated man holding up the threaded needle and my mother poking at my damaged organs, saying, "It's perfect!"

I felt numb, shut off within. I wondered if my aunt Ubax ever loved me. What about my sister Amal? Why did everybody know about this celebration except me? The pain was unbearable, like bullets piercing my heart. Again I saw the image of a dead lamb, lying on our kitchen table as Xaawo cut its stomach and filled it with rice and vegetables. Her short fingers stitching the dead lamb's stomach tightly back together.

"Say something," Aunt Ubax said.

Nothing made sense, and I didn't see the point of talking when they could see that I was in pain. I was not even going to pray. Why would I pray when God and my father had forsaken me? Why would I speak to Aunt Ubax when her words were like scissors ripping my skin?

I longed for Grandmother. I called to her silently, and my pain was so great my mind escaped into dreamy memories. I saw us as we used to be, Grandmother sitting under the full moon arguing with God while my older brother Asis and I lay beside her, begging her to show us God.

God is all around us! Grandmother exclaims.

I don't see him, Asis answers.

Grandmother lifts her arm up to the sky and smiles. Look up into the moon and find his big head, she says.

Why would he have a big head when we have a little one? I ask.

Grandmother wraps her shawl around us, sheltering us from the cool, windy night. She asks, Wouldn't you have a big head if you could see all the rubbish floating around us?

Like what? I say.

Grandmother gestures toward the sky and says, Stare into the moon and find his face.

Today, I wanted to lie under the full moon, find God's face, and ask him to let me die. My hands felt the soft sheets, and I wanted to sink into the firm mattress and disappear into the depths below. I wanted Grandmother to wrap her shawl around me.

Mother used white sheets when tending to Grandmother's body, but she would not waste any white sheets on my body. My shrouding would not be that elegant because I was just a child. Nor would it be wise for Mother to insert cotton pads into my ears and nostrils because, although my body had died, I could still hear and smell, especially when she released that corrupted breath of hers.

Aunt Ubax did not need to stack white towels, soap, shampoo, cotton pads, or the box of white gloves; I did not need water dissolved with camphor to wash my dead body. Aunt Ubax and Amal did not need to waste a moment holding a white sheet above my body to avoid seeing my mutilated vagina. One white sheet, instead of five, to cover my dead body and what was left of my private parts was enough. The only thing Mother needed to do was to make the head veil by tightening the white sheet above my head, then cover my bare feet by tightening it below.

She should not waste any time putting my lifeless body in front of the White Turban Man. He knew I never trusted him, and his prayer would only sink my body deeper into the grave. He had no permission to stand by my shoulder and look down on me.

No one should waste time by forcing my face to lie toward Mecca. Instead, they must let me gently face the Himalayas. That way I will see the three-eyed one who wears a snake garland on his neck. I remembered Grandmother telling me that Shiva's eyes represent the moon, sun, and earth.

And they must not waste time putting the ritual stone under my head; they had already installed one in my heart. The dead mind never forgets.

Through my dream images, I heard the joyous chants blasting at my open window. Giggling classmates poked their faces through. This was the perfect moment to send me off to the moon, while the celebration was still in progress. The guests would only need to switch their multicolored garments to bright whites. My death would not change anything. They would continue their feast. Their white garments would blend perfectly with the rich and lustful greens of the flower gardens that surrounded our white brick home.

Aunt Ubax's soft hand landed on my face, then moved down and squeezed hard with two fingers by the side of my lips, attempting to force me to speak. But I pushed my tongue forward and sucked in my cheeks.

Amal took Aunt Ubax's hand from my face. Looking at her, I saw Amal was ready to cry. She got up and opened the other window, then turned back and stared at me. I motioned to her to bring me a pen and paper. She rushed to the desk and hurried to me with them.

I took them from her and wrote, *I will not speak until Father gets back.*

"Speak now!" Aunt Ubax yelled.

Frustrated, Aunt Ubax got up and went to the door. She stopped and looked back at me. "Now it's time for your friends to bring in your gifts." She walked out, closing the door behind her.

Amal returned to the window and stared out. I heard her crying. I wanted to crawl, but moving my body caused too much pain. I picked up the pen and threw it at Amal.

She did not turn but continued to stare out the window. Then I watched her body slowly drop to the ground as she let out a painful cry.

I didn't know what to do. This was making me forget my own pain. Amal never cried, even when she had painful menses and threw up into the silver bowl filled with sand. Amal placed her chin on her knees and wrapped her arms around her legs, just to stop shaking.

"I can't feel my legs," I said.

Avoiding my eyes, Amal got up and walked over to me. She checked the rope tied around my legs.

"Your legs will remain tied together for two weeks," Amal said.

"Two weeks!"

"You will learn how to walk again."

"How did you stand the pain?"

"The pain will wear off, and you won't remember this day."

There was a knock on the door. Amal jumped up, wiped her tears away, slapped her face, and went to the door. With a smile, she opened the door. Fatima, our servant, carrying a full tray, entered.

"This is the herbal mixture your mother asked for," Fatima said.

"Thank you," Amal said.

"She will need to pee soon."

Amal nodded her head. "Yes."

Without looking at me, Fatima placed the tray beside me and exited the room. I threw my notebook at Amal, my body twisted in pain.

Amal read my note, which said, *How long am I going to be invisible?*

She advised that I should pee soon and let the wound heal so that the stitches could fall out easily. "Think about ways to forgive Mother."

Furious, I wanted to leap up at her and scream *Never!* I struggled hard not to open my mouth and let the air out, hoping to stop the pain.

"Stop choking the air in, or you'll get asthma!" Amal exclaimed.

My classmates and playmates walked into the room and lined up in front of me. They held gifts in their hands, grinning at me. I was like the future mother-in-law waiting to inspect their worth.

And like a dreadful mother-in-law, I began spitting at them. Their bodies jammed in the doorway as they rushed to get out all at once. Only after my gifts crashed to the tile were they able to get out of that door. Amal shot me a horrified look.

But why should I greet them when not long ago they wouldn't touch me or play with me? I was made to suffer, and I didn't want their love or admiration.

That night, I woke up soaked in sweat as I lay on the firm mattress. Hearing the loud arguments outside the door gave me a headache. I couldn't understand who was fighting. The voices got so loud and violent, and I realized my parents were arguing. Father was finally home.

Instead of crying for joy, I was mad and wanted to shout out, *You're not my father!*

Then I heard Mother yelling, "She is my child, too!"

And Father shouted back, "Stop justifying your life—it's wrong—a wrong act against God!"

Not able to get up and turn the light on, all I wanted to do was crawl into the bathroom, get into the tub, turn on the water, and drown myself. I struggled to untie the white rope around my legs but couldn't. I would have to do it with my legs tied together. I pushed and crawled until I got into the bathroom and dragged myself to the tub, where I painfully raised my arm to turn on the water. I was trying to get up and slide in, but as I was about to do it, I heard the bedroom door open. I froze in the darkness.

"Soraya!" Father called out my name, and I heard him approaching.

He came in the bathroom, turned on the light, and saw me sitting beside the tub with the water running. I looked up at him and saw a broken man who was wearing the body of my father.

"Why, Father—why did you leave me?" I sobbed.

Suddenly, Father rushed to the bathroom closet and yanked out a towel. I wasn't wet and could not understand why he wrapped the towel around me as he lifted me. Avoiding my eyes and struggling to hold back his tears, Father held me close to his chest and walked to the bathroom door but stopped at the sight of Mother.

I had never seen my parents this angry with each other, and I felt terrible thinking that I might be the cause of a divorce. Mother burst into tears as she let Father and me pass through the door toward the mattress.

I was confused. Were her tears for me or out of sympathy for Father?

10

learning to walk again

For the next two weeks, my body twisted in pain, and I would whimper even at the idea of walking. I was fearful that I might never learn how to walk again. My life had changed so dramatically that I did not want to see any friends or classmates. I refused to speak even to Father now, and I would not eat. I felt like I was losing my mind.

Asis, Shams, and Raha would come into my room to try to cheer me up. I couldn't help but notice Shams holding back the tears as she nervously squeezed my hand until it hurt. I was not sure if she was fearful for being next in line to be mutilated, but I was not ready to talk about the pain. She forced a smile, and all I could do was stare back as I felt the painful waves in my stomach. Shams was ten, only three years younger than me, so unlike me she would remember her older sister's anguish. I lacked any memory of my older sisters' mutilations, and the secrecy surrounding mine had effectively kept me from acknowledging what I did not want to know. But Raha was too young to understand and was kept in the dark, just as I had been.

They told me about a mysterious Italian man who had been hanging around Father. Father and this mysterious man would stop at the Casa d'Italia country club to get gelato before heading home. Father had not only gotten fat, but he also wouldn't eat the delicious meals Mother planned for him. Mother flipped when she found out that this man was rumored to be a spy. But Father laughed, saying that most foreigners were spies, but this man was his friend, and there was nothing to worry about.

I listened as Asis described how upset Mother was with Father, but I couldn't tell him that I had known Father's Italian friend for a long time from visiting him at his office. To make Mother happy, the Italian man was helping set up our home movie theater.

Asis explained how simple our home movie theater would be. It wasn't going to be like those big movie houses, like the Shaneema Centrale or the Equator, but we would be able to watch the big American films dubbed in Italian. "A projector will shine a picture on the big white wall—you just need to drag a chair and sit in front of it."

"You can bring food and watch the film!" Shams said excitedly.

They told me that Aunt Ubax missed the opening night of the movie theater because she was late.

Before the movie, the Italian man decided to show short clips on health and hygiene. The clips showed African children learning how to wash their hands before they ate. Angrily, Mother told him how much he disrespected her family and threw him out.

Asis then described the nasty medicine that Mother would give them and how she later inspected their feces.

"What was she looking for?" I asked.

"The snakes living inside our bodies," Shams said.

"It's *parassita*!" Asis said, referring to parasites.

"Did she find any?" I asked.

"I don't remember," Asis said.

Mother walked into the room to help me pee. Asis picked up Raha and took her to bed.

"I'm hearing that sound, Mother," I said.

"What sound?" Mother asked.
"The sound of the scissors cutting my flesh."

A few days later, my stitches fell out, and my wound was healed. Slowly, I had to learn how to walk again. One evening, Asis guided me out of the room, toward the courtyard, and into the movie theater, where he already had set up a mattress, pillows, and a blanket on the floor. I lay down on the mattress and stared at the white wall, eager to see the new film. Asis covered me with the blanket and started that evening's movie.

Shams and Raha walked in, dragging their blankets, and dropped next to me and snuggled up to watch *Pillow Talk* with us, dubbed in Italian. This film marked a healing period for me.

"She is smiling toooo much!" Shams commented about the blond star.

Raha snored loudly. Asis squeezed two fingers over her nose, and she woke up crying.

"We're watching a movie!" Asis yelled.

Annoyed, Raha rolled over to the other side, got under my blanket, and went back to sleep. I became fascinated watching the yellow-haired, blue-eyed woman with her color-coordinated ensemble who smiled so easily. Shams continued complaining and carelessly described each scene. Asis told her to leave, but she wouldn't. She lay down next to me, threw the sheet over herself, and went to sleep.

As I watched the movie, I felt waves of laughter rushing through me. Every time the blue-eyed actress smiled, I felt the pain fading away. I didn't understand why, but her smile made me temporarily forget I had been damaged. I forgot about the marks the ropes had left on my legs; I forgot about my mutilated vulva, which I had been looking at with a tiny mirror. I had nothing to compare it with, because I had never looked at myself before, but as I held the mirror to myself, I would count the stitch marks left behind. All of these bad memories faded as I watched the beautiful actress who smiled like an angel. For many nights after that, I watched the film over and over again, until the movie disappeared. I realized the healing effect Doris Day had had during my painful rite of passage.

⚜

Life began to return to normal, and I went back to school. But one morning I awoke with painful cramps, and I was rushed to Madina Hospital. In the emergency room, the doctor explained to Mother that if he didn't open my scar, I would accumulate menstrual blood in my uterus, which was a health risk. But Mother refused and demanded that the doctor ease my pain. Soon after, I was given a shot and put on medication that would stop the painful cramps. I asked the doctor why my period smelled like soured blood.

"You're fine—everything is fine," he said.

Later that day, Mother walked into my bedroom with a plaster incense holder burning frankincense. She asked me to get up, and I stood above the incense burner. I lifted up my long dress and spread my legs. The sweet smell of incense wafted between my legs and rose up to my head and all around. Soon the infection healed, and the sour smell of blood disappeared. I felt better and was no longer ashamed to be around people.

But the medications had a side effect—vomiting when I swallowed cooked food. I had to stop taking the medications, and, soon after, my moods got worse. I never knew what I was taking and what kind of shots I was getting until years later.

At times I felt numb and didn't care about anything. I became a regular at the hospital, and my body was on constant display for the doctors. No one attempted to help me understand why I was getting worse, and the pain and the confusion caused me to panic and have fits of anger if someone just looked at me the wrong way. I would flail my hands and attack anyone near me. Mother insisted that I was just angry and this was the only way I would express my anger. As if I were possessed by the devil, I would scream and scream, hitting myself.

Father and my twenty-two-year-old brother, Malik, with whom I had never had a close, comfortable relationship, pinned me to the bed while the rest of the family crowded in the doorway, horrified. Trembling, I burst into tears as cold chills ran down my spine. I felt violated and traumatized all over again.

Like a madwoman, I struggled and fought back until Father let go and took Malik's hands off me. My family believed that a bad spirit had taken over my body and that I had lost my mind. News got out of our gate, and many in the city heard that I was going crazy. It was the pain that was causing this insane behavior, but my family had wanted only to numb me with medications that had caused me additional problems. When the pain continued and my mood got worse, Mother simply asked the doctor to prescribe different meds. At night, I would wake up seeing myself tied to the table and scream. Nothing like this had happened to my older sisters when they were mutilated, so my family concluded that my hysteria was a spirit possessing me.

In reality, I was losing my sense of self as my body became a constant display to the men wearing white coats. Most of them didn't understand my body or my pain. I would faint, and it was the only time I could get relief.

Finally, the family got the *wadaad*, a highly respected religious man, to come into our home and chase the spirit out of my body. I don't remember how it happened, but the story ended like this. I was unconscious, lying in bed, when the gate opened. As the *wadaad* stepped into the courtyard, I woke up and hysterically shouted, "No!"

Father and the rest of the family gathered around as Malik tried to calm my rage by pinning me back onto the bed. The *wadaad* entered, and that's when the spirit, a man's voice, spoke through me. Decades later, I watched a film that reminded me about this day, but my body didn't rise up from the bed and hop onto the roof, unlike the young girl in the film. In fury, I spat and spat, until the *wadaad* shouted Allah's name so loud that the walls shook, and he climbed up onto the bed and inserted an animal horn into my left ear.

"In the name of Allah, I order you to get out of this body."

The *wadaad* lifted the horn, moved to my right ear, then blew air. This repeated for what seemed like hours, until I fell unconscious.

My problem continued, and I developed an infection and had pain in my legs. Father brought the Chinese doctor, who told my family that pain possessed my spirit, that I was not crazy. He did ease the pain by giving me herbal drinks, but the next morning, I awoke with swollen legs, and I was rushed back to the emergency room. The doctors told Mother that the swelling was caused by inflammation around the wound and that my urinary tract was infected. I closed my eyes and silently prayed to be removed from this darkened world.

11

mysteries

Two years after I received my gift, Asra fell mysteriously ill and was rushed to the hospital. Nothing was found, but Mother insisted that something was wrong. Asra refused to see the sunlight and stayed in bed all day, staring at Father's picture. She was depressed and wouldn't swallow any food. One day my siblings and I peeked through the window and watched her as she talked with Father, trying to hear their words. But when he turned and saw us at the window, we fled to the nearest room to hide, which took us to brother Malik's bedroom. We stood still at his door and watched him listening raptly to the BBC Somali Service.

"Anybody being shot or arrested today?" Asis asked.

Malik was a mystery. He didn't like to talk and was very particular about where you sat in the room. The longest we had heard Malik speaking was the time Mother expanded Asis's bedroom into Malik's. She built them a living room, feeling that Malik needed to spend time with his younger brother, Asis. He talked to her for an hour.

Malik looked up at us. "The government is forcing the nomads out of their lands!"

"Why?" Asis asked.

"Didn't Father answer this question?" I asked.

"I'm talking to your brother," Malik said.

"I didn't know they were chasing them out," Asis said.

"Stop hanging with the girls and find out why the nomads are being fed *kaluun*—fish!" Malik's impatience with Asis was rising.

I remembered Malik asking Father the same question: *Why is the government forcing the nomads off their lands?* Father told Malik to go over to our neighbor Kulmie's house to get some answers. Kulmie headed the National Drought Relief Committee. The drought had killed many nomads and their livestock, and many more were starving. Father thought it would be better if Malik helped the general instead of complaining about the government's actions.

But Malik had become frustrated and acted as if he were the spokesperson for the nomads. For a time, he had lived with the nomads in the dry lands. He and hundreds of other privileged students were chosen to teach the Somali language to the nomads. The government's mission was to fight illiteracy and make Somali the national language.

So Malik stopped asking questions and spent three months teaching the nomads how to write Somali and learning their ways of life. For those months that Malik was away, Mother never stopped weeping, which caused her to get raccoon eyes. Every day she would tell Father about her dream that Malik was being eaten by the lions. Day after day, she would talk to Father about the lions, and he could not calm her down.

"Enough!" Father said finally.

Malik came back a changed man, and this is when his silence began. Mother wanted to buy him the foreign car of his choice, but he refused. He would retreat to his room, distant and quiet.

At night, fresh after our baths and wearing striped pajamas like the prisoners, my siblings and I would climb up to Malik's bed and ask him about the nomads. Instead of telling us fascinating tales about the lions and nomad life, Malik would stare for a moment, then say the strangest things.

"What would happen if angry clan men burst through the gate . . ." he said one night, his voice trailing off.

"Our gate?" Asis asked.

"Through that gate," Malik said.

"Why?" I asked.

"I'm talking to your brother!" Malik shouted.

"Why would they do that?" Asis asked.

"Yes—why not go to Villa Somalia, where the president lives?" I asked.

Raha distracted Malik by falling asleep on his lap. He covered her with the sheet and looked at me.

"Are these clan men your age or Asis's?" I asked.

All these great moments flashed before me as my siblings and I stood by Malik's bedroom door. Malik paid no attention to us as he listened to the BBC.

"Can we come in?"

A bell rang. This indicated that Abdulqaadir, Father's personal chef and assistant, was on his lunch break and one of the children should serve Father. None of us liked this chore. Malik looked at his watch. Quickly, my siblings and I hurried into the room and climbed up onto Malik's big bed. Raha struggled to find a comfortable position to lie down, while Asis, Shams, and I pretended to snore. I felt my body moving with the rhythm that was creating the beautiful music. The volume of the radio went up and drowned the ringing bell and our snoring. Asis demonstrated different types of snoring, which gave us the idea to sound more like the secret police's car engines stuck on the red mud on their way to Afgooye town. We were roaring and getting louder, surpassing the BBC Somali Service and Father ringing the bell for lunch. We heard Malik slamming the door behind him and opened our eyes, clapping our hands wildly in celebration of Malik's selfless service to Father.

The dark alleys in our neighborhood were the hot dating spots for many, including my sisters Sakiya and Asra. Frustrated teenage girls would jump off the white brick walls behind their homes and escape into the dark alleys. Sakiya, the oldest sister, appeared to act like Mother, giving orders, but she was hard on me, and I couldn't understand why. Asra, second in line, said that I was a disturbance by being Father's favorite and that I had an annoying air of importance.

Tonight, Xaawo informed me that Sakiya would be going out with her boyfriend. His name was Mahamuud, and she told me the exact time his car would sneak into the dark alley. I got ready and busied myself around the courtyard, trying to look inconspicuous. But my closest siblings, Asis, Shams, and Raha, realized I was up to something and joined me.

Before they asked any suspicious questions, I told them that I was creating a short play about the stories Grandmother told us.

"How are we going to do this?" Asis asked.

I told them that it would be a mixture of *hiwaayado* (story-telling) and *xerdhaanto* (folk dancing). Shams's and Raha's eyes lit up with excitement as they tried to choose among the stories. Asis was quiet and crossed his arms in front of his chest.

"What's wrong?" I asked.

"It's not going to work," Asis said. He turned to Shams and Raha to exchange a glance, then stared back at me.

"You will control everything!" Shams said.

As we argued about the whole idea of putting together this play, I noticed Sakiya peeking through her bedroom door. She watched as the driver brought a car into the driveway and parked. He got out and waved to the guard as he exited the house.

"Perfect!" Shams shouted, realizing our parents were going out.

Our parents, dressed casually, exited their quarters and headed for the parked car in the driveway.

"We can stay up late!" Raha said.

"Shhh!" I admonished.

We probably had about two hours to do anything we wanted in the house while they were gone. But it would all depend on whether or not they left on time. Mother was usually the one who delayed the departure by insisting Father change the cassette tape they listened to in the car. He would turn off the engine and lean his head back against the seat. Armed with her favorite cassette, Mother would remove Father's prayer tape from the player.

"I need a break!" we now heard Mother say.

Calmly, Father turned on the engine on and looked into the rearview mirror.

"God, too, loves listening to beautiful music!" Mother said.

We knew what to do as our parents sat in the car and argued about what was in the cassette player. Asis divided us into two groups. Shams and I would sneak toward Mother's side of the car, while Asis and Raha would go toward Father's. They wouldn't notice us. Mother removed Father's cassette from the player and put in hers. Father took hers out and put in his own. It became a game.

"It's me you're taking out, remember?" Mother said.

As usual, one of them would look to the side and see us.

"*Enough!*" Father said.

"You think this is funny?" Mother said.

"No . . . ," Shams replied.

"We're putting a play together," Asis said.

"What about?" Mother asked.

"About this." Asis laughed.

The enchanting voice of the beloved singer Magool blasted from the car speakers.

"God likes music and beauty," Mother said.

We wanted to nod our heads in agreement, but Father glared at us, and we didn't want to hurt his feelings. Listening to prayer was music to his ears.

He kissed Asis on the forehead and opened the door to kiss Raha. "Go to bed, now."

We obediently moved away. The car moved forward, and we watched them leave. My plan was to pretend that I was going to go to my room and sleep. I looked over and saw Sakiya's bedroom door closed. Ignoring Asis and Raha's frustrated pleas for me to come back and work on the play, I rushed into my bedroom and waited until everyone got in bed and was asleep.

When the time was right, I sneaked out of the house and into the back alley, hoping I hadn't missed Sakiya and Mahamuud. There were no cars, and not much activity was going on. I ran toward the other dark alley and saw Sakiya and Mahamuud sitting in the car. They were not hiding—the car lights were on, and they didn't care as other cars flashed their lights on them. A few young men were walking into the alley. They stood at the corner and lit cigarettes. A car door opened, and the light illuminated the tall and lean young woman getting out.

It was Asradheer, our neighbor, known to be a man-killer because of her shining gray-black-blue eyes and her honey-glowing face. She shut the car door and walked out of the alley. A loud whistle erupted from the young men smoking in the corner; she stopped and looked at them for a moment.

"You are a horse built with grace!" one man shouted.

I thought she walked like a lion, bored from killing too much. But Malik's friends would argue otherwise, saying that Asradheer walked elegantly. I saw Asradheer as a sad young woman who found it hard to break a smile.

I sat by the edge of the alley and waited for Sakiya to get out of Mahamuud's car. I watched as cars entered, lighting up the dark alley, exposing the men standing at the corner smoking cigarettes.

I caught glimpses of their splendid dark eyes and thin shoulders, their shapes like silhouettes of stringed musical instruments. But it was getting late, and Sakiya refused to get out of the car. I stood up and decided to go to my warm bed and sleep. I had learned nothing new about the mysteries between men and women.

12

the sheikha

On one Saturday morning just before summer, Mother took me back to the hospital for another checkup. I was seventeen, and this was to be my final year of high school. I wanted my health to stay good. I had been through so many attempts to relieve the pain, with meds started, then stopped, and Mother asking for new meds. Most recently the doctor had given me some miracle pills, and my mood swings and cramping both stopped. If, by any chance, I forgot to take the pills, I was back in hell, as the hysteria and fainting fits and pain ripped through my body.

Father decided to send me to Europe to see a specialist and determine if the pain resulting from my mutilation and causing my hysteria could be stopped. The trip was arranged, but before we left the country, Mother tried, as a last resort, to find someone to heal me.

About six weeks before my trip to the European doctor was to take place, Mother came to me while I sat in the garden. She leaned close to me.

"I am taking you to a spirit dancer, the Sheikha," she said. "This priestess removes the dark spirits that possess people's bodies and souls."

That night, I lay in the back of the car as we headed toward the Sheikha. Mother's anxious eyes stared back at me.

"It will be a quiet ceremony . . ." she began, then waited for my response.

I thought, *Why should I speak? She thinks I'm possessed by a dark spirit. She does not believe or understand that the pain brought on by the mutilation of my body is causing my anguish.*

"She'll communicate with the spirit," Mother said.

I could not hold my tongue any longer. "And find out that I tripped over the jinn's body and lost my sanity!" I shouted, taking her comment to the point of absurdity.

Mother simply turned away and stared into the darkness. We traveled more than an hour in silence.

"The spirit will talk through me as I go into a hysterical trance!" I yelled at her as the car stopped in front of an *aqal*, a traditional collapsible hut made from poles covered by hides and woven fiber mats.

My legs were swollen, and I was in pain, and the driver carried me behind the hut and laid me on a quilt that covered the ground. I heard a cackling sound and turned to see a white chicken jammed into a wire cage, struggling to escape. I looked out into the courtyard, where incense burned in four corners. Under a large tree, the burning fire glowed. Mother stood under the tree, watching me.

Looking up, I saw burning coals in a large earthenware brazier. A drum was above my head, next to burning incense. The heavy frankincense in the air soothed my aching head, and I inhaled deeply. I wouldn't mind being locked in a room full of incense smoke. It lifted my mood.

Lying there surrounded by the scent of frankincense, I wondered how Mother could have brought me to a witch doctor. I knew many women attempted to release emotional pain through rituals, but I could not believe Mother would bring me to such a person. The Sheikha frightened me. I could not remember the last time I yawned, which would indicate a spirit had entered my body though my open mouth. And I was getting a little better since the medications had filled my nightstand. Mother monitored them, and I had become used to her throwing pills into my throat. It wouldn't take long for me to feel the magic in these bottles, as they turned me into a legless giraffe. The pain disappeared for a while, and I would become a tolerable person. I became quiet and just stared out the window. No more hysteria and screaming rage.

The outside seemed peaceful, but I was still hearing the slamming doors in my head. At any moment I might break down and scream wildly. It didn't take long; the pain and the memories would come suddenly and forcefully.

As I lay there, I recalled one morning about four years earlier. I woke up and heard my legs complaining about how long they had been bound by the rope tied around them. They were furious about my weak hands, because they hadn't untied my legs for three long weeks. Then my vulva interrupted them and shouted, *Shut up!*

You shut up! my legs retorted.

I sat there, feeling I truly was losing my mind.

I'm the one crippled for life! said my vulva.

This became a daily battle, and when I told Mother she said, "You mean the lips are not tightly shut?"

Horrified, I stared at her for a moment.

"Can I look at it?"

"Mother!"

I stopped telling her about the fights my lips were having with my other private parts. But even with the medication, I could not stop the internal noise. In the classroom, I would hear the arguing inside my head. Ashamed and frightened, I would look around to see if the students could hear what I was hearing. Some would stare, waiting for me to go into hysteria and run wildly around the classroom.

Whenever the pain, the shame, and the fear became unbearable, I got up and stood in front of the teacher. "I need to pee. . . ."

Stunned, the teacher would watch me rush out of the class-room. Instead of going to the bathroom, I would run into the street and to the huge Catholic church in the heart of the city. Inside, in the semidark quiet, I could sit and watch a peaceful nun kneeling in front of her God. Staring at the red, burning candles, I could feel everything quiet down. My face would become like the nun's face; I would find peace. Sometimes, she would take too long kneeling, and I would get back to hearing my organs asking my legs and my vulva to stop the shouting.

But I brought my mind back to the present. I lay on the quilt belonging to the Sheikha and observed Mother. She stood under the big tree and watched the Sheikha step out of the hut, wearing a white *toobi* (robe), white scarf, silver ornaments, and silver bracelets. Her body moved like that of a well-fed elephant as she stopped at each of the four corners and sprinkled something into the burning incense.

Suddenly, smoke shot up and released tiny fire balls from the incense burner, as if there were an invasion of fireflies. She picked up one of the incense burners and walked toward me. Fear rose inside me at the sound and sight of the rattling shells around her ankles and her dark, haunting eyes aiming at mine. Sweat poured from her forehead, washing over her face. I remembered Grandmother telling me about her friends who went to the beach to offer flowers to Waaq, the sun god. Some possessed healing powers, like the spirit dancer known as a witch or a Sheikha. Grandmother had said the Sheikha believed in the African goddess AySitu, known elsewhere as Isis. The Sheikha possessed the spirit of AySitu, and that is how she became the best healer. Some felt the Sheikha practiced the good magic, but some thought differently, saying she was a witch practing *sihr*, the black magic. Seeing her before me, I believed her to be a witch.

The Sheikha stood over my head with an incense burner. Her eyes were agitated and fishlike—she had no eyelids. The excessive sweating smeared the kohl around her eyes, and it dropped to her cheeks. Her skin shone like the moon, and her camel nose opened and closed as she began to mumble something in Swahili. Thinking this was the end of me, I stretched out my long giraffe neck and surveyed my life.

Feeling overcome by fear, I looked down and saw myself still lying on the ground, terrified by the sight of the Sheikha. What scared me the most was her open mouth, which looked like an elephant's mouth. The Sheikha had four teeth, like an elephant, but long and sharp looking.

She held up the burning incense and circled around me three times. She put down the incense and sat above my head. I felt her rough, dry hands covering my ears as her forehead touched mine. Her head shook like fast drumming, and I could hear the whispers. Her sweat ran onto my face, and her smell of sandalwood was overwhelming. The Sheikha removed her hands from my ears and clapped them violently above my left ear. I felt a sharp ring echoing in my head. She moved her hands to my right ear and clapped them violently again.

The noise hurt my head, and I wondered: *Am I cursed by those I keep in the secret files of my head?* I closed my eyes for a moment to think, and in my mind's eye I saw my brain opening, spilling all the secrets I'd kept from those close to my family. Their glaring eyes wanted me to admit that I was not a normal child.

But I'm not a child at all, I thought. *I am possessed by something I have no control over, and my life belongs to them. They took away my innocence.*

Overwhelming heat rose all around me. I opened my eyes to find myself lying in the middle of a ring of fire. The Sheikha stood in front of me holding the white chicken. Mother still stood under the big tree, watching me.

In terror, I pushed my body to get up, but I couldn't move. An invincible force, with strong arms, rose from the depth below and held me to the ground. I couldn't move my limbs. The Sheikha moved forward and held the chicken above my head. She lifted a shining silver knife and quickly slew the chicken. The night sky opened and showered me with fresh red rain. The blood vessels seemed to pop in my forehead as fear tightened my neck. Unbearable pain shot through my abdominal area, sucking the blood out of my thighs. I was having a terrible cramp.

The Sheikha declawed the chicken and released the feathers soaked with blood, covering my body with them. I made a mewing call to Mother. But she would not hear me.

"Close your eyes . . . prepare for the purification ceremony," the Sheikha said.

I did as she said, and after a while I felt the hands of the Sheikha lift my body and move me away from the circle of fire. She sat me on a low wooden stool with my eyes still closed. I heard Mother and the Sheikha talking.

I was too scared to open my eyes and tell Mother that nothing had changed. I felt the same as when I was brought to the Sheikha, but I didn't want to have the ceremony all over again. The Sheikha wiped the chicken blood from my face, then grabbed my hands and told me to get up and open my eyes. I did not respond; I sat there. She tried again, but this time pushed me upward, and I stood. Suddenly, warm water scented with oil washed over my body as the Sheikha prayed. She splashed the water over me three times and then, without drying me off, dressed me in clean clothes.

The smell of the oil was not pleasant, and I thought I would vomit. I felt Mother's hand rubbing my back, and I opened my eyes. She wrapped me with a shawl and guided me toward the car, helping me into the backseat.

As I lay in the car, all I could think about was the Sheikha releasing the chicken feathers soaked with blood and my body lying in the ring of fire. For days, I would have nightmares about the ceremony; I could not rid myself of the vivid images of the Sheikha's haunting eyes.

13

asra's elopement and mother's pain

I was trapped in a nightmare—I was back in the ring of fire with the Sheikha clapping her hands and dragging me into the blood pool again—when I felt a body leaning against my side. A hand clamped over my mouth. As I struggled out of my dream state, I heard Asra breathing heavily.

"It's me!" she rasped.

She got up and turned on the light. I grabbed my pillow and hit her hard with it.

"How do you climb up the back wall?" she asked me.

"Why?" My aware giraffe eyes circled the room and saw a suitcase sitting by the door. Fear ran down my spine.

"Can I trust you with a secret?"

I nodded.

"Mother is planning Sakiya's engagement!"

"But she felt Mahamuud wasn't good enough…"

"Mother gave in but still thinks Hassan isn't good….I'm cutting my ties with the family."

"What do you mean?"

"I'm running away with Hassan!"

"To where?"

"To Riyadh." Tears slid down her soft cheeks as she started to leave.

"But women there wear an *abaya*. . . . And what if Hassan marries you, then goes to those secret houses?"

Asra stopped and looked back at me. "Are you going to help me climb over the wall?"

I reminded Asra about the neighborhood cookie maker's daughter who ran away with her boyfriend. He happened to be a Somali Bantu, living in the Jubba Valley. She was Barawane. It was said that Barawane are the Arabs left behind in Somalia centuries ago. The Bantu are called Wagosha, meaning People of the Forest, and are the descendants of people from Malawi, Tanzania, and other parts of Africa. They got upset when the Somalis called them Habash, which was offensive, and said that was exactly why the other Africans call the Somalis and Ethiopians the bastards of Africa. The first time I heard people wagging their tongues about the Bantu was when I heard Halgaan arguing with another man who talked about gypsy blood running in Halgaan's veins. Halgaan objected, "I'm a noble Isaaq!" Isaaq is a large Somali clan from the north; they are proud people.

When the cookie maker's family discovered that the daughter had eloped with the Bantu boyfriend, they staged a funeral. The Barawane have strict rules and are known to resist intermarrying with other Somali groups, especially minority groups such as the Bantu.

"What's wrong with you?" Asra asked.

I continued with the story, telling Asra that, a few years later, the young Barawane girl gave birth to her second daughter. That same day her husband brought another Bantu wife to the house because he wished to have sons.

"What makes you think Hassan wouldn't do that?" I asked. Hassan was not Bantu, but I feared his disappointing her.

Angrily, Asra stomped to the door and opened it. Quickly, she jumped back into my room, shut the door, and gave me a terrified look. I rushed to the window and peeked. Mother, wearing a shawl, stood talking to the guard.

"I think Amal is sleepwalking again," Asra said.

"It could be Mother sensing your plan," I said.

We peeked through the door and watched Asis and the guard bring Amal back from her sleepwalking adventure. Mother rushed toward them and wrapped her shawl around Amal.

Asis guided Amal by the hand and took her back to her room. Mother walked over to the marble chairs and table and sat down.

Asra asked, "What is she doing?"

I peeked through the door and saw that Mother was gone. "It's safe!"

Excited, Asra got up and hugged me. She frantically grabbed her suitcase and purse. "Someone will call you when we leave Hargeisa."

Asra said that a woman would tell me, "The lamb is no longer tied to the tree." Then I would know Asra and Hassan were able to travel to Riyadh, and I could tell our family. I helped her escape through the back door and into the dark alley behind the house. A car started flashing its lights.

I rushed behind Asra toward the car. She opened the back door and shoved the suitcase in, then shut the door. I opened the front door and looked at Hassan. "I don't like you at all!" I said, looking directly at him.

"Soraya!" Asra exclaimed.

"He didn't even get out of the car to help you!"

"Would you like to see me thrown in jail?" Hassan asked.

"Be happy for me," Asra said.

I nodded my head yes, but sadness covered my face. This might be the last time I would see my big sister. Asra got into the car and rolled up the window. I grabbed the handle and opened the door.

"Do you know Halgaan?" I asked.

"Who?" Hassan asked.

I told Hassan that if he ever tried to hurt my sister or take another wife, Halgaan would travel to Riyadh and break his legs. Hassan softened as a smile broke out. Asra shut the car door, and I watched them drive away while arguing. This didn't sit well with me, and I started to worry, but I couldn't stop her. All I could do was keep my promise not to tell her secret until I got the call. I went back to my room and thought about my acupuncture session tomorrow with the Chinese doctor named Heng.

The next morning I awoke hearing the bell ringing and Mother crying out. I sat up in bed, feeling the pain in my stomach. I went out and found the whole family sitting around Mother in the living room. Father was on the phone while observing Mother, crying and gasping for air. I joined the circle and knelt before Mother. I felt a sharp arrow piercing my heart and rested my head on her shoulder, smelling her heavy frankincense. I wanted to tell them that I knew where Asra and Hassan had gone, but I couldn't. Asis leaned over and pinched my cheeks with his sweaty hands. I lifted up my head and met the frozen stares of Malik and Amal. Mother looked into my eyes with intensity, and I was afraid that if I opened my mouth, the words might spill out and cause havoc. I gave her a look of disbelief and just shook my head no.

"Were you aware when Asra visited the dark alleys?" Mother asked.

"She wasn't the only one," I said.

Everyone turned their head and looked at me. Their eyes were like tiny needles piercing into my skin. I told Mother that I watched neighborhood girls climbing up the white brick walls and jumping into the dark alley.

"Her imagination is unbelievable!" Sakiya said.

Mother got up and hurried into her bedroom.

Walking like a camel, Aunt Ubax entered, leading the big-eyed cousins. As usual, they spread themselves around the living room and looked at the new curtains Mother installed.

They made themselves comfortable, ignoring the annoyed looks on our faces. This time, they didn't bother to even notice Father.

"What Asra did is horrific and shameful!" Aunt Ubax shouted.

I could see Aunt Ubax forcing emotions as she squeezed her eyes, trying to cry. But no tears fell onto her soft, honey face. Without a word, Father got up and walked out of the room. Suddenly, the phone rang.

Malik grabbed it and said, "*Pronto.*"

I felt my heart sinking with a need to flee.

"Is it Asra?" Aunt Ubax asked.

"It's Khalifa. She is at the airport," Malik said.

"She is here?" Amal said.

Khalifa, our cousin in Brussels who lived with her husband and children, had a habit of showing up in Mogadishu when she felt bored. She was the daughter of Mother's sister, who had passed away in childbirth.

Abdulqaadir walked into the living room and told me that Dr. Heng arrived early and wanted to see me. I got up and followed Abdulqaadir out of the room.

Dr. Heng liked to stick thin needles into my ears and legs. Sometimes his wife, a woman with a ready smile, would come with a bowl of fresh noodles and vegetables. I bowed, took the bowl from her, and put it aside. I had gotten sick after eating the last noodles she brought me, but I did not want to tell her and hurt her feelings.

She was also a doctor and helped get my body ready for the treatment. Gently this time, Dr. Heng stuck hot needles into my legs, feet, hands, and forearms, and I didn't feel any pain. I began to feel the warmth penetrating my body. I closed my eyes and took a mini-journey in my mind.

I hadn't been visiting around the Secret House lately, but my mind took me back, and I remembered the cries I heard coming from the Ghost House. I tried to shift my thoughts away from this image, and I tried to think about Jasira Beach.

After a while, Dr. Heng placed his hand over my face and, in Italian, asked me how I was feeling. I opened my eyes and saw the needles removed from my body. I didn't feel it this time.

"I'm fine, thank you," I answered.

"Rest for a while," Dr. Heng said.

I did as he said, and eventually I woke up and saw Sakiya sitting in a chair. I could sense her nervousness; I saw her restless eyes and her finger playing with her gold earring.

"I know everything . . . ," Sakiya said.

I knew immediately what she meant. "It's too late," I said. "Asra is on her way to Riyadh."

Sakiya slapped me so hard that I lost my vision and got an instant headache. She jumped up and ran out of the room.

I knew this would hurt everybody deeply, especially Mother. All the relief I had felt from the acupuncture was replaced with anxiety, and I stood up. But suddenly, I felt the earth shake, and the cries of the women of my family seemed to shatter the white brick walls. I felt like I was choking as my heart rose up to my throat. I dropped my body to the ground and let out a sorrowful wail.

14

boots marching to ogaden

As time went on, Father more and more frequently locked heads with Siad Barre and vowed to resign over the president's intention to create Greater Somalia and recapture the Ogaden region from Ethiopia.

When Barre came to dinner at our house, Father usually started a heated conversation, but this night was different. Father didn't explain why he wanted to resign, but he got right to the point and said he intended to lead a civilian life. Barre tried to make Father feel guilty by saying how well they had worked together for those long years and how he wanted him to continue wearing the general uniform. But Father held firm, and Barre said he could keep his title but think about what kind of life he wanted.

Father realized that I was still in the living room, listening to their conversation. He stood up, and when I saw him lifting his hand with the missing fingers, I fled the room. The door closed behind me.

I hurried toward the hallway, passed through Mother's bedroom, and sneaked to the other side of the living room. I hid behind the strange-looking room divider that Mother had gotten from Japan. With everything else, this piece made the decor over the top.

Feeling something huge was about to happen, I wriggled under a table and listened to Father and Barre argue. Father talked about the Somali National Army helping the guerrilla group Shifta in the Ogaden region. Tension was building between Somalia and Ethiopia, and war was imminent. Barre would not stop until his Soomaaliweyn—Greater Somalia—was achieved and the three regions of Ogaden, Djibouti, and nothern Kenya reunified with the north and south of the current nation of Somalia.

Although Barre refused to let Father retire, he allowed Father to oversee businesses rather than actively join the battle with Ethiopia. Still with the title of general, Father managed several public-owned entities as tanks shook the earth and aircraft blasted the Ogaden region shortly after our army went to war.

The Somali army made many attempts to achieve Siad's goal of reunification, but one particular battle seemed encouraging because the army had captured Gode town, by the Shabelle River. Sakiya's husband, Mahamuud, and Uncle Hussein went to the frontline to fight. Even though Sakiya had just delivered her first baby, she was proud her husband was going to fight.

The possibility of a Greater Somalia now seemed real, and Mogadishu was on high alert. But when Father received a phone call and appeared troubled, we knew something bad had happened. Later, we found out that the Ethiopian army recaptured Jijiga, the capital of Ethiopia's Somali region. Most people living in Jijiga are Somalis and wanted unification. But we lost, not only the war but three thousand lives, and the death toll included Mahamuud. Sakiya had been struggling with postpartum depression, so Mother withheld telling her of Mahamuud's death.

The whole country was in a state of fear, and problems were brewing, making everyone lose trust in the government. A group of army officers turned against President Siad Barre and attempted to overthrow the government, but they failed.

✤

Early one morning shortly after the failed coup attempt, I saw Father pacing at the back of the house. I sat by my door in the guest house behind our main house and watched him. Suddenly, in the distance we heard gunfire ripping through the air. I cringed and cried in fear. Father stopped in midstep and looked up to the sky as if asking God a question.

We heard Mother yelling out for Father. "Where is my Mohammed?"

The house was in total chaos as everyone ran to the back and crowded around Father. I had never in my life seen Mother devastated like this. Sobbing, she knocked everyone away from Father and locked her arms around him and cried. There were no dry eyes, and the sound of weeping surrounded me. Even the stern-faced guard seemed to be crying.

What Father had predicted the previous night had happened. The seventeen army officers who attempted the coup had just been executed.

That night Father refused to greet President Siad Barre at our house for dinner. Barre and his entourage waited for a brief time, then left. I had known something was wrong; earlier, an army tank had burst into our neighbor's house, and soldiers dragged the general from his home as his family watched in horror. I was afraid that the same would happen to Father.

Father immediately decided that my siblings and I had to learn what to do in case Mogadishu was attacked. For one thing, my eight siblings and I were to learn different languages in case we needed to leave the country, and he hired tutors.

The first thing Mother wanted to do was to freeze all the property papers and send Malik and Sakiya overseas with plans to start new businesses. But Sakiya refused to leave the country until her husband returned. I moved into Sakiya's house to help with the new baby boy. Early morning, Sakiya would get up and prepare Mahamuud's tea and bring it to the dining room. She would sit there and stare at the cup for a long moment.

"Do you want to hold the baby?" I asked one morning, as usual.

"Tell me again what he was wearing when you saw him the last time," Sakiya said.

Sakiya didn't listen to the radio, but I had a feeling that she knew in her soul that Mahamuud was dead. Each morning I would sit in the dining room next to her and describe the clothing Mahamuud wore the last time we saw him. I would tell her that his uniform was well pressed, and he carried his son into the hallway and kissed him all over his face. "I'm your father," Mahamuud had said.

"What else?" Sakiya asked.

"That was the last thing he said," I replied.

"What else?" Sakiya asked again.

"He handed me the baby and walked out," I said.

Mother walked in leading Aunt Ubax and the rest of the female relatives. Slowly, Sakiya put her forehead on the table. Her hands lifted, and she started hitting the table over and over again. I did not hear her cry as Mother wrapped her arms around her.

I got up with the baby and went into my bedroom. I shut the door behind me and got in bed with Sakiya's baby. Quietly, I watched his beautiful smile as he forced his tiny finger into my mouth. I couldn't stop the tears, but I felt the need to tell him about what happened. "Your father taught me how to play Ping-Pong."

The baby smiled and grabbed my earring.

I told him about the night he was born. I said, "Your mother screamed like crazy, shouting, 'I dropped my baby!'"

The baby's smile faded as he fell asleep. But just then I heard Sakiya crying so loudly that her son woke up. I realized Mother and Aunt Ubax had confirmed Sakiya's fears and told her finally that her husband was dead. I picked up the baby and rushed to the backyard as he began crying, too.

Gradually, Sakiya realized she needed to get better and take care of her newborn baby.

In the meantime, after the Ogaden War, Khalifa opened a business in Gabon and asked the family to invest. Malik thought we should look into Kuwait and other parts of the Middle East. Amal wanted to move her company's headquarters to Baghdad. But Father said no. She needed to finish college at Benadir University. Sakiya and Malik, with degrees in economics, were the only ones who had graduated from a university so far. Despite Mother's desire to send them overseas, both started working in Mogadishu.

15

arousal transactions

Not long after Khalifa opened her Gabon business, she came for a visit, and Mother threw her a dinner party. Father was away, but everyone had an enjoyable time, even though I could feel the strain of the unstable political situation outside our gates.

After the party I went to my room, but I could not sleep and decided to get some fresh air. I stepped outside and took a deep breath of the cool air, looking up at the sky and thinking of Grandmother.

I noticed a government car parked in the driveway and frowned. Whose car was sitting in our driveway when Father was not at home? I looked for the guard and saw him standing near the gate. I ran up to him.

"Whose car is that?" I demanded. Something did not seem right. "Where is my cousin Khalifa?"

The guard informed me that cousin Khalifa had company, and everyone else was asleep.

I scanned the rooms to see if the lights were on. But all the windows were dark. A chill ran down my spine as I walked toward Mother's bedroom. I tried to open the main door, but it was locked. I rushed to the living room doors, but they were also locked. I couldn't get to my parents' quarters. Then a light flashed in my head, and I decided to check the back room, Mother's *asilo*. This was her own special room, a sanctuary where she entertained her girlfriends.

I stepped to the door and noticed the light was not on. I moved to the window, and just as I was about to peek in, I met the smell of heavy incense rushing through the wooden window. I heard soft moaning coming from inside the room. I couldn't see anything, but then I heard a voice softly saying "Allah!" followed by heavy breathing.

A light broke the darkness, and I came face-to-face with my worst nightmare. Mother had decorated this room with a colorful rug and Indian cushions, just like the ones I saw in the Secret House. In shock, I watched as Khalifa sat next to shirtless General Ali, a friend of my family who had been at the dinner party, and poured a cup of tea while he pulled up his *macawiis*. He picked up the cup of tea, sipped, then sighed. He seemed to be content as he leaned back against the pillow. Ali was a father, husband, and well-respected general who was very close to Father. What's more, Khalifa and Ali's wife were very good friends and often met for lunch.

My own house had become the Secret House. A bundle of qat shrub sat in front of them, and the plaster incense burner with a handle released the frankincense.

"I'm going to take a shower," I heard Khalifa say.

She got up and headed for the bathroom while Ali began chewing the qat. I was confused and horrified; Mother must have known about this union because this was her guest room, her *asilo*. Father was clear about not wanting qat or cigarettes around. The reason Mother didn't allow me or anyone else in this room was because it was her own private sanctuary.

Khalifa, carrying a bar of soap, walked out of the bathroom. "Smell it," she said, handing the soap to Ali.

Ali sniffed it and seemed to be intoxicated by the smell. "It's orange blossom."

She sat beside him and poured a cup of tea. She picked up her cup and sipped, leaning back against the pillows.

"How many houses would you like to build?" Ali asked.

"How many can I build?" she asked, with a smile.

"Start with two," Ali said.

He leaned forward and kissed her neck. She opened the bundle of qat shrub and snapped each leaf with her manicured fingers. She popped them into her mouth and chewed. I could not understand this. Khalifa had grown-up children. She was married to the most fun man, even though he was kind of strange because he liked to share the bathroom and take showers with her. Father was wealthy, too, but didn't act in this strange way. If Khalifa needed to build homes, she could easily afford it with all of her money. Or she could ask for help from Father instead of selling her body.

I had become distrustful and depressed, and this new discovery left me hopeless and wishing to die. Uncle Hussein's habit of showing up looking for Mother at odd hours, after Father left the town or the country, only made me feel worse. One night, I found him in Mother's bedroom chatting with her and saying that he had gotten some qat. They were so involved with each other that they didn't notice me standing by the door. My mind flooded with the images of the Secret House and how Uncle Hussein acted toward the young woman. But what I saw now was Uncle Hussein lifting his long arm and resting it not in the young woman's lap but in my mother's. She picked up a cigarette and put it between his lips, grabbed a lighter, and lit the cigarette for him. He shut his eyes, deeply inhaled, and then blew smoke onto Mother's face. Standing before them, I felt the sob rising in me and my body shaking. I knocked on the door and startled them.

"Uncle, you should leave."

Quickly Mother sat upright on the bed and pulled the bedsheet up, covering her shoulders.

"What's wrong?" Uncle Hussein asked.

"Father is away," I said.

"That's why I'm here. I'm checking in. . . ."

My eyes swelled with tears. Speaking was difficult. Mother fixed her eyes on me as her face filled up with anger. Uncle Hussein got up and walked over to me.

His hand touched my shoulder, making my body cringe painfully, and I sobbed uncontrollably. Uncle Hussein kissed my forehead and walked out of the room without a word. Mother's fiery eyes told me more than I wanted to know about the bond between her and Uncle Hussein. I told Mother it should stop or I would tell Father.

That was the last time I had words with Uncle Hussein. When Asis or Father asked why I was not speaking to him, before I could answer Mother grimaced and turned her unwavering stare on me.

"What did he do?" Father asked.

"Did he touch you?" Asis asked. All eyes turned toward me in disbelief.

"No!" I shouted.

But Asis's expression was hardened and resolute. After this, he told Shams and me we could not ride in Uncle Hussein's car or go to his house unless he was with us.

This was not the first time Asis had become madly protective. And he had good reason to be suspicious. When I was five years old, one of our guards told me that he wanted to show me something. I followed him into the laundry room, and he closed the door behind us. Suddenly frightened, I cried so loudly that he put his hand over my mouth, and I couldn't breathe. His other hand lifted my fluffy blue dress and brought pain inside of me. No one had ever touched me this way, and I found myself chewing on his sweaty hand. I screamed and screamed, until Xaawo hurried in, almost knocking the door down. She grabbed me by the hand and spit on his face.

"You're dead!" Xaawo yelled.

Within hours, the guard was escorted out of the house, while angry Asis shouted, "Shoot him!"

I never found out what happened to him, and I did not want to know.

⁂

The political situation continued to deteriorate, and leaving Mogadishu became imminent. My health had gotten worse as well. I developed more infections and blood clots. My legs were swollen, and for days I could not walk. With difficulty, I completed high school. Soon after, Mother and I left for Bonn, Germany, for my hospitalization.

16

the da vinci hotel

On the way to Bonn, we stopped in Italy. At Rome's airport, we were greeted by the embassy staff, who drove us to the Leonardo da Vinci Hotel. At the hotel, Mother and I situated ourselves in our rooms and called Father to let him know that we had arrived safely. Mother was hungry and wanted us to change and stroll around the neighborhood restaurants. But I didn't feel well and asked Mother if she would go alone. The phone rang, and Mother answered, telling whoever was calling to come up.

Mother went to take a shower, and I took my luggage to the next room. I was so tired that I threw my body on the bed and closed my eyes. I ignored a knock on the door, feeling the aches of my body. The knock persisted, and then I remembered Mother had mentioned she was expecting someone and went to answer.

It was Intisar, a young woman who worked for the government in Mogadishu. She looked weaker than the last time I had seen her.

"Mother is in the shower," I said, watching her carefully. She took off her shoes and lay down on the bed.

"Did you just turn seventeen?" she asked, her hands caressing her plump stomach.

"Yes," I said.

"My advice to you is never become man's towel," she said.

"How do you become man's towel?" I asked.

"They are empty and problematic!" she said, still rubbing her stomach.

I stood there, trying my best to figure out her words. As I was about to question her further, Mother got out of the shower, and Intisar got up from the bed and hugged her.

I walked back to my room and lay down on the bed, thinking about what Intisar had said. In all my years of investigating the Secret House, the Ghost House, other houses, and our own family compound, I heard many things that described men, but nothing about a woman becoming his towel.

Then I remembered Xaawo getting upset every time she heard someone talk about men being allowed to marry up to four wives. I wondered if it had to do with that.

Xaawo would argue that men were downright awful and their heads were fried by chewing too much qat. Most of them had erectile dysfunction and became very angry at women.

"What do you mean?" I had asked one day as we stood outside the gate saying good-bye to Halgaan.

Xaawo ignored me and kept eyeing Halgaan, who was getting into his car and trying to avoid Xaawo's talk. She continued on about men getting big heads and building fences, not to herd their livestock but their wives.

Halgaan fought back, saying that chewing qat actually improved his sexual drive.

Xaawo shook her head in disgust, mumbled something, and then said, "Your seed is useless!"

"Nothing is wrong with my seed!" Halgaan shouted.

"Then why is nothing sprouting?" Xaawo asked.

She grabbed my shoulders, turned my body toward the iron gate, and pushed me toward home. With his face twisted in frustration, Halgaan turned to Xaawo, then hit his hand against the car door. The engine roared, and he drove away, throwing a blanket of hot dust on us.

I knew Intisar was not married, and I wondered about her pregnancy. I didn't have a chance to question her further, but I continued to watch her caressing her stomach.

⚜

When we arrived in Bonn, the people from the Somalian embassy met us at the airport and took us to our hotel, just as the embassy people had done in Italy. The next day I was taken to the hospital and met the doctors who were to find me some relief from pain. The embassy sent a young man, named Hersi, to translate the German for us.

We met in the doctor's office. One of the young doctors said something in German, and suddenly Hersi seemed to blank out, and sweat dripped from his forehead. I knew something was wrong. The doctor placed his hand on Hersi's shoulder and spoke again.

Hersi removed the handkerchief from his pocket and wiped his face.

He turned to Mother and said, "Do you want to talk about what happened that day?"

"Why does he want to know?" Mother asked.

"He wants to know why she's numbing herself with all of the medications."

I was as bewildered as the two doctors as Mother and Hersi continued their conversation above me, their words batted back and forth. I had become invisible. I had allowed this horrific experience to take all the life out of me. And I refused to watch. I got up and walked to the door.

Mother hurried after me. "Where are you going?"

"Is this really my arm that you're holding?" I asked in defiance.

The doctors spoke up, saying that I needed to come back the next day for an X-ray. I had to drink a special liquid later that day, but I was not to eat or drink anything further after midnight.

I turned and left, with Mother trailing after me.

⚜

The next day, Hersi picked up Mother and me at the hotel and took us to the hospital. When we got there, I discovered I had to have a CAT scan. I was nervous about being closed in. They said all I had to do was close my eyes, be still, and breathe normally.

I was given a liquid to drink, and then a young woman took me into a cubicle and handed me a hospital gown to wear. I put on the hospital gown and followed her into a room. A machine with a tiny bed sat in the middle of the room. It looked like a tunnel, and I lay down on it, making myself comfortable. She said something to me, but I didn't understand.

"Do you speak Italian?" I asked. The young woman shook her head, then put one finger on her throat and swallowed. She shook that finger and said, "No." She coughed, then shook the same finger and said, "No." She extended her arms along her side, stiffened her body, and closed her eyes. Then opened her eyes and nodded her head, "Yes."

I lay there on the X-ray table, not knowing whether to laugh or cry. She didn't have to put me through this horrible routine again, since Hersi had translated everything beforehand. He had said close your eyes, lie still, breath normally, and don't swallow or cough. But I knew she was trying to help me.

After the exam I returned to the hotel with Mother. Hersi called and said the radiologist examined my results and would like me to visit a gynecologist. A warm sensation flushed through my body, and my breath came hard.

Mother said, "It will do you good to go out to dinner with my friends."

But panic was taking hold of my heart. "I don't want anyone touching me!" I sobbed.

"I understand—you are here to get better," she said, going through my clothes to pick out an outfit for me to wear.

Suddenly, I felt my heart swishing. It was getting louder, and I grabbed my chest. Mother rushed to the bedside table and brought my pills. She handed them to me and poured a glass of water.

I felt lightheaded as I swallowed them. "No one will touch you. I promise," she said, rubbing my chest.

The phone rang, and Mother answered. It was the ambassador's wife calling to ask if we were coming to dinner. Mother said we had had a long day at the hospital and that we would visit them tomorrow night. The last thing I remembered was Mother ordering room service for us.

17

the overpriced vagina

Hersi picked Mother and me up and drove us back to the hospital to see the gynecologist. A giant blond woman with a thick body welcomed us to her office. She was taller than my mother, and her hands were strong, like the hands of the white-coated man who had mutilated me. Avoiding looking at Hersi and Mother, I focused on the blond woman's pale face. That's when I noticed the light—her eyes were full of light, and her smile brightened the room.

She said my test came back and it indicated an abnormality in my abdomen. She asked if I was having difficulty urinating. I noticed Hersi directing the questions to Mother, as if I could not speak Somali. Mother turned to me, and I nodded my head yes.

"How long since her last period?" Hersi translated the doctor's words.

"It's been six months," Mother said, taking my hand and holding it on her lap.

The doctor glanced at me and stared for a moment. She wrote something on a piece of paper. She picked up the phone and dialed a number. The doctor was on the phone while Hersi explained to Mother, "She wants to examine your daughter."

Looking at her thick hands brought fear, and I had difficulty breathing. I put my hands between my legs and crossed them tightly. Suddenly, I felt a hand over my neck, and the never forgotten smell of blood and rotten flesh overwhelmed me. I was back in Mogadishu, reliving the pain my body endured. I could not go through that again. Everything became blank, and I don't remember what happened.

⁜

Hours later, I woke up. I was lying in a hospital room, and I could hear the doctors speaking. I saw two doctors standing with Mother and a young Somali woman. I realized that I had had another panic attack.

The young translator introduced herself as Fardowsa and said that I would remain in the hospital for the examination. Mother stood quietly and watched.

"I don't want anyone touching me," I said.

"These doctors want to help you." Mother walked over.

"They will look but not touch you," Fardowsa told me.

Drowning out the voices, I closed my eyes and saw myself pouncing healthily around in the snow. I became a galago blessed with night vision and energy, and I found myself chasing the German autobahn sign to escape from the hospital.

⁜

Over the next few days, the doctors discovered that I had a vaginal obstruction, which caused the blockage of my menstrual flow, which in turn cause the fullness of my abdomen. The sealing of my vagina, and the surrounding scar tissue, was the reason I had difficulty urinating.

The doctors wanted to operate on me. They wanted to open the outer lips of my vulva, which had been sewn together the day I was infibulated. But Mother refused the operation, saying that the scar, sealing the vagina, was proof of my virginity. Only when I got married would I be opened. It was not a pretty sight to see Mother and the doctors arguing. Mother's words spilled like water as Fardowsa raced to translate as best as she could.

"Is it better to have your proof or to lose your daughter?" Fardowsa translated the doctor's question.

"Tell these doctors I respect their opinions, but they have to show respect for our way of life," she stated firmly.

With eyes blinking fast, Fardowsa translated Mother's words. I saw heat waves wash over the doctors, turning their faces red.

Mother did agree to the abdominal surgery, and within days a small incision was in made on the side of my belly button. I was shown a glass jar full of the disgusting stuff they removed from my body.

After my recovery, I was sent to behavioral therapy and prescribed another antidepressant. During the session, I refused to allow Mother to join us. I did not want my words to hurt her. I had been feeling angry and confused for so long, but I could not express that in front of her. The young female doctor said her presence would help my healing process.

"No," I insisted.

After completing the hospital tests in Bonn, Mother needed to meet her own doctors in Heidelberg, so I went with her. Some years before, Mother and Aunt Ubax had gone to Mecca for the Festival of Hajj and had a terrible automobile accident. Mother's back was never the same afterward, and as her back got worse, she began having treatments.

In Heidelberg, I had no peace. At the hospital, I watched Mother get into a pool of hot, dark mud and work with the medical team. The doctors stuck a thick, ugly needle into her back to drain accumulated liquid. She felt better for a while but then suddenly was struck with crippling pain.

After her treatment, Mother began to talk about my cousin Yusuf. Yusuf's father, Khalifa's mother, and my mother were siblings. Khalifa, though, had helped in raising Yusuf, providing him with opportunities in Europe.

She told me how much he wanted to help me find the best college in Geneva, where he lived.

"But, Mother, I was five years old when I last saw cousin Yusuf!" I replied, then said emphatically, "I want to go to Rome for college."

"We think Geneva is better," Mother said.

Mother and I toured the beautiful city of Heidelberg. My favorite place was the castle; it took hours to walk through the grounds. She continued to mention Yusuf and Geneva, but I would not let that spoil my fascination with the historic landmark.

We had been in Bonn for months, and in Heidelberg for three weeks, and Mother needed to stay in Germany. I acquiesced to her wishes and headed to Geneva to look at colleges. The arrangements had already been made for me to stay with cousin Yusuf.

PART TWO

an imprisoned wife
1979–1984

My womanhood is robbed
I have become a woman . . .
My future
—Hilda Twongyeirwe, "Threshold"

18

the limping one

I would not be able to recognize Yusuf, so Mother had given me his photograph, which I stuck into my passport, then forgot all about. When I landed in Geneva, I went directly to the immigration booth. My passport was quickly stamped and handed back to me.

Yusuf's picture fell from the passport, and I looked at his sharp suit, short mustache, and dark curly hair. I picked up my suitcase and walked on, looking around the crowd. I didn't see any Somali faces.

I set my luggage on the floor to wait. In case he didn't show up, I had the embassy phone number, and so I was not worried. A few minutes later I noticed a young Somali man dressed elegantly in a dark blue suit. I looked at the picture, then up at the handsome man walking through the crowd. It was Yusuf.

I picked up my luggage and walked to him. Our eyes met, and he flashed a big smile as he limped over to me. He carried flowers.

"I'm Yusuf—welcome to Geneva!" he said with excitement.

I stared at his feet trying to figure out why he was limping.

"No one told you that I had a deformed foot?"

I shook my head no, and I felt the knot in my stomach.

He handed me the flowers. "These are for you."

"What am I going to do with them?"

He shrugged. "Put them in a vase."

Yusuf picked up my luggage and led me out of the terminal as he told me the story about his Saudi clients, for whom he booked entertainment. His work seemed shady to me.

Yusuf and I got to his elegant, expensive house. Bookshelves surrounded the entrance.

"I need to call Mother and let her know that I'm OK," I said.

He put down the luggage, led me into the living room, picked up the phone, and dialed a number. He said something in German, then hung up.

"I left a message with the concierge," he said.

A young woman, wearing a French maid uniform, walked in. Her face was pale, she wore red lipstick, and her dark hair was tied back. The woman spoke in French, saying her name was Ana, as she picked up the luggage and signaled me to follow.

I told Ana that speaking Italian would be better but promised to learn French.

"The music blares loudly at night," Yusuf said as I turned to follow Ana.

A gut feeling of fear took root inside of me. I nodded my head at his statement and followed Ana to my bedroom. It was painted yellow, white curtains covered the windows, and dark wood furniture filled the room. A mirror hung on the wall, and a prayer rug was spread next to the fireplace. A picture of Mecca hung above the fireplace, and an angel painting hung above the bed. The bathroom door was open.

Ana walked out, shutting the door behind her. Suddenly, the angel painting fell off the wall and crashed to the floor. I got cold chills all over my body.

There was another door in the room, and I tried the doorknob. It was locked. I peeked through the keyhole and saw nothing. I walked over and sat on the bed, feeling uneasy. I was nervous and scared to be alone with a man, even a close relative. I stood up, then went to the door, opened it, and peeked into the hall, then realized there was no lock on it. I rushed to the bathroom. There was no lock on the bathroom door either.

Later that night, I jumped awake, hearing the blaring music. I turned on the light and looked at my watch. It was 11:00 PM.

I stepped out of my room and into the dimly lit hallway. I noticed light coming from under a door, and I crept up and put my ear to it. I heard voices, so I opened the door and saw two blond men and Yusuf stuffing something into briefcases, but they didn't see me.

Just then the phone in the room rang, startling them. Yusuf looked at his watch and let it ring another time. He grabbed it and listened, then wrote something on a piece of paper and handed it to one of the men.

Slowly, I backed away and hurried to my room. I lay in bed, thinking, unable to quell my curiosity.

I got up again and walked out of the room. I met Yusuf coming down the hallway. "What's wrong?" he asked.

"I can't handle loud noises," I said.

"This is not noise—you will get used to it," he said. His demeanor made me very skeptical. "I'll turn it down."

I nodded my head and walked back to my room, questions whirling in my mind.

19

the twisted tongue

Early the next morning, Yusuf took me out for breakfast and a little sightseeing. We stopped at different colleges and met the administrators. I called Mother when we got back, and I told her about feeling a little uneasy.

"Mother, I don't feel right for some reason. I'm not comfortable here with Yusuf. He wants to hold on to my passport and money," I said.

"Give them to him," Mother said.

"I'm not going anywhere with him!" I yelled.

"At the moment, he's all you have."

Fainthearted, I hung up. Once again, my life was changing in an instant. I picked up the phone and dialed the embassy number, hoping to talk with the ambassador's wife. A man answered, and when he heard my name, he put me on hold.

He came back on the line. "Shukri's family is in town. I believe you know her? We would like you to come to dinner at the ambassador's house. We will arrange for a car to pick you up."

I agreed readily. Shukri's father was a former ambassador to different countries and would ride his horse around the neighborhood and stop at our house. He dressed like an Englishman going on safari and was the most handsome man I had ever seen.

He usually came to our gate, sitting on his well-groomed horse, and chatted. Watching him, I always would be reminded of the night I met Haile Selassie, the emperor of Ethiopia until 1974.

As I got ready for the dinner, my mind went back to happier times and that wonderful night. At school, Amal, Malik, and I were among those chosen to be in a play at the National Theatre for visiting African heads of state. After the show, an officer came backstage and took me to a room where I saw Father standing with a skinny man in a uniform. His hat was too big for his face and hid his eyes. Father moved me closer to him, and I looked up and saw his deep, penetrating dark eyes. I stared at him for a moment. He smiled and pinched my cheek. He extended his hand, and I took it.

"I'm happy to meet you," Haile Selassie said. He took my hand and walked me through the door where a crowd gathered. I looked back to find Father, who was right behind me. Excitement rippled through the group, and I saw nothing but smiles. When we got back home, Father told me about Haile Selassie. After that, whenever a new building was to be opened by the president, I would be in attendance, carrying a tray with the flowers and scissors for the president to cut the ribbon.

I took one last look in the mirror, bringing myself back to the present. I prayed Yusuf would not come back until I left. I wrote him a quick note telling him where I was going. Sure enough, the embassy car arrived, and I left for dinner. At the door, Shukri greeted me, and I heard loud Somali conversation, the first since leaving Mogadishu four months ago. Suddenly, I felt alive with nothing to worry about. I walked into the living room and met the whole family. It was like being back at our home, with so many relatives and workers.

I even forgot my frustration with Mother and my uneasiness about Yusuf. During dinner, I was told that Lausanne had great colleges, but Shukri said Leysin was better and she would be moving there. It was up the mountain and too cold, her brother insisted. We went on, talking and laughing, planning our futures. How wonderful to be among friends again!

╬

When the embassy car dropped me off at Yusuf's, I walked in quietly and found him broiling in anger. He lifted up my note and glared at me.

"Nothing goes on around here without my permission." His voice trembled with his effort not to lose control completely.

"I'm sorry," I said. A rising fear immediately pushed away my happy, hopeful mood.

Yusuf walked away without saying a word. I picked up the phone to call Mother, then I remembered she was on her way to Frankfurt.

I put down the phone and went to find Yusuf. A bit of the high spirits of the evening came back to me, and I decided to try to make the best of things.

I found him in the living room watching a sports show on TV. It was a sport I had never seen before. I sat down and looked at the television. Big men with helmets, big shoulders, and tight pants ran up and down the field after an oddly shaped ball and pulled each other down. Under their eyes, some had what looked like black shoe polish. It could be kohl.

The game was violent and very hard to watch. The ball passed through the legs of one man, and another man took it and ran like a cheetah while players created a barrier and threw others to the ground painfully.

Yusuf turned and saw my face twisting in pain.

"What kind of game is it?" I asked, hoping to restore the peace.

"It's American football . . . ," Yusuf went on, saying that each team was trying to get the ball into the opposing team's end zone. His body moved with the players as he explained the game to me.

"Is that kohl or shoe polish under their eyes?" I asked.

Yusuf stared at me for a long moment.

I felt my discomfort rising again and tried to explain. "Mother uses kohl to darken her eyelids. . . ."

"Are you also wondering about their tight-fitting pants?" he asked.

I turned to the television.

"Think about that ball hitting them right between their legs!" Yusuf talked about the pads or cups that protect the players' sex organs and how they make them look bigger down there. "Look at that one!" he shouted, as the whole audience jumped up, watching the man fleeing with the ball.

I walked away and decided to never look for Yusuf when that game was on again.

⊹

Mother left Frankfurt and was coming to stay with us for two weeks.

At the terminal, Yusuf and I met Mother. She and I walked to the car while Yusuf dragged the luggage out.

She looked at me, her eyes holding mine firmly. "Yusuf is the one who will guide your life," she stated emphatically.

"Mother, I'm not comfortable living with him. I am not going to trust that someone who does not know me can guide my life."

During the drive from the airport to Yusuf's house, I made sure Mother understood that I was going to college and wanted to move to Leysin.

"Mother, I saw Shukri, and we had so much fun talking. I want to go to her college in Leysin."

Yusuf was in the car, listening quietly.

"Yusuf has a better plan for you. You do not need to worry." Mother patted my leg.

I did not respond. I stared out the window at the streetcars passing by.

⊹

Within a week, Mother had planned a huge dinner party. In the kitchen, I watched as Mother prepared the dough to make the *sambuus*, telling Ana she wasn't fast enough to chop the vegetables. Ana could not understand Mother's language but observed as Mother demonstrated. I walked away to get ready for the party.

When I returned to join Mother, Yusuf, and the guests for dinner, I was wearing a short burgundy dress, black boots, and my hair loose at the back. Horrified, Mother rushed toward me.

"Get back in your room and change into the red silk *dirac* and matching scarf I gave to you!" she shouted, her eyes flashing with anger and distress. But as she continued to argue with me, her attention turned to Ana, walking out of the kitchen carrying a silver plate filled with yellow rice mixed with meat, raisins, onions, and other vegetables.

Seeing Mother's face twist in frustration, distracted because Ana hadn't followed her instructions for properly presenting the food, I stepped away, watching the tall men with elongated heads standing around Yusuf. None of them looked familiar. Like Yusuf, these men had soft curly hair and wore suits and shining shoes. Well-groomed women wearing colorful *diracs* sat in the living room away from the men. The intoxicating scent of their Somali rose oil wafted throughout the house.

As I moved toward the living room, one of the women rushed over to me. "Congratulations," she exclaimed. "May you have a long life and many sons!"

It was as if I had been hit by the falling sky. "What are you talking about?" My voice was quavering. Shocked, I looked at the other women, my eyes desperately searching each face for information.

Was this a wedding dinner party, *my* wedding party? But there was no loud ululating chant, no traditional drums, no prayers from the White Turban Man, and no *buraanbur*, the wedding dance in which women form a circle and choose someone to dance in the middle. If this were my wedding, Mother would have washed my body with water full of sweet scents and herbs. She would have put fresh henna on my feet and hands and combed olive oil through my hair. Mother had not removed the furniture to make room for the Persian rugs and patterned cushions, where the guests would squat on the floor and eat the delicious food with their fingers. No, the dining room table was set with silver forks, white plates, and crystal glasses.

"What is happening?" I shouted in fear.

Mother rushed into the living room, pulling me to the side. Her face was close to mine as she spoke in a harsh whisper, "The *nikaah*, the wedding contract, has been made, and the other formalities have taken place back at home." I could see she was trying to control her voice. "This is your party to honor your marriage to Yusuf, who will provide for you for the rest of your life." She said that Father agreed to shake Yusuf's father's hand and give me to Yusuf in marriage.

Stunned, I stared into Mother's eyes. Once again, she had shaped my destiny without my knowledge, and the familiar sense of childhood betrayal rose within me, tingling nerves tightening my muscles. Something horrible had been decided for me, and my only choice was to follow my parents' wishes. After all, as children, we learned the parents' responsibility was to look after their children's welfare. The parents' words had the power of swords, and death was better than disobeying them.

Traditionally, marriages were arranged to strengthen family ties. It was common to see marriages to a cousin from the mother's side, but no one in my family had ever practiced this system of clanship. Tonight, nothing appeared like the wedding my parents had thrown for Sakiya and Mahamuud, the wedding that showed off Mother's style and extravagance. Those tall men with elongated heads were not singing the *dikrisalaan* to Yusuf to praise the Prophet, Muhammad.

One thing was certain: Mother expected me to remain calm so this marriage would succeed for the family's sake. She envisioned that Yusuf and I would remain in the house for the traditional seven days to prove that my sealed vagina was worthy of the mutilating pain. It would prove the family honor, the one I was carrying between my legs, my virginity.

With the blessings of my family, and without my knowledge or agreement, I had become Yusuf's private property, an object for his pleasure. At the end of the seven days, Mother would organize *shaashsaar*, inviting only the married women. They would gather around and prepare me for the role of motherhood. Each woman would get up and place a scarf over my head and give me a gift such as jewelry. As the bride, I would change outfits until the *shaashsaar* was ended. Would Mother have the courage to tell me how much *sooryo*, or bride price, she and Father had received from Yusuf in order to buy me as a wife?

I looked across the room at Yusuf, and I felt the numbness of my vulva. Marriage reminded me of that horrible day, the day I felt the thick, rough fingers running all around my genitals as Mother watched while the white-coated man sealed it for Yusuf to break through to prove my virginity. I had been sealed since the day of my mutilation for my wedding night, for Yusuf. In my mind's eye, I saw myself at age nine, fixing my gaze on the bride to see the smoke rising from her ears while the groom lay on top.

Would Mother be watching tonight when Yusuf lay on top of me and I twisted my face in pain like that bride on her wedding night? Would she watch when my right arm shook with fear as it tightly grabbed the white silk sheets? Would Mother cry when she witnessed my pain?

I had become an orphan, a child abandoned by her family.

I stormed to my room sobbing and began packing my luggage, pausing to rest each time my body writhed in pain. It was better to run into the streets of Geneva than become Yusuf's wife. Mother burst into the room and wrapped her arms around me. I struggled to push her away, but she wouldn't let go.

"Most of your classmates are married while going to college," Mother said.

"You're throwing me away!" My body burned with anger as I choked on my tears.

Mother did what she was good at, bringing me pills to numb me. "You'll come to love him," Mother said as she handed me the pills.

I realized this had all been planned for a very long time, the purpose of the trip to Geneva willfully kept from me. I would later learn that I was promised to him when I was five years old.

"Yusuf is family," Mother said, taking on a soothing tone. "He will take good care of you. . . . You know you must think of your family. Where would you run to? You cannot sleep in the streets. . . ."

As I swallowed the pills, she continued explaining how and why I had to obey their wishes and what my fate would be if I didn't. Her voice became a distant hum.

That night, I awoke with Yusuf hovering over me, touching my body, which turned to ice beneath his hand. He reached up to my face. In horror, I lay still and stared at him.

"Your body moves with my touch, and I'm sitting in here." His finger pressed into my forehead as he spoke. "You are under my control."

He stood above me and stared for a moment. Then he walked out.

I jumped out of bed and barricaded my door, turning my bedroom into a war camp. Mother knocked on the door and said, "You must come—Father is on the phone and needs to speak with you!"

I remained silent.

"No one escapes destiny," Mother said, persisting with her knocking.

As I stood in the middle of my bedroom, staring at the door blocked by the furniture I had pushed in front of it, all I could see was the image of the white-coated man standing between my legs asking Mother, *Would you like to look at it?*

And Mother's response: *Perfect.*

Remembering the tray full of my sacrificed flesh, I now understood my destiny. I had become Yusuf's wife; I was a branded lamb, and my scar was my worth.

20

the smoke screen

Yusuf stopped harassing me for a few nights. It was so quiet that I could sleep without clinging to the bedsheets. Before closing my eyes, I looked over at the chair blocking the door. It didn't do much good because with one kick the door would slam open. But at least I was fighting and trying to protect myself.

Feeling the cool air rush through the open window, I put my head on the soft pillow and closed my eyes. Ever since Mother arrived, there had been none of the noise and blasting Spanish folk music. Also gone were the two yellow-haired Swiss men with alert eyes and pursed lips who had been stuffing packets of what looked like sugar into briefcases. Yusuf had also removed all the expensive alcohol bottles from the kitchen and his bedroom.

Walking into the living room alone, the only time I was able to let down my guard, I saw how Islamic scrolls and photos of Mecca had taken over the walls. I sometimes glimpsed Ana staring at them as she dusted the furniture. At dawn, I would be awakened by a roaring voice shouting for prayer—"*Allahu akhbar!*"—and the sweet smell of incense burning, just as in our house back in Mogadishu. Slowly, the voices in my head stopped, and I could sleep.

⁂

One night, I woke to find something softly caressing my face. As I opened my eyes, Yusuf put his hand over my mouth. He lay beside me, and I felt frozen. My teeth began to chatter uncontrollably. His hand squeezed my chin and pushed upward, as if to stop the chattering. I bit my tongue and tasted my blood.

Horrified, I felt as if my teeth were crashing inside my mouth, sliding one by one to the back of my throat. In my head, I heard the sound of my body hurtling into the darkened world once more. I had never felt a man's body against mine, and Yusuf's strong hand touched places I refused to acknowledge existed. His touch was no longer soft.

"I'm not here to hurt you," he whispered.

As I looked at his eyes, I again saw the image of the white-coated man and felt the prick of the sharp needle, the hands plucking my lips like a giraffe feasting on thorny branches. I heard the sound of the scissors cutting through my flesh. Yusuf's wild eyes searched mine. He shifted his body on top of mine, and, in a flash, I saw myself at age nine, but now standing before me, with eyes focused on my ears looking for any sign of smoke rising up. His hands traveled over my body.

I kicked him wildly and screamed, "Stop!"

His hand clasped over my mouth, but I kicked and kicked, trying to free myself.

Yusuf pinched hard on my cheeks. "Never use that word again!"

I remembered the water glass placed on the nightstand with my pills. I held my body still as he touched me everywhere, but my right hand snaked around the bed, trying to reach the glass. I couldn't find it. I screamed again, hoping Mother would hear and rush to my rescue. She didn't. My body was numb, but my mind raced like an engine, struggling to produce the power I needed. I had to reach the glass before Yusuf forced open my legs and the smoke rose from my ears.

In one sudden movement, I pushed my hand toward the nightstand, grabbed the glass, and, with all my strength, hit Yusuf. Blood spurted from his forehead and ran into his eye. Frantic, he jumped off the bed and screamed.

With his hand covering his wound and one eye shut, Yusuf began shouting. I was sure this time that Mother would run into the room and rescue me. Again, she didn't. His voice echoed as he vanished from sight.

But I now fully understood why Mother would not break down that door. I had been sold; I was Yusuf's property. Questioning what he paid for my worth was not even necessary at this point. What was important to me was to let Mother know that I would not be the only one living in hell. I stomped out of my room, my feet hitting the floor in anger as boiling waves rolled through my stomach. Storming into the guest bedroom, I found Mother sitting on her prayer rug, staring at the Islamic scroll.

"Didn't you hear my cry for help?" I shouted. My voice shook, and I breathed deeply, trying to regain control.

Mother continued to ignore me and stared at the scroll.

Pain and confusion took hold of me. I told Mother the bite marks on my tongue were my proof that it was he who sparked the trouble. Mother bent her head down and refused to look at me.

With bowed head, Mother told me about my aunt—her sister—dying in childbirth and, according to tradition, Mother being forced at age fourteen to marry her brother-in-law, her sister's husband who was much older than she. Growing up, I had heard whispers about Mother's past and that she had given birth to sister Sakiya at age fifteen. Her second pregnancy, with Asra, gave her the strength and courage to run away from her older husband. After she was divorced, she met Father, and they were married.

No one ever talked about her history or how Mother married Father. I knew something painful had happened to Mother but could never bring myself to ask about it.

"Mortified, I would sit in bed and watch this grown man approaching," she said. "I couldn't close my eyes because, if I did, I would see the image of my sister lying in a pool of blood."

Mother lifted her head and again stared at the scroll on the wall. She turned and stared at me as my eyes locked with hers, and I could see the writhing pain in her eyes. Wordless, she fled from the room.

I found out the next day that Mother had taken the first flight home. Like a door shutting, my heart closed with a jolt. I stared at the meds on the nightstand. I opened a bottle and began swallowing pills, one after another, begging Grandmother and the Angel of Death to take me to her.

Please, Grandmother, please, let me come to you. I want to sit with you on the moon, not to face God's big head but to put my head on your feet. Angel of Death, come and take me to Grandmother. . . .

When I awoke, the hospital's white walls surrounded me, and Yusuf's dark, curly hair fell on my face. Yusuf had become my eternal ghost, like the soul of a dead person who would not rest. My signature word—*why*—disappeared, along with my fire inside.

I listened to him mumble words that pained my ears: "Do you know how many blonds would jump at the chance to marry me?" I simply listened as he threatened to travel to Mogadishu and bring back three women who would feel blessed to be married to him.

Watching Yusuf, I saw dark and angry clouds circling above me. From now on, I would be walking in foreign lands without a destination. I saw Yusuf's face fading away as I felt my body enter a shallow trancelike state.

After leaving the hospital, it didn't take long before Spanish folk songs once again blasted through the walls as Yusuf jumped into my bed. On one particular night, the fire inside the soul I had lost was ignited. Yusuf's body pinned me to the bed, and my right hand clung to the bedpost as I writhed in pain. Yusuf tried to force himself into me like a large screw penetrating a wall. This was no ordinary wall. It consisted of branding scars and bleeding wounds—the vivid images of the lamb tied to our cotton tree. To show his manhood, Yusuf pushed his *belino* into the chastity belt made of my flesh. This was the price of my self-worth, which he now owned. But pushing the large screw into me, he met nothing but pain. Now *he* screamed, feeling the pain of his skin being removed from his *belino* by his forceful attempts at penetration. He would need fourteen days of pushing if he wanted to have any success in breaking my wall.

I finally understood what it meant to have smoke passing through my ears. The pain was unimaginable. My whole being was crawling six feet under. I would put an end to this misery and be very happy to leave this darkened world.

I lost any ability to think or make choices. Every time I picked up the phone, I found myself crying like a madwoman. A dark cloud was draining my spirit; I was a defeated soldier without a map, holding an empty gun without any bullets. When I dialed home, I struggled to speak coherently, all wise words slipping away.

"*Pronto*—Mother, please, please help me!"

I heard Mother roar at the end of the other line. "Stop fighting and listen to him! It is your fault," she shouted, "for this emotional tailspin!"

21

the quelling *pene*

Yusuf and I were on our honeymoon, but I felt as heavy as the luggage we were dragging from one European port to the next. Our extensive honeymoon voyage had been his idea. I was just grateful that our touring kept us busy, and he mostly kept his hands to himself.

On our way back to Geneva, we stopped in the beautiful town of Grenoble. We decided to eat in a restaurant in the Notre Dame district, and during our meal, Yusuf talked about his last trip to this town. He told me about meeting a beautiful, lean blond woman. He said he was fascinated by her hands.

"They looked like the hands of a fine violinist," he said. "I told her how magnificent she was and asked if I could escort her to my hotel room, and she agreed." At the hotel, after a few drinks, Yusuf couldn't help but want to tear off the woman's clothes.

Was this what new couples talked about on their honeymoon? I flashed to the image of Fadwa and me giggling under the bed of the bride and groom many years before. Now Yusuf's intense eyes were fixed on his hand as it moved slowly over the wineglass. He picked up the glass, drank the wine, then continued with the story.

As his hands gently stroked the blond woman's body, they touched something firm. When his eyes saw what it was he was touching, he leaped out of bed.

"I felt like a nomad without his walking stick," he said.

"What happened?" I asked.

"The words cannot pass through my lips," Yusuf said.

"Was she bleeding with her period?" I asked this because Somali men don't touch women during menstruation.

"I saw the *pene*—the penis!" Yusuf said.

"You mean she had three legs?"

Annoyed with my questions, Yusuf waved to the young waiter and ordered another red wine.

"It was a man, wearing a woman's clothes!" he said.

Stunned, I stared at him. This was the strangest thing I had ever heard. I opened my mouth to say something, but Yusuf stopped me.

"Nothing happened!" Yusuf said emphatically. His hands were now up in my face as he gestured wildly.

"Did she tell you how she got a penis?" I truly did not understand, and Yusuf was getting increasingly agitated.

"He was *pede!*"

"What is that?"

"*Omosessuale*—a homosexual!"

"*Omosessuale?*"

Quickly, Yusuf drank the wine and stared back at me.

"He—she thought you were one, too?"

He asked if I understood the meaning of the word, and I told him I didn't know what they did, but I had heard about men slapping each other on the butt. I felt terribly naive. I told him about the night I saw two young men who appeared to be kissing sitting in a car.

Yusuf's hand hit the table hard, making his fork fly down to the ground. His eyes looked at me in anger. "Liar! That would never happen!"

"It happened to you!"

"I was kissing a woman!"

"Yes, but she had three legs—"

"Stop!"

I continued with my story, telling Yusuf that, when I approached the car, I saw the men's heads separate, and they quickly began eating.

"Where did you see this?"

"On my way back from Jasira Beach. The restaurants there serve people in their cars."

"Did others see the men locking lips? In Mogadishu that's a death wish."

"I stood by the window and—"

"Were they Arabs?"

I told him they were Somalis.

"What a lie!" he exploded.

I had no idea why he was so angry about homosexuals, and since I understood so very little, I kept my mouth shut. On our honeymoon, I saw how powerless I was out in the world as well as at home. He held my passport. He controlled the medicines I needed for my abdominal pain. Living under his autocratic rule, I feared my plan to enroll in college would never come to fruition. After a long silence, the waiter returned to our table, and Yusuf paid the bill.

He decided we would stop at a friend's house nearby. When we got there, many people were gathered around a long wooden table covered with bottles of wine, strong-smelling cheeses, and colorful dishes. The man next to me poured Yusuf a glass of wine. He smiled at me, then stuffed food into his mouth, chewing like a camel eating a thorny twig. I could see the veins on his face and his large, purple nose.

Laughter rang all around as one of the women talked about her dog kicking her boyfriend out of their bed and taking his place. Yusuf laughed like a madman, and I realized they were all drunk. To prove it, the woman's boyfriend jumped up and lifted me out of the chair like a rag doll. I shrieked as my hands grabbed his skinny shoulders. Like a helpless child, I found myself sitting on his neck, stomach against his head, feet dangling on his chest. His hands were under my armpits. As he ran around the table, I heard loud cheers and clapping.

"You're the queen of Sheba!" he shouted in Italian.

A scream was burning in my throat, but I just begged him to put me down.

"My wife eats nothing but grass." Yusuf laughed.

"She's a goat then, not the queen of Sheba!" the purple-nosed man yelled out.

After we had been there a while, I came to enjoy these peculiar people and their delirious ways. Maybe because of the shouting and everyone talking at the same time, I was reminded of home, when Aunt Ubax and Mother would compete to tell strange stories about the nomads.

It was getting late, and Yusuf told me it was time to go back to the hotel. As we headed for the door, I asked the man how he got the purple nose. Hands hit the wooden table as loud laughter erupted. Bodies dropped off the chairs and rolled around the floor, like mindless children having tantrums.

Not knowing whether to laugh or cry, I watched as the purple-nosed man held a bottle of wine up to his mouth. He drank the whole thing, then dropped the empty bottle on the table and said, "I'm a drinker from Viareggio, Italy. That's why I have the purple nose!"

22

incapacitated state

Yusuf and I returned to Geneva after our trip, which marked the last time I would have a belly laugh. Things began to deteriorate further soon after we arrived home. Yusuf locked my medications in a cabinet and said to me and anyone who would listen that I'd lost my mind. He gave the key to Ana and told her to monitor my meds.

This drove my anxiety and fear beyond my previous panic attacks. When I got an unbearable cramp, the earth opened; I wanted to jump into the abyss and die. If I didn't get my meds in time, the air rushed out of my lungs, and I would shake, then faint.

I didn't know enough French or have enough time to explain to Ana that she needed to drop the vacuum cleaner and get my medications immediately. I now was her prisoner as well as Yusuf's. The situation was intolerable and risky. My cramp came on full blast, and in frustration, panic, and fear, I slapped her hard and screamed wildly. She fled from the house.

I ran to the kitchen and knocked everything from the shining table, looking for the cabinet key. Yusuf walked into the minefield and to try to get me under control pulled me by the hair, like a hungry camel grabbing higlo leaves. Screaming like a lunatic, I threw anything within reach and made Yusuf run for his life. I heard him shout, "This is madness!"

I don't know how many hours I lay on the cold tile, but I awoke with Yusuf hovering over me.

"The cabinet is open," he said.

It was strange because I didn't feel any pain in my abdomen, but I had the urge to vomit. He rose to a standing position, dropped all my meds on the floor, and walked out of the kitchen.

⚜

The next morning, Yusuf walked into my room and handed me a jewelry box.

"It's your Mother's gift to you," he said.

I opened the box and found a gold necklace, earrings, and a ring with a ruby stone. I didn't feel happy or sad; I did not feel anything.

Yusuf handed me another box and said, "I hope you like it."

I opened the box and found more gold jewelry than one person could wear.

"Is this my *meher*?" I asked. *Meher* is the compensation a groom gives to a bride. It's symbolic and is supposed to be the bride's security.

"You'll come to love me," he said.

Yusuf told me that I had to wear the gold wedding ring, just like his, if I wanted to go to school. I agreed and put it on, and I could see the muscles in his face relax. He also said that before I enrolled in the private school to learn French, I had to visit a doctor to open my scar.

"No," I said.

"No?"

I told him about the German doctors who wanted to do the same thing to try to relieve my pain. Mother would rather see me suffer than open up my costly scar.

"Leave my scar alone!" I snapped.

Yusuf looked at me for a long moment, then left the room, shutting the door behind him. My knees trembled and my muscles tightened as the fire rushed though me. Like a flame, I could feel my spirit fighting to enter my body.

Just for this time, Yusuf did not touch me or force me to go to the doctor.

23

the kohl eyes one

In 1980, soon after our honeymoon, I started taking French classes. It was snowing the first day when Yusuf and I arrived at the private school I would attend. The school building was nothing like the beautiful old structures that we saw in Geneva. This was a simple gray-colored structure with odd burgundy windows.

As I got out of the car and followed Yusuf inside, he whispered, "Don't be rude."

With a smile, a woman extended her hand to greet me. "*Beinvenu à Geneve!*" she said.

Instead of shaking hands, I folded my hands over my chest and bowed. She did the same. She turned to Yusuf, talked for a moment, and then led us out of the office, toward the classrooms.

"Are you planning to sit in the class *with* me?" I asked him.

"No need. I'm all you've got," Yusuf said as we stopped in front of the classroom door.

The woman knocked, then opened the door into a classroom where a teacher was writing on the board and seven women sat in rows. Some wore a *hijab*. The teacher signaled me to a seat.

"*Je suis Madame Bedelia, et toi?*" she asked.

"Madame Soraya," I said.

Laughter erupted, probably because of my accent. I felt a great urge to look back, and when I did, I met black sparkling eyes staring at me. A young woman, wearing a dark *hijab* and probably around my age, sat alone at the back of the room, unblinking. As I caught her eye, she got up and sat in the chair next to mine. She seemed familiar, like those Somali Arabs running around the old port, watching as the camels were being shipped overseas. I didn't smile at her but turned and focused on the closed door in the classroom.

The young woman leaned over and whispered in Arabic, "The price is too high."

"What?" I asked.

"There is a reason that the door is closed."

"Are we in prison?"

"Eyes are watching us."

I turned my attention to the teacher and realized that I shouldn't be speaking any language other than French. I was determined to learn French so that I could have a tiny bit of freedom.

During the break, the young woman introduced herself as Sahir from Lebanon. I needed to practice my French, but I found Sahir to be a firecracker and wanted to hear her wisdom.

She called women "private properties" and said that in our culture women belonged either in the house or in a grave. This was a saying, meaning the house belongs to the man, and when he takes a wife, she belongs in the house as his property. If a woman is not married, the shame is so great that death is better, and therefore she belongs in the grave. When I asked her why she said such things, she said because God didn't have a mother, he did not know what to do with women. I told her that I trusted men more than women because at least I knew when they were going to attack me.

"That's the stupidest thing I ever heard!"

I told Sahir that I called men "matadors" after seeing the tape of a bullfight once. I said that my husband, Yusuf, was a matador and that at night my room became the "Plaza del Toros." Like a matador aiming at a bull, Yusuf would aim at me. My history followed me into the bedroom, and everybody was watching me. Like a bull, I would not back down. Yusuf's long white robe would cross the foot of the bed like a matador's cape. He would stand still, glare at his folded hands rising up to his face, then pray. At that moment, I would lift the bedsheets up to my neck and prepare for the imminent fight. It wouldn't take long to see the killing sword rising up through his white robe. Soon he was trying to penetrate me, and I was screaming like a wounded bull. He knew I was still stitched closed. Why did he do this to me?

"He's a ponce, stripping your dignity!" Sahir exclaimed.

"Ponce?" I asked.

"He's a pimp!"

Sahir and I became friends and, during the break, would meet in the school bathroom. She would check every stall before she gave me instructions on how to abuse Yusuf back. I would listen, then shout "No!" because some of the instructions seemed foreign and I didn't understand them.

"If he's raping you, what makes you think he won't do that to your daughter?"

"Rape?"

I had heard stories about men fighting with their brides on their wedding night, but no one ever said anything about rape. Sahir told me that if the wife said no and the husband continued, that was forceful penetration. That act made him a rapist, not a husband.

This understanding left me in a cold sweat; it was as if a hand was squeezing my heart. I dropped to the ground and cried. Instead of rushing to my side and being kind, Sahir turned to the mirror, took off her *hijab*, and admired herself. Without looking back at me, she said I had two choices. I could either burn Yusuf with boiling water seasoned with salt and pepper or put a knife between my legs.

I could only stare at her as she quickly put the *hijab* back on and, with those stunning dark eyes, glared right back at me.

I was starting to wish I had never met her, but she was my only friend and confidante. The knife idea pained me. It reminded me of the man with the white coat, and as always when I thought of him I heard the sound of the scissors cutting my flesh.

But I could never burn Yusuf with the seasoned boiling water because it reminded me of a young girl back in Mogadishu who slipped into the hot ghee and burned to death.

I took a deep breath, then said decisively, "I will try the knife."

"OK, then. . . ."

I was already out of the bathroom before Sahir finished her sentence. I was thinking about Aunt Ubax's story about Caraweelo, who loved to emasculate men. In my defense, I decided that putting a knife between my legs was better than letting Yusuf try to pierce my scar.

✢

That night I placed a knife between my legs, covered myself with the sheets, and lay flat in bed.

Yusuf strolled in, dressed in his white robe, and stood rigidly in front of me. He forgot to fold his hands in prayer, and the killing sword didn't rise up between his legs. Slowly, he got into bed and lay next to me.

"I'm not here to hurt you," he said.

I looked up at the ceiling, thinking about how awful the yellow paint was. Then I noticed the long-haired angel staring at me from above the bed. I would have bet she was one of those spectators at the Plaza del Toros, cheering Yusuf on. I felt a hand gently untie my hair, and Yusuf's fingers run through it.

"Can I look at it?" Yusuf said.

I slapped him. I completely forgot about the knife, and it fell from its perfect position between my legs. Yusuf's body slowly moved up and fell on top of me, his face above mine. I could smell the alcohol on his breath, and it was unbearable.

"Please, don't rape me," I begged.

"You're my wife!" Yusuf shouted.

His hand landed on my throat as his tongue danced around my face. I shut my mouth tight and struggled to reach for the water glass sitting by the nightstand. Yusuf forced his tongue into my mouth. I pushed my teeth forward and closed my lips tightly, making it impossible for his tongue to sneak in again. I felt his legs become as stiff as iron as they spread mine apart and prepared me for another piercing episode. Like a horned beast, I roared with madness and, just as I had two months ago, grabbed the water glass from the nightstand and smashed it on his forehead.

Blood poured from the cut. He screamed, put a hand to his forehead, then jumped off the bed, and, with a frenzied look, shouted, "You have gone mad!"

My head was whirling with images as if I were watching myself in a movie. *The crowd watched as the horse dragged the wounded matador toward the cleaning area. Some were glad not to witness cruelty in the ring, but others were upset and felt the show had started wrong, since I wasn't stabbed with the banderillas. They couldn't cheer Yusuf or lift up their white handkerchiefs because the horse didn't have my lifeless body to drag out of the arena. Suddenly, a voice blasted from the crowd, and it sounded like Mother. She was upset, shouting about how unwomanly I behaved by disobeying my husband and asked if I had taken my medications. I told her they were not strong and couldn't paralyze me. Mother didn't need to be in the Plaza del Toros and watch Yusuf's tongue invade and rape my mouth because she had already seen my flesh and blood ripped from me in honor of Yusuf. I wondered if Mother, before entering the Plaza del Toros, brought her own seat cushion or rented it like the locals.*

24

moving away from bedlam

Back in school, I was told that another Somali woman had registered, and I rushed out to find her. In the hallway, I met Deeqa, a beautiful Somali woman around my older sister Sakiya's age, and I introduced myself. Deeqa worked at the embassy and was at the school that day just to translate for the new student and help her register. She knew about me and wondered why I had not been in touch with the office since the night of the dinner party.

I was ashamed to tell Deeqa anything about my life with Yusuf. I was in a vicious circle of fluctuating and conflicting emotions—shame, fear, rage, confusion, self-doubt. Whenever I called back to Mogadishu for support, I was told my feelings, perceptions, and instincts were not real, that Yusuf's reality was the true one and I must follow his instructions and desires. Mother insisted he was not a violent man and denied it when I reminded her about seeing an alcohol bar in Yusuf's room in Geneva. She said I was hardheaded and my temper would drag me into the grave. I still had not spoken with Father. I could not understand why he had allowed this arrangement and why he had not warned me.

Deeqa was very pleasant, and I longed to spit out all the stories about the Secret House and tell her that I had become what I witnessed as a young child. My own mother sold my body, like my cousin Khalifa sold hers for a piece of land. But how could I tell that to someone I had just met, even a woman who reminded me of home? Sahir had become my confidante, although I saw her only in class, and she was the only one to know about my twisted life with my family and Yusuf. My shame and distress were such that I was not able to confide in anyone else. Sahir had even given me the name of someone who could help if I ever wanted to get out or needed support.

Warmly, Deeqa hugged me; I smelled her Somali rose oil, and tears welled up in my eyes, and waves of emotion rippled through my stomach. I remembered the day when I was five years old and I wanted to put the rose oil in Grandmother's hair. Grandmother lifted me onto a wooden stool and told me to stand still while she knelt in front of me. She poured Somali rose oil in my palms, and I waited, watching her untie her thick, gray, horselike hair. I smeared the oil on top of her hair and awaited her next instruction. I watched as Grandmother parted her hair and her fingers glided smoothly through it. This seemed to take forever, and I thought she had forgotten about me and my tired legs waiting on the stool.

Impatiently, I jumped down and rushed to her side. "Did you forget about me?"

"Never!" She pulled me close and snuggled me against her warm chest.

Deeqa's warm hug brought a rush of memories, and I burst into uncontrollable wailing.

"What is it?" Deeqa asked, confused.

"I miss my father!"

It felt good to cry and cry as the powerful emotions washed over me. Quietly, she sat me down and let me complete whatever I was going through. Without a word, she passed me paper napkins to wipe my face, and her hand rubbed my back.

"We cry when we fear seeing the possibilities of what could be right in our lives," she said as the teacher stepped out of the classroom and asked me to come to the class.

"I will see you?" I asked.

"Very soon," Deeqa said.

I rose and hurried into the classroom.

"Very soon" was sooner than I had expected because Deeqa was smart, found our address, and showed up at our house. Several days later Ana called me into the living room, and I was shocked to see Deeqa standing there. She wore a light blue suit, and her reddish glow made it seem that she bathed in henna.

"I've come to take you out for a bit." She smiled and walked toward me.

I was struck by the fact that although Deeqa wore a business suit, she managed to walk as in the old days, when women were carried by the regal wind and their feet bounced softly from the ground. Nowadays in my country, women's hips rolled sideways as their long arms danced freely with each step. But Deeqa's hair didn't fit the style of the old days, when women looked like they were wearing a Sufi dancer's hat. Some were experts and had a style that could double for Marge Simpson's hair. Painfully, the women would gather all of their hair onto the top of their head, pulling it tightly, experiencing a sudden facelift. If they didn't have long hair, they would simply add a sheer material that they draped around their head to create a high, thick style, then cover it with a beautiful scarf. But Deeqa neatly tied her glowing hair tightly back.

Just then, Yusuf rushed into the living room, stunned to see Deeqa.

"*Salam alaykum,*" she said. Peace be with you.

"What prompted this visit?" Yusuf asked, signaling her to sit as Ana brought the afternoon snacks and placed the tray on the table.

I sneaked out to my room to change while he was distracted with the conversation. When I returned, I was surprised to find Yusuf and Deeqa laughing and talking about the men who sneaked qat across the border between Switzerland and Italy. Like bandits, these men parked their cars in front of the Somali houses in Geneva and sold the qat. I thought this was the perfect time to ask Yusuf about the yellow-haired Swiss men, loading up all that white sugar at night. But Yusuf and Deeqa seemed to be catching up on the old days and laughing. All Somalis in Geneva knew one another.

Yusuf turned and stared at me. "Where did that coat come from?" he asked.

"I brought it from Bonn," I said.

Yusuf watched Deeqa and me as we walked out of the house.

When we got to the car, Deeqa told me that some people were wondering about my arrangement with Yusuf and why my mother would leave without consulting the embassy.

"I'm OK," I said hesitantly.

She said family might not always know what is right for us and went on about forced marriages and how in this country my marriage was considered incest. People don't marry their first cousins because they are too close and it is illegal.

"Incest?"

Deeqa said that, in our culture, most people marry their first cousin to protect the family lineage, and the groom negotiates with a family for the bride's price.

"But, here, in the West, these practices are called child endangerment," she said. "They are not healthy."

I bent over, put my head into my hands, and sobbed.

"I'm going to help you," she said soothingly.

Soon after, I was spending more time with Deeqa, learning all the tricks on how to chase the phantom spectators out of my room and demolish the Plaza del Toros. One day she showed me floating silk nightgowns with lots of lace, then said I should watch how movie actresses seduce the men and get away with everything. I felt betrayed by her words and thought I made a mistake in confiding in her. She believed my options were few and that my fighting Yusuf would only cause me more pain.

"I have a plan of my own!" I shouted.

Deeqa grabbed my hand and sat me on the edge of her bed. I listened to her long stories about how, after ending her marriage, she ventured out and dared to mingle with men who had a different heritage.

But I interrupted, telling Deeqa that I grew up with Arab and Italian men who took young Somali girls in cars, then dropped the wailing sinners at the street corner, and that I was not wearing a laced-up gown for Yusuf.

"Forget about the Italians. . . ."

"I'm not going to wear those clothes."

Deeqa offered to take me to the doctor and help me get birth control.

"I will not get pregnant!"

"You will if you don't take precautions."

I stormed out of the room, and Deeqa rushed after me.

"I want to go home, please," I said.

When I got back to the house, Yusuf was in the kitchen making dinner and said that Ana had taken the night off. The smell of fish was too strong, and I covered my nose with my hands. Yusuf informed me that he talked to my parents, and Father was now officially back to eating lamb. He had stopped when he learned that I couldn't stomach meat and started eating fish and lamb again only after I left home. I did not have the energy to fight and really did not care if my father was eating meat again. He had abandoned me during the mutilation and allowed Yusuf to rule my life. I did not want to speak with him. That said a lot in my heart. Before falling asleep, in the darkness I would cry silently under the pillow, thinking about the good days when I would visit Father in his office and watch him work.

Battle is much more than picking up a rifle and hurting someone physically. My defense was to hold on tightly, survive until better days, and still be able to love my father.

25

time to burst forth

I had been living with Yusuf for eight months, and he had become relentless in pressuring me to start a family. I finally told him I would agree to let the doctors open my scar, hoping to buy myself some time while I tried to figure out what to do. Sahir continued to talk to me about the woman she knew who helped abused women who feared for their lives. I was desperate to escape, but I was not emotionally ready to cut ties with my family, which I had to do in order to save myself from Yusuf.

One day just as I finished getting ready for class, Yusuf, with a trash bag in his hand, marched into my bedroom and opened the closet door. He said he had decided to upgrade my clothing style. He removed my clothes, threw them into the bag, and walked out.

When I got back home and found the closet still empty, I was so upset that I screamed Ana's name at the top of my lungs. She rushed in and, when she saw my eyes blink rapidly, said the new clothes Yusuf bought were in the room next door. Calmly, she signaled me to open the other door in my room for the surprise.

Furious, I yanked the door open and was stunned by the red paint covering the walls of the room. It was so red it seemed all that blood from the Plaza del Toros was stored in there. The colorful spring clothes—pants, shoes, shawls, and jewelry—were neatly stacked in the room. Nothing had been chosen by me. My husband was denying me a voice in even the most basic of decisions. I began to sob and begged God to get me out of this prison. But my passport and money had disappeared right after we had returned from our European tour.

⁂

After many conversations with Sahir and many painful and lonely nights, surviving nightmares, the onslaught of images of the Plaza del Toros, and encounters with Yusuf, I had formulated a plan to escape. The day after Yusuf threw out all my clothes, I slipped out of school to a phone booth and called the number Sahir had given me. I did not know the woman's name or where she lived, and I was not to say my real name and had to choose a color that would become my name. I had chosen the name Red.

I took a deep breath as I heard the phone ringing on the other end, and finally a woman answered. I told her my story, trying to keep my emotions in check.

She listened in silence, and when I finished speaking she spoke up. "You are not yet serious enough to escape and cut off your family for good. You understand that leaving your husband means leaving the country and possibly never speaking with any of your family members again."

She began to say good-bye, but I interrupted just before she hung up. "I will call again—I am not ready to give up. Please, please, you must help me escape my prison."

⁂

After several talks with the woman, she finally agreed to help, and I listened to her instructions. Excited and hopeful for the first time since being abandoned in Geneva, I looked forward to going to school so I could talk with the woman.

The fights with Yusuf started again because I refused to go to the doctor and be opened up. When I told the woman about this, she said I should be patient and try to gain Yusuf's trust and find a way to put my name on his account.

"I want a way out," I said.

"This will be your way out."

The woman wasn't interested in hearing that I was going to find a job wherever I might end up and that I didn't care about getting onto his account.

"Call back in a week," she said. "By then I will know if your escape can be organized. But meanwhile, don't change anything. Do everything your husband asks. . . ."

But she didn't live my life, and a doctor wasn't waiting to cut her private parts with a scalpel. Nonetheless I would do what she told me to do.

When Yusuf picked me up at school, I asked him to forgive me because I wasn't doing my duty as a wife. I asked if he remembered the night I was at the hospital and woke up with his face hovering over me.

"No."

I told him I remembered because he said if I didn't behave he could pick up two blond women, take them back to Mogadishu, and marry them. His wedding ceremony would be the envy of the president himself because it would be a spectacular event.

"Do you remember?" I repeated.

I asked him how long he could withstand poking me and, instead of affection, be met by my pillow knocking him out of the bed. Yusuf said my problem was that I couldn't face the fact that I really loved him, and I was playing a hard-to-get game. It had been two weeks since I saw him drink, and I did notice his kind words and that he was trying to make me feel safe. He said I was teaching him how to appreciate the love in his life.

But it was too late to turn back and to imagine how it could have been better for both of us. I did not want this life; I wanted to escape.

The day finally came for my last call to the woman who was helping me escape, and she gave me the final instructions. I was to wear all white clothes and a red scarf to school the next day. I would go to the train station to meet a woman wearing a red scarf who would have a message for me. I should take from the house only my schoolbag—nothing else. I would be beginning a new life with a new name, "Surer."

When I got back home, I put all my meds for my mood swings and painful cramps into a paper bag and selected the white coat, pants, hat, and red scarf, but I couldn't find white shoes. Yusuf was getting ready to entertain guests from Saudi Arabia and said I should greet them before dinner. I refused to come out of my room until I heard the Spanish folk music blasting through the walls. I knew by now Yusuf was with the two Swiss, yellow-haired men, loading up the "white sugar" into the black briefcases. I stood in the middle of my room and waved at the imaginary spectators who watched Yusuf transform this spot into the Plaza del Toros.

The crowd stood still and understood when I said I was no longer a bleeding bull with spiked sticks hanging on my neck because, as a matador, Yusuf couldn't kill my spirit. Clutching the roses in their hands, the crowd watched as Yusuf's baffled hooligans circled around the arena, not comprehending that he wasn't going to be rewarded. I winked and waved at the crowd, knowing the hooligans' forceful efforts couldn't tie another rope around my legs.

The next morning, while I was getting ready for school, Yusuf walked into my bedroom and was shocked to see me wearing white clothes.

"Did someone die?" he asked.

"I feel like wearing white," I replied.

He stood in front of me and watched me put on the white coat. He said the doctor would be able to meet me by the end of the week. I listened to him explain how the doctor described the corrective surgery and the healing process. I said yes to everything he asked.

As he drove me to class, he seemed to sense something was not right. When he pulled the car up to the school, I could feel his eyes on me as he watched me get out and walk into the building carrying my schoolbag. I entered the classroom, and a sharp pain pierced my lower back, a result of the anxiety growing inside me.

This could be the most important day of your life, I told myself as I took my seat. *You must find your courage, stay focused on the schedule. You must get to the train station during the second class break as planned. You must stay in control.*

Just then, the classroom door inched open, and I was horrified to see Yusuf peeking through the crack. The teacher walked over to him. Quickly, I rose and followed Yusuf into the hallway.

"Is there still time for me to say the *shahaadah*, or are you planning to recite something at my grave?" he asked sarcastically.

"But you're not dead," I said.

"It looks like you're in mourning!" Yusuf yelled.

I decided to not argue and go along with this request to recite the *shahaadah*, which a dying person is encouraged to say to strengthen his or her faith.

"Do you want me to recite it out loud with you?" I asked.

"*Laa ilaaha illa allah*," Yusuf said. There is no one other than Allah.

"That was powerful—do you feel better?" I asked.

"I bought you the most colorful clothes. . . ." He shook his head.

"Are you scared that I will dig a small grave site for you, making the visit of the angels Nakeer and Munkar impossible?" I asked. In Islam Nakeer and Munkar question people at their death to determine if they've lived a good life and would go to heaven. Because Yusuf drank alcohol and abused me, I believed he would find himself in hell.

"I lead a perfect life," Yusuf said.

I wanted to say that it wouldn't be such a perfect life if those angels went to his bedroom, where the prayer rug and the photo of Mecca faced the shining alcohol bar.

But then a smile broke on Yusuf's face as he moved forward and hugged me. He whispered into my ear, "You begged me to stop being a matador and throw away that white robe, and now I have. I have some fancy pajamas." He thought a new chapter was beginning for us.

I agreed never to wear white clothes as long as he was still living. "Good-bye," I said, then turned and walked into the classroom, feeling Yusuf's burning eyes on me.

During the break, armed with my medicine and schoolbag, I went into the bathroom and stared in the mirror, trying to see my new life ahead. I watched myself take a deep breath, then left the bathroom. I walked out of the school, never looking back.

Once outside I did not pause to think but ran down the streets dodging traffic until I reached the train station. I rushed through the crowd to find someone else who was wearing a red scarf and who had a message for me. I did not know what my new destination would be; all I cared about was getting the hell out of Geneva.

I noticed an elderly woman wearing a red scarf, sitting on a bench. In her hands she held an envelope, and a white suitcase sat beside her. I approached her, and before I had a chance to say anything, she put the envelope on top of the suitcase, got up, and walked away. I grabbed the envelope, opened it, and found money, a passport, and a note.

The note said that I should go to gate 7 and take the train to Grenoble, France. There I should take a taxi to a place called Alecht Dormitory at Domain University. I picked up the suitcase and hurried to the gate. I followed the other passengers onto the train, placed the suitcase in the proper place, and found a seat by the window.

My whole body was shaking. I was scared, surprisingly not because Yusuf might find me but because I was going to a place where I did not know anyone. I took a pill, put the bottle in my coat pocket, and held tightly to the paper bag, telling myself the medications would be helpful during this new journey.

The train pulled away from the gate, and I looked out of the window and watched Geneva slowly disappear from my view.

26

grenoble

The cold weather hung over Grenoble, France, and the city wrapped me in a blanket of sadness as the train pulled into the station. Why couldn't I feel joy for being set free? I should have been happy; this was what I had yearned for. But now all I could think was *This is not the right choice*.

The passengers grabbed their luggage, rushing out of the train, and I found myself stuck in my seat, paralyzed by fear, unable to move. My silent tears kept falling. I watched families and friends embrace and welcome one another. I was alone, the opposite of those reuniting with loved ones. While I had consciously and deliberately chosen the pain of detaching from my family and my culture, I felt like at least I could return to using my own name, Soraya.

I was the last to step out of the train onto the platform. A young man approached and asked if I needed help with my luggage. I had learned French in just eight months living in Geneva with Yusuf. I said yes and asked him to tell me how to get to the Domain University dormitory. I followed him out of the terminal. He was kind enough to stop a taxi for me and said I shouldn't let the taxi driver circle me around the campus.

The taxi stopped in front of a high-rise building, and I went inside. A man in his late fifties stood behind the counter. Behind him was a board full of hanging keys. He greeted me with a smile.

"I'm Jean-Pierre. I was expecting you." He grabbed an envelope and a key and handed them to me.

Inside the envelope I found my room number, the class schedule, and a campus map. I signed the registration book as he picked up the campus map and underlined the directions to the orientation office, library, restaurant, and lake.

"*Merci bien.*" I picked up the luggage and went to the elevator, but Jean-Pierre hurried after me and said that I needed to call my mother. Stunned, I stared back, not sure I heard him correctly.

"My mother?"

"She called. . . ."

After my initial shock, I realized that the caller must have been the woman in Geneva who helped me come here. He directed me to the mailroom, where I found a phone booth. I dialed the woman's number.

With relief, I found she was the one who called. She was glad that I had arrived in Grenoble safely and said that an envelope was coming with money and that would be our last contact.

I expressed my gratitude for all she had done and promised to pay back all the money. She said the money would last for six months while I focused on my new life. When I got a job, I should save some money and help another woman who was in need. I cried, feeling the intense fear of starting this new life. She was my only remaining contact with my past, and when we hung up, the door would close. I would be on my own.

"You have made hard choices, and your new world will be beautiful." Her voice was calm and reassuring. "Do not give up. Make your mind stronger. You have come so far, and you *will* find a way to put your life in order. And you will go on to help other women. . . ."

I did not want her to leave. I wanted her to keep talking.
"He will find me!" I cried.
"Then get ready before you hear the footsteps."
I felt a sharp pain in my abdomen, and I couldn't stand still.
I thanked the woman, and we hung up. I checked my luggage,
but I couldn't find the bag full of medications. I checked my
coat pocket and found one bottle of pills. I took a few; then,
dragging my luggage behind me, I set off to look for my room
and my new life.

As I walked down the hallway, I heard the American music
that Mother loved to play in her *asilo*, her private room. It was
Ray Charles's "Set Me Free." A young African man yanked
open his door and brought out a drum. He started playing in
what seemed a protest. Another door opened, and a young
female with dark spiked hair and lots of makeup dragged a
chair into the hallway. She climbed up on the chair and hung
the American flag on the wall, instructed the whole second floor
to shout in protest against it, then dragged her chair back into
the room and slammed the door behind her.

I found my room, which faced the young woman's room. I
thought the loud music would surely damage my hearing, and
I feared again that I was not fit to live in this new world. The
young African drummer started knocking on the doors, making others come out, gather in the hallway, and stare at the red,
white, and blue flag. Some students were upset and argued over
the American flag posted on the hallway wall.

I walked into my room, which had a tiny bed, chair, table,
bookshelf, closet, and sink. I sank onto the bed and lay down as
arguments that seemed to be political erupted in the hallway.
Exhausted, I covered my ears with the pillow.

⁂

I must have slept a long time because I awoke in darkness. Panicked, I jumped out of the bed, not knowing where I was. In my
mind, I was hearing the Spanish folk songs at Yusuf's house. As

I searched for the light switch, excruciating pain stabbed my abdomen, intensifying like never before. I turned the light on and swallowed the rest of the pills, emptying the whole bottle.

I took my clothes off and saw the blood. It had been only a week since my last period, so I couldn't understand why I was bleeding. A wave of panic passed over me. I told myself that if I could take a shower, everything would be fine.

I left my room wearing a towel and found the large bathroom with shower stalls. I stepped into the shower and let hot water wash over my body, imagining it washing away my fatigue, my pain, my fears, the ghosts of my past. But I was so dizzy, everything was spinning, becoming confused in my mind—the hot water, the train, the voice of the woman who helped me, the students in the hallway, the faces of my mother and father, Yusuf, my sisters and brothers. . . . I lowered my body—I would sit in the warmth of the water just until the spell passed.

27

the feared mutant

I woke up in a hospital emergency room in chaos, a white-coated crowd gathered around staring down at me. The gurney I lay on lurched into motion, the nurse pushing it down the hallway. I clutched my abdomen as we raced beneath small lights that grew brighter as we sped along, as if the light were coming from the background to the foreground.

I heard a woman with a heavy accent shouting behind me, "What's wrong with her?"

A door slammed opened, another bright light flashed, and the nurse rushed me into a room. I was struck with a horrible smell that nauseated me. It was like a nightmare, reminding me of the day I woke up in pain years ago at the house in Mogadishu, sickened by the smell of a hospital, burning blood, and rotting flesh.

In agony, I was placed on a table, and a tube was shoved into my throat, then pushed to make me vomit. I descended into a kind of madness, feeling suffocated. I kept pushing people's hands away, and a nurse put a hand over my forehead.

Suddenly, in my mind's eye, I saw Mother gazing into my eyes as she put a wet towel over my forehead. The white-coated man's hands were pushing upright on the syringe, then disappeared under the white sheet covering my legs. Gasping for air, I tried to stifle the panic and screamed, "No!"

A white-coated man approached and asked if I had severe abdominal pain.

"Where am I?" I asked.

"This is the maternity hospital emergency room in Grenoble," he said. "May I examine you?"

"No!"

Calmly, the white-coated man said nonetheless he was going to examine me and would help to ease the pain. Suddenly, a crowd of white-coated men and women poured into the room and stood around him. The room was pulsing, intense with very strange energy, and I felt like a lamb being prepared for slaughter.

Cotton was wiped between my legs, and a hand painfully tried to examine me. Everything was moving so quickly and my pain was so intense I wasn't able to tell these French doctors about the time in Bonn when the German doctors could not do a pelvic examination, and they had to cut into my stomach to drain the debris of blood that had built up inside me since my mutilation.

But the German doctors were gentle, kind people who didn't act like these French doctors. I was shocked to witness, for the first time, a white-coated man who seemed lost, confused as to what he was seeing. When he looked up, I saw the distress covering his face, and his astonished eyes pierced me. The room was buzzing as bewildered people stood in full view between my open legs.

It's difficult to express what their wide, horrified eyes did to my already damaged heart. I felt like a caged monster locked in a mental hospital. I struggled to fight, to push my body off the stainless table, but I couldn't. A new burden the size of a mountain descended on my shoulders at their expressions of disbelief and anxiety.

A white-coated woman clapped her hands over her mouth, then looked over at a giant white-coated man with a beard cutting his way through the crowd. "Dr. Omar!"

"What happened to her?" Dr. Omar looked at what everyone else was looking at, then threw the sheet over my legs. *"Everybody out!"*

"The blood has no way to leave—" the first white-coated man said.

"Move along, please!" With brown skin, high cheekbones, and large arms, I knew Dr. Omar was an Egyptian. His eyes were beaming with warmth and kindness, but a sharp pain went through me as he stood at my side and spoke Arabic, saying to nod if I understood.

But I hated speaking Arabic, and the language brought back more bad memories. As a child, I had attended an Egyptian-run school from kindergarten through eighth grade, and the teachers punished us with long sticks that made me wish that they would go back to their own country. My teacher had come to Mogadishu before I was born, but he still would not speak Somali, and that made me furious. In class, he would ask me questions in Arabic, and I would respond in Somali, which made him furious. He would shout, "Grab the table!" I would get up, turn my back, and hold the table. I faced the class as he smacked my behind with the long wooden stick. When Father heard this, I was removed from the school, and I remember Father having a very serious talk with my new principal about breaking the family trust and abusing the children. I don't remember what happened to my stick-loving teacher.

Now, I felt the gentle hand pressing on my abdomen. Dr. Omar continued to ask me questions in Arabic, and I would respond in French, which made him frown. Still traumatized by the reactions of the white-coated crowd, I told him that I had been around doctors but none who looked at me like I was a feared mutant.

"Their horrified eyes burnt my skin like acid," I said.

"I apologize for their unfamiliarity. . . ."

He said that many of them had never seen a genitally mutilated patient and that I could teach the young students and doctors a lesson. A panic wave continued to build inside me, along with my sense of being a deformed person.

After examining me, he said the occlusion of my vaginal opening caused the painful menses, and he could fix it. In Egypt, he had witnessed many patients suffering from a similar condition. He talked about how he eased their pain and how he wanted to do that for me, too.

I agreed and allowed myself to be cleaned up and moved to a room where he talked to me for hours about how he would help me.

"Have you had any alternative sexual relations?"

I thought about it for a moment, then realized this alternative could mean the "brushing of the vulva," a term I had heard back in Mogadishu, meaning a man's erect penis would brush the sealed vulva without penetrating the girl. When the young girls jumped off the walls into the dark alleys to meet up with young men, some would remain in the cars and experience "brushing of the vulva." Little was known of this secret until some of the virgin girls got pregnant because the sperm had found a way to swim inside the vulva and catch an egg. The distraught mothers rushed their daughters to hospital, and the white-coated men proved their virginity. They explained the mysterious pregnancy, and the mothers learned the meaning of the "brushing of the vulva." Some girls swore they kept their underwear on during the sinful act and blamed the young men for the misfortune. The mothers planned the rushed marriages, life returned to normal, and everyone forgot how the whole event started.

I watched how eagerly the giant white-coated man waited to hear whether I had had any alternative sexual relations. I didn't know where to begin, but I wasn't ready to speak about Yusuf forcing himself on me.

I asked Dr. Omar the most profound question. "Who am I?" Mother had told me she asked God the same question while giving birth.

He began to explain the reversal surgery he wanted to perform. He described cutting the scar tissue that blocked the opening of my vagina and widening the opening, which would release the debris of the accumulated blood.

"You mean with scissors and needles!"

"With nerves intact, I would carve around the clitoris—"

"Forget it!"

In his experience, Dr. Omar had seen women like me, but I was confused and did not really understand the reversal surgery.

He said the surgery was very beneficial and that it would be free, but I had to attend sessions with a therapist, a sex therapist.

I again asked my profound questions. "Who am I? What kind of woman was I?"

He did not give an answer but wanted to know everything about my family and what age I had been when I heard the sound of the scissors cutting through my flesh. I began to describe my childhood, but I grew weary of talking and made another decision that would change my life. I agreed with his recommendation to undergo the corrective surgery and meet with the sex therapist.

Lying in the hospital room, I thought about running away in the middle of the night. But to never have painful cramps again sounded really wonderful. I felt I was splitting myself into two people. One was heavy in grief about her alien body, and the other wanted to reeducate herself about all her body parts and have a positive outlook on life.

I was trembling, remembering the day my sister Sakiya's husband, Mahamuud, brought home a young servant from the nomadic area. Sakiya opened up her closet and gave the servant new clothes and showed her how to take a bath. But the young servant insisted on continuing with her own way of doing things.

Early one morning, I heard Sakiya screaming at the top of her lungs, as if Mahamuud had been caught and dragged away by the armed forces men. I ran to the back of the house where I found Sakiya watching the young nomad taking a shower.

Completely at home with nature, she saw nothing wrong with using a bucket of cold water. But Sakiya's shriek arose from her shock at the sight of the servant's large-winged labia.

Concerned, Sakiya called a doctor. After examining the young woman, he said that definitely her clitoris and the inner small lips were excised, but the labia majora were left intact. He could not give any reason as to why. Then he told the servant he would make her normal. She was shocked to be told that her genitals were once again strange and needed correction.

Tonight, lying in my hospital bed, I couldn't help but feel just like that servant whose vulva was already amputated once, but she still wasn't quite a complete woman in the eyes of others.

28

distorted body

The next morning, I met with Dr. Omar and confirmed that I wanted to have the reversal surgery and was willing to go to therapy if he could prescribe medication to ease the panic attacks. He said the therapist would evaluate me and prescribe sedatives in accordance with the treatment.

Before the surgery, I was visited by the young woman with spiked hair who lived across the hall from me in the dormitory. Her name was Jane, and I discovered she was the one who had found me lying on the shower floor and rushed me to the emergency room. I was again alarmed by her appearance; she looked like she could start a fight at any moment. She wore all-black clothes, boots, and fire-red lipstick and had raccoon eyes. I remembered the day I moved in that she was putting an American flag on the wall in the dorm hallway as a protest.

The nurse came in and asked Jane to leave so that I could be prepared for the surgery. Jane put her hand on my shoulder.

"I'll be back later to see how you're doing," she said kindly.

I closed my eyes as fear took over my body. Dr. Omar entered. I told him I wanted my eyes shut before I was taken to the surgery room. He said I would be given medication and that I wouldn't feel the pain at all.

"I want my eyes shut!"

"OK," he said.

That last thing I remembered was someone holding my hand before I was taken out of the room.

⚜

I woke up in the hospital room alone. I felt a tingling of pain, but there were no ropes tied around my legs, and I wept. I finally was taking charge of my life, and being responsible for my new body was overwhelming. This was the first time in my life that my body was my own. Now I understood what being free meant. The nurse walked in and, seeing my emotional state, gave me a pain-relieving shot. I told her that I wanted to see Dr. Omar.

"He'll be in shortly." She walked out of the room.

I dozed for a time—I wasn't sure how long—but I was awakened when a young white-coated man entered. He looked sick and had blotches on his mouth.

"I'm Nigel."

"Nigel?" I was groggy, having a hard time focusing.

"It means the Dark One."

"The Dark One?" I detected a British accent. He had red hair and was handsome enough to be an actor.

"Something like that—how are you feeling?"

I was cautious; who was this man? I simply said, "Fine." I asked if Dr. Omar had sent him.

Nigel explained that he dealt with stress and guided people through painful situations. He was leaving the hospital post but told Dr. Omar that he would like to offer his services.

Before I had a chance to respond, a white-coated woman, carrying a file, entered the room. She seemed surprised when she saw Nigel in the room. Feeling uncomfortable, Nigel got up and said hello to her. She forced a smile at Nigel and looked at me.

"I'll come back later to ask you some questions," Nigel said.

"About what?" I asked.

Nigel didn't say anything and left the room, closing the door behind him. The white-coated woman stared at the door for a moment. I watched as she pursed her lips and nodded her head in agreement with something that I didn't see. She opened the file in her hand and leafed through it. She looked up at me.

"Why didn't you sign a consent for Dr. Omar to share the before and after photos of your surgery?" She said the other surgeons and students wanted to view them and asked if I would sign the paper now. "It would be a great thing if you released them in order to share the information."

"They are for my mother," I said.

"Your mother?" she asked.

"I can't release them to you," I said. Because of the way the doctors behaved in the emergency room, I did not want to share my bloody photos with them.

⁂

It was very difficult to adjust to my new world, where I was seen as a different kind of woman. The good thing about the corrective surgery was at first it made me forget Yusuf's ghost, if only temporarily. My mind was occupied by thoughts of how to see the good side of my mother and the reason she did what she did. I began to mourn for Mother and how, at the age of fourteen, she was forced to marry her dead sister's husband, and my oldest sister was born when Mother was only fifteen, four years younger than I was now.

Dr. Omar said I should focus on healing and building my new self-image. He ordered me not to avoid looking at my body, but this kind of talk would only lead me to depression because this was the body I had since the mutilation, and I had never seen it differently before. To him, I was a brand-new woman, the one God intended before Mother and her minions decided to "correct" my body. That Mother had thought God made a mistake, that she needed to alter parts of my body, had always been confusing and painful.

And, indeed, I found myself falling into depression. I was fearful of how my new world would judge me, and I imagined how I would shake when I told those Frenchmen, with their soft voices that greeted me with *bonjour*, that I was deformed, a mutant woman in their land. I thought about the imminent rejections, then promised myself to be wise and keep my mouth *shut* about my history.

I was thankful that Dr. Omar had prescribed painkillers, which helped my mind focus on school and finding a job before I ran out of money. He had told me that Nigel had once worked in a hospital in Sudan and had helped other women like me. I anxiously awaited my first therapy appointment with Nigel, the Dark One.

29

the black swan

In the distance I heard church bells as I walked through the cemetery, headed toward my first therapy session. A stone house sat nearby. I stopped and looked around to make sure I was in the right place. I was; it was the right address. I walked up to the door and knocked. Nothing. I knocked again. No response.

I tried the knob, and the wooden door opened. Hesitantly, I entered, seeing a long hallway ahead. No one was there. I shut the door behind me and walked down the hallway.

"Hello," I called.

Bright paintings covered the walls, and the beauty was over-whelming. Slowly, I moved along a section of the wall as if I were in a museum, each step revealing more breathtaking art.

A black-and-white photo caught me off guard. I moved closer and was stunned to see naked men's butts. They were smooth, plump, round, and firm, like those of well-fed women. Closely inspecting it, my face almost disappeared into those butts, breaking the glass. I had never seen anything like this, and I felt these derrieres were saying something to me. I observed how well the bodies were positioned as the legs snaked together comfortably. I stood admiring the photo, thinking how great it would be to meet up with the owners of these firm butts and ask them advice on how to love my new body.

Suddenly, a voice blasted from behind, startling me. "Hello!"

I turned and saw the young man who had paid me a visit at the hospital. His appearance shocked me because the dark spots had spread to his forehead. He was thinner and did not look well, and only about two weeks had passed.

Nervously, I said the door had been open so I came in, and I told him how much I liked his paintings.

"How are you feeling?" he said. Nigel looked at me for a moment, then said the hospital informed him that I was hearing voices.

"I'm having nightmares."

"What are your nightmares about?"

"I hear voices. I can't sleep. . . . I'm afraid to fall asleep."

I followed him into the living room, where I saw a large mirror by the window and colorful pillows on the floor next to a desk full of papers, books, and medicine bottles. I watched Nigel walk over to the desk and flip through a file, and then he said he was very good at chasing ghosts.

"Ghosts?" I asked. Of course, by living near the cemetery, he could become an expert about spirits and play with the ghosts.

Nigel went on to say this meeting was informal and a way to see if we could stand each other's sense of humor. He would listen and guide me to know more about myself so that I could deal with stress. "We'll figure out the best way to help you feel better."

"How?"

"You'll come here twice a week."

"And do what?"

"We'll just talk."

I asked if he knew anything about women and their problems.

Nigel said he knew many things about women, and, in fact, a woman's vagina blessed his head.

"How?" I asked again.

During his birth, the midwife believed his mother would not survive because Nigel was taking too long to come out. After a while, he poked his head out, which made it easy for his mother to make the final push. She said he was quiet, and she didn't notice him pass through her gate.

"Gate?"

"That's how the vagina blessed my head!" He laughed.

I found Nigel to be strange, yet his voice was a kind of medicine that took me up to the clouds. He turned toward a beautiful nature painting and stared at it, seeming to forget that I was standing right before him. After a long moment, he turned back and gave me a surprised look. His piercing blue eyes deeply penetrated my skin. I felt like I was staring into the eyes of those qat-addicted and delusional Somalis who behaved so oddly. Like them, Nigel had dark circles under his eyes as if he, too, struggled with insomnia.

"Do you have goals in mind?"

"Find a job and do well in college. What are we going to communicate about?"

Nigel said that we would talk about any problem I might have, and his guidance would empower me. He would be my psychiatrist and sex therapist.

He asked about my classes and schedule, saying it was important that I set aside a quiet time just for me.

"What would I do with all that quiet?"

"You'll go over the exercise lists and do your best to follow them."

"Exercises?"

Nigel said that my body had been through a very traumatic experience, and I must learn how to overcome my anxiety.

"Do you believe the act of sex is only for procreation?" he asked.

"Sex is the only way to stop the sinful roaming thoughts and the scanners wasting their seeds."

"Scanners?"

I explained that the scanners were young men who came to people's living rooms looking for ways to satisfy their urges and find a wife. They got lucky and married, but soon after one woman wasn't enough. Instead of taking the second, third, or fourth wife, these men created the Secret House, where they would find other women willing to be used as waste disposal pots for them.

"Here we call them courtesans."

"Courtesans?"

"Women providing sexual companionship for wealthy men," he said, then changed the subject and went over what I should expect in the sessions and the work I had to do at home. His goal was to help me learn how to work with what I had and find ways to heal from unspeakable pain.

Nigel thought stimulating my mind with books would help me understand human sexuality, make it easier for me to trust, and make it possible for me to create a deep relationship with myself. He would recommend books that would widen my world and would help me cope with the past. Talking about the past was the key to opening up my mind, which would lead to healthy sexual functioning.

His subject matter was shocking, but it would be worth it if he helped me learn how to find and love myself.

"You said lists of exercises. What kind?" I asked.

"Mirror exercise. . . ."

I knew right away what he was suggesting. "You mean holding a tiny mirror or standing in front of a full-length one?"

"I would suggest that—"

"I'm not going to look at it!" I interrupted.

"Why?"

"Here? You expect me to sit naked in front of that mirror?" I pointed to a mirror in the corner.

Nigel quickly cleared up my misconception. He would be only a talking head, and I would do all the work at home.

"Why wouldn't you stand naked in front of a mirror and admire your beauty?" he asked. He said that if I found the exercise to be hard, I should stop and reward myself with something special, like reading a book that would help me relax. Then I should get up the courage to try the exercise again and study the functions of my body parts and inner organs.

"In that mirror, when I look at myself, will I feel like a real woman?"

"You are one. . . ."

"So now I'm counting stitch marks left by a French surgical device that will empower me to say, 'I'm a complete woman!'" I told Nigel about my thirteenth birthday when I held a tiny mirror and counted the stitch marks left behind.

My aunt Ubax, with the scent of her Somali rose oil, carried me to my room. She leaned over and proudly smiled, saying, "Today you have become a woman!"

"Now the difference is you're holding the destiny in your hands," Nigel said.

"No . . . my private pain is leading the way."

"You will have an intimate communication with your body."

"What about the nightmares?"

"I will listen carefully, chase the demons away, and you will feel better."

"Where will the demons go?"

"They will go back to where they came from." He removed a piece of paper from the file and looked at it. I felt it was the right time to ask about my medication refills.

"My medications are getting low. When can I get the refill?"

He didn't reply to my question but said, "Was she there?"

"Who?"

"Your mother—can we talk about her?"

"No!"

"Do you know how the sperm travels into the uterus?"

"Uterus?"

Nigel said, during the fertilization process, the sperm swims into the vagina, into the womb, and up to the fallopian tubes to meet the egg. It's the egg that has the choice, not the sperm. The sperm will invade anything and is known to get frantic trying to find an egg that will accept it.

I was fascinated by the whole process, and it reminded me about when I heard Xaawo tell Halgaan that he was wasting his seed by going to the prostitutes. I asked again about the refill, but Nigel wouldn't answer and continued talking about more of the exercise assignments. I expressed my willingness to come to talk and learn more about my new body and how to deal with it, but I needed the medications.

"What about your head?"

"My head?"

"Do you want to remain a body without a head?" He picked up a pen, wrote something on a piece of paper, then handed it to me. I noticed the red-pen-circled words at the bottom of the page, words like "rhythmic breathing," "gender," "sexuality," "bustier," "iron hoop," and others. I wanted to know what they meant.

"Iron hoop?"

Nigel said that in Italy around the fourteenth century women were known to wear iron chastity belts. Some had iron hoops that gave men a choice to either tighten or loosen the belt. He went on about corsets, Chinese foot binding, and how the well-known Victorian obstetrician Isaac Baker Brown tried to treat epilepsy and masturbation, which many believed caused women's mental diseases. Feeling that he had dazzling hands, Dr. Brown performed hoodectomies on young patients, removing their healthy prepuces and thus violating their rights.

Suddenly, I felt a burning spear hit my gut, and I knew where this conversation would lead. I was not ready to open up my wounds; I was looking for ways to numb them. In my mind's eye, I saw the day Mother said to me, "After today, no one will ever call you the girl with three legs." I remembered the young girl around seven years old who was rushed out of the surgery room, her mouth open in a silent scream. What would she say if, instead of me, she were sitting right here in front of Nigel today? What would she do with this kind of luck and opportunity to open the wound in order to heal mind, body, and soul?

I folded my hands, slid them between my legs, and stared down, reminding myself that with Nigel I would not be alone in this journey. It was at this moment that I decided to learn and observe everything, even if I really didn't understand it.

I saw Nigel's face twist in pain as his hand grabbed his stomach. He got up and rushed toward a room. I started after him, but I was met by the door slamming, and I heard the phone ring in the living room. I decided to go back to the living room and wait.

A few moments later, Nigel returned, walked over to desk, and took some pills. It was clear that he was sick. I didn't want to leave, but it was the right thing to do.

"I have a class. . . ." I got up and hurried out of the house, feeling overwhelmed.

30

mending the wounds

Instead of going to the campus, I rushed to Dr. Omar's office. He wasn't there, but I would not leave without seeing him, so I sat to wait.

When he walked into the office an hour later, he wasn't surprised to see me. He sat down in his thick leather chair.

"What is wrong with him?" I asked.

"Who?"

"The therapist."

"Why do you ask?"

I said that I did not want to open up and trust someone who wasn't well and then find myself transferred to an unfamiliar therapist.

He said Nigel had left his hospital practice and transferred his patients to other therapists but insisted on helping me heal.

"He's sick!"

Dr. Omar said not to worry; he would find me another therapist.

As he spoke the words, a sudden attachment to Nigel paralyzed me, and I burst into tears.

"Do you like him?"

"He's eccentric. . . . He has a healing voice." His voice had had the same effect on me as classical music the first time I heard it. In the midst of pain, fear, and anger, I saw beauty and smooth colors decorating my soul with hope and joy. The eight months that I lived in Yusuf's house, the classical music did for me what Doris Day's film did while my legs were bound by a rope.

Dr. Omar asked about the session and how it went. I told him it was OK and showed him the list of books Nigel recommended and those circled words.

"Why read stories about the unpopular king of France?" I asked.

"Maybe it's background information. . . ."

"You mean into your culture?"

I took the piece of paper from him and looked at it again. Some titles and words were circled, but two had question marks—"rhythmic breathing" and "bustier." I found I couldn't wait to get back to the library and look them up to prepare myself for the next session. Nigel reminded me of our family employee Halgaan and how exciting it had been to go places with him that children weren't allowed to go. Those adventures had increased my natural curiosity, which sometimes got me into trouble.

This was a very trying day, and I needed to think about something else, to give my mind a rest. As I left his office, Dr. Omar rushed to the door and said, "I'm very proud of you. See you next week for your checkup."

I shifted my focus to class and trying to act normal, but Nigel's circled words kept coming into my mind. My thoughts shifted back to his advice; I felt he was out of his mind to ask me do these types of exercises. After class, I hurried to the library and spent long hours reading books recommended by Nigel, forgetting to eat.

⁜

I went to my first literature class, where the teacher was reading an amazing book by a famous female writer. I had never heard such words: "If destiny had me go from the domination of my grandmother to my husband, it's possible—I should never have been myself."

George Sand's words seemed to be tailored for me. The teacher went on, "Fate decided that from seventeen, there would be an interlude between the exterior forces, that I would belong to myself—for better or worse, essentially what I would be the rest of my life."

After class, I returned to the library to find books that would help me understand more about what my body had gone through and how. I wanted to know how to deal with the healing process.

The good thing about the reversal surgery, and talking to Dr. Omar, was that my world was turned upside down. In the midst of my profound sadness, a new world opened up for me. I wanted to remain awake, but the most disturbing and traumatic things began to happen every night right after I fell asleep. I would find myself hearing the folk music blaring at Yusuf's house and see my room turning into the Plaza del Toros as once again he became a matador. I would jump out of my sleep, yank the door open, and run down the hallway, thinking I was still at Yusuf's house. Frantically, I'd knock on the door where music was blasting and shout, "Yusuf, stop the noise!" I would hear someone say, "I'm not Yusuf!"

By the time I regained my sanity, I would realize that I was standing in front of my dorm neighbor's door, not Yusuf's library. I would apologize and hurry into my room and stare in the mirror, trying to figure out what was happening to me. Eventually, I would get back into bed, but a surge of panic would overcome me. What if I had left the door unlocked? I'd jump up, run to check the door, then I'd move to the sink, splash water on my face, and stare into the mirror again. The voice of the white-coated man in Mogadishu would fill my head, shouting, "Hold her and grab the rope!"

After many nights of lying awake in bed, fearful of falling asleep only to be confronted with the voices and to relive the fights with Yusuf, I began to hear the sounds of young girls crying.

I needed help; I could not be afraid of devoting myself fully to therapy. Maybe I would get lucky and find ways to put together my distorted mind and body.

31

moving away from
perdition

When the time came for the next session, I was eager to
cut through the cemetery and shout angrily at Nigel. I
walked into his house and found him sitting behind the desk,
looking a little better.

"Hello," he said.

I couldn't greet him properly because I wanted to spit the
unthinkable words out of my mouth. I was embarrassed to say
them aloud, but I forced out the question that had been occupy-
ing my mind: "What is the purpose of inserting a finger?"

"To see if your vagina tightens involuntarily. . . ."

"And these are serious medical exercises?"

He didn't really answer the question except to say how
I must train that part of my body against any fear and pain.
Looking at my naked body, touching it, and strengthening the
muscles inside it would help.

I had a problem with this both emotionally and physically—
how could I stop the flow of the urine to tighten those muscles
when, in fact, I had had corrective surgery to let everything flow
easily down there?

"I simply said strengthen your muscles by squeezing that area."

"This is not normal!"

Nigel said that if touching my body was hard, he would recommend medical tools of different sizes to help train that part of my body to relax. I would insert the tool inside at home while lying in bed and reading a book about female anatomy and human sexuality.

"Sex is not dirty. You need to open your mind," he said.

"Why don't I just go to the red-light district?"

I removed a piece of paper, a full list of the exercises he had given me, and read aloud those words he circled in our session last week—like "rhythmic breathing." The exercise was to imagine the rhythmic wind blowing kisses all over my body. The tingling feeling should build up, and it should be easy for me to tighten my muscles.

I told him that after our last session, and after I had gotten over my embarrassment, I had thought about how fun it would be to wear the bustier. I dove into my new world with confidence. I told Nigel how strongly the muscles inside of me were tightening and that I imagined being with my first French lover.

I stand in front of the open closet and admire the red bustier and the glowing belly-dancer outfit that makes me feel inside like I am blessed with an opulent body. But I choose the tight-laced bustier with a garter belt and, as I put on the thigh-high boots, I gasp for air. With a constricted body, I move toward the bed with cracked ribs because my breasts are pushed up, and I manage to climb up on the nightstand, which seems like a shelf. In full display, I stand there while my lover trembles with the anticipation. He is fascinated by the lusty lingerie, and before our bodies press against each other, I think about ways to prolong this moment. Suddenly, his hands wrap around my tiny waist, and as he lifts me off the shelf, my shining brown Somali skin blindsides him. I then begin those long African-history lessons. While breathless, I tell him how the Dinka in Sudan initiate their children by tattooing their foreheads and how the Mursi women in Ethiopia wear beautiful plates in their lips.

Before the French lover opens his mouth and shouts Quelle hor-
reur! *I ask if he's seen how the Wodaabe males in Niger prepare for
their Geerewol dance before they line up in front of strong women
judges. By the time I get to the feared mutant story, and how many
times my body has been reincarnated, the bewildered French lover is
too exhausted to untie the tight-laced bustier and work on my inside
muscles.*

I finished narrating my imagined scenario and shouted, "I'm
not going to be an object!"

I was still too close to my experience as Yusuf's property and
believed that no matter what I did, a man would always think
of me that way. I did not want to do these exercises because I
still saw them as a way to please men rather than as a way to
accept myself.

Nigel remained calm. "You are here to learn how to please
yourself, not someone else," he said. He explained how the
Masasi in Tanzania have a long tradition: the young girls are
taught to self-stimulate by stretching their labia every day.

Quietly, I walked over, sat on the couch, and noticed the
horse painting leaning against the wall next to the window. I
closed my eyes and quieted my mind. I sensed Nigel getting up
and walking away. I opened my eyes and saw him bringing me
a glass of water.

"Thank you."

"Was she there?"

"Who?"

"Your mother—did she watch you struggle?"

"She couldn't see me." I told him I didn't want to talk about
anything from the past because Dr. Omar had already asked all
the questions about the day I was mutilated and if I struggled.

"What happened after you struggled?"

"They chopped off my flesh and fed it to the dogs."

"It was your mother, then, who stole your body." Nigel said it
would be helpful to understand how the culture had tied Mother's hands and forced the cutting. Now, by focusing on school
and therapy, I could heal and learn about women's oppression

worldwide. Nigel said he would be gentle, listening to the traumatic experiences in my life. I should not feel like my body was separated from my mind.

"Forgive your mother," he said.

"How?"

"Detach yourself from her."

"I came from her, but I was never attached to her." Waves carrying anger rushed through me, and I didn't like it. I had so many conflicting emotions about Mother, but I never allowed cold words to come out of my mouth. I had a bitter, sour taste, and it didn't feel good at all. I told Nigel my mother had given birth to twelve children, and nine of us survived. With each birth, her vagina was restitched—twelve times, trying to return her to the state of a virgin—and she never complained at all. "That alone should make me want to forgive her," I said.

"You should, if that will help you move forward."

I asked him if he could summarize the sessions and what his role was going to be.

"I will listen and teach your mind and body how to communicate."

"How? Are you going to do something to me?"

"You'll do the simple home exercises," he said.

I told him that I had problems doing these exercises, especially the touching and the masturbation.

"It's the healthy way to explore. . . ."

"Forget it!"

Nigel said it would be amazing if I took the time to know what my body can do and find ways to get familiar with those sensory nerve endings and the muscles inside. "It's you getting to know how you would like to be touched."

"I don't want to be touched." My body moved back on the couch as I slid my hands protectively between my inner thighs, something I do unconsciously when I'm nervous.

He went on about the self-awareness exercises to awaken my sexuality, but I was more focused on the tingling, sharp pain rising between my legs.

"Stop!" I shouted. "This kind of talk is too hard for me to take." I put my hands over my face as I spoke. "Please do not repeat words like 'muscle relaxing' and 'masturbation.'"

"Do you know what the plateau phase is?" he asked.

"Yes," I answered, and I went on to describe the house in Hargeisa high above the cliff and the beautiful nearby lake. "Those were beautiful times!"

He looked me in the eyes. "I'm talking about sexual arousal."

I listened carefully as he explained the whole thing about how the senses elevate the body and how I should watch when my nipples become erect and write down the exact cause, like what was I doing? What was the time? Was this the first experience noticing their erection?

"You mean I should carry a notebook?" He was serious when he said I should write down every movement my muscles, nerves, and body made. I would have to bring in those notes, share them with him, and together we would analyze the progress I had made. Nigel said this journey was not about me learning how to give pleasure to someone; it was about taking my power back.

"And where do you expect me to put the notebook while I make love?" I asked sarcastically.

His stare, those piercing blue eyes, told me he didn't know. I grabbed my bag and got the hell out of there. I could feel Yusuf's firm hands grabbing my arms as he yelled, *You're my wife!*

32

the diderot restaurant

I walked into the campus restaurant, called the Diderot, and saw the huge line. I was too hungry to leave and find somewhere else to eat, so I got in line and waited like everyone else.

I noticed a handsome student's brown eyes transfixed on me, and I turned back to see if he was looking at someone behind me. My suspicion was confirmed when I looked up again, and his eyes were racing over my body.

I opened my backpack, thinking this was the perfect time to go over the class schedules for languages and political science. Reading over the information, I realized the Hebrew class was full, but the English and Russian classes were open. When I looked up, I saw the brown-eyed student standing in front of me.

"I like a woman with a wide forehead."

"Is that all you see?"

The line started moving forward, and I went back to reviewing the choices for language classes. I definitely did not want to take Russian because it reminded me of home, when Mother had her Moscow friends visiting. If Father made remarks or didn't say nice things about the guests, Mother would threaten to leave, telling him how fast she could pack up and go to

Moscow with her friends. Instead of English, I decided to take Latin, which would help with my literature classes.

"I'm Raj."

I stared into his intense eyes, wondering if I should say something. Suddenly, two male students rushed in and stood in front of Raj. They dropped their bags on the floor between their legs, completely ignoring my space.

One of them leaned over to Raj and said, "I used my white tantric magic on her!"

"She is hooked!" the other said.

I really didn't understand what tantric magic was. I folded my paper and put it into my bag and tried to ignore their conversation.

"You mean the red tantric?" Raj asked.

Finally, the line moved up again, and students started picking up the lunch trays. Raj grabbed a tray and handed it to me.

"Thank you, but I don't need it." He locked eyes with me as I handed back the tray. He watched while I observed the food choices in front of me.

"You're holding up the line," Raj said in a teasing voice.

The potato salad looked good, but, to be sure I could eat it, I asked the man standing behind the counter how the potatoes were cooked. Annoyed students got out of the line behind me and moved forward, filling up their trays with food.

The man behind the counter glared. "They're boiled."

"Did you use butter or olive oil?" His attitude reminded me I should be making my own food; most dorms had kitchens. To be safe, I grabbed the fruit bowl, bananas, and water. I walked off and found a table.

Four girls sat at the table, busy planning a party and what clothes they intended to wear. I didn't turn my head to see what Raj was doing. I ignored him and enjoyed eating the delicious fruit.

Suddenly, like impatient stoats, the girls turned away, their gaze fixated on the food line. Curious, I looked over and saw Raj picking up a dessert from the counter. The girls' glazed eyes followed Raj back to the table and watched him sit down and begin eating the dessert. They dropped their forks as their faces turned bright red. They seemed to be worked up and giggled nervously.

Finally, they looked at me and asked, "Are you from India?"

I shook my head and started eating my second banana. I couldn't speak because I was focused on my plan to visit the red-light district and needed to come up with questions to ask the prostitutes.

33

the coffee shop

To forget about therapy and everything about my body, I went out with Jane, my neighbor across the hall in the dorm. We walked into a packed and noisy coffee shop filled with college students. She knew most of them and found a place for us to sit.

She wanted to know what was wrong and what kind of surgery I had had. I talked about how I felt when I had my first menses and asked Jane if she celebrated when she saw hers. She talked about her abusive family relationships and how much she wished for her father's passing in a painful death. I couldn't help but notice her face turning bright red as tears welled up in her eyes. She was angry, describing the night she broke a beer bottle on her father's head, trying to protect her young sister. Her words made my skin crawl; I couldn't understand why a father would hurt his own child like this.

I jumped when suddenly a hand came down on my shoulder and I heard a voice asking, "Is this seat taken?"

Before I could turn to see who stood behind me, Jane yelled, "Raj—hello!"

I looked up and locked eyes with Raj, the brown-eyed student from the Diderot. Excited, Jane told him to sit down before I had a chance to say anything. Raj sat down and flashed a smile.

"Please tell my friend the meaning of your name," Jane said with a smile.

"*Raja* means 'king'—call me Raj, please."

Jane talked nonstop, and Raj listened politely until she asked about hearing rumors that his bride-to-be was being shipped to Grenoble.

"Don't spread rumors," he exclaimed.

"Well—"

"Does your friend have a name?"

Jane said that she called me Peace because I like quiet and don't like loud noises.

"The king likes peace within his kingdom!" he quipped.

Jane asked how he could say that when he was surrounded by wildflowers.

"But do I smell them?"

"You do with your eyes," Jane said, then asked, "What is the king's favorite flower?"

Raj responded, "Rose."

"With thorns?"

"So delicious!"

It didn't take long to notice the flood of breasts rushing to our table. Girls talked over one another, asking Raj which party he was going to attend that coming Friday. I leaned over to Jane and said I was going to the bathroom.

Instead, I left the coffee shop and decided to walk around town and enjoy myself.

⊹

The next day, I awoke feeling anxious. I did not want to go to the hospital for my checkup. I decided to visit Nigel and talk about the progress I had made since my last session.

When I got to Nigel's house, I heard a woman shouting. "You haven't stopped your dogging lifestyle!"

"Parking lots were never my style."

"Then what formed your bonds?"

"You're not listening!"

Slowly, I walked down the hall and then peeked into the living room, where a slender woman with long red hair stood in front of Nigel. I remembered her as the woman who visited me at the hospital room, asking me to sign a release of the surgery photos.

"Take your horse painting, please," Nigel said.

"Why would he leave me a horse painting?

"Go to the lake and ask him why."

"I gave him seven years of my life, and you ruined it!" The woman stormed out, leaving her violent energy to knock me out of balance.

I crashed into the round table, and pain shot through my knee. Sure enough, Nigel stood in front of me.

"How long were you standing here?"

"Not long. I'm sorry. . . ."

"What happened to your checkup?"

I told Nigel I had something to talk about that was more important than the checkup, something that showed I was not a mutant. The night before, while walking downtown, I realized most French women were not different than me; we had something in common.

"You found out they, too, have endometrial linings and bleed?"

"Most of them had an episiotomy!" Nigel didn't say a word. He just crossed his arms in front of his chest and kept staring. I said these women experienced cutting and, during the healing process, did exercises by tightening their pelvic muscles. I had read about it and talked to women who experienced the surgery.

"Are you hungry?" he asked.

"Yes."

I followed Nigel into the kitchen where two plates, cups, and forks sat on the table. A bottle of red wine sat in the middle. He pointed me to the chair on the other side of the table, and I sat down, thinking that Nigel was expecting another guest. I watched him reheat a pot, and the smell was very strong. He placed a plate and a wineglass in front me. I asked what he was cooking, and he said it was mutton soup.

"I don't eat meat."

"I can make you something else."

I asked if all his pots were used to cook meat, and his reaction, especially his serious facial expression, was very interesting. Nigel said that every pot, fork, spoon, and everything else in the kitchen had touched some form of meat. He uncorked the bottle and poured the wine into the glasses. He walked away and brought in a plate full of smelly cheese and fruit.

"I'd like to know more about your family, your culture—especially the arranged marriages. Do women have a choice in these arrangements?"

"Choice?"

Nigel tried to be funny and said the woman should test-drive and decide if the groom is good enough for the marriage, like they do in the West. "It's called sex before marriage," he said. "It's acceptable because people want to get to know each other and share love. What's unacceptable is when two people are forced to marry and intimacy becomes a battle. This is called rape—it's sexual assault."

Before Nigel had a chance to ask about my life in Geneva, Yusuf's voice emanated from my mind, *It's me.* I flashed back to the night I woke up and his face hovered above me as his hand clasped my mouth. *It's me.* Panic shot through me. Yusuf said, *Your Mother is home—be quiet and do not fight.* I reminded him that she was the one who arranged for him to torture and fuck a child, and all I could offer was a fight.

By the time I shook off the flashback, Nigel was sitting across the table eating the mutton soup. I was frantic, waves of emotion overpowering me.

"Abuse is not a destiny," he said.

"I'm not abused. . . ."

"Why did you shove pills down your throat?"

"I was frightened."

I told Nigel that when I fully realized how alone I was in my new life, I did not feel I was courageous enough to move forward. I told him about my life with Yusuf and how I could still vividly see the night when he got the most violent. I narrated the whole scene like a movie so that Nigel could understand the depth of the scar that it left in me.

I hear the Spanish folk music blaring from the invisible speakers, and I know Yusuf is in the library, loading the white sugar into the black briefcases. Ana is performing her nightly ritual, carrying a glass of warm milk down the hallway to the guest room where Mother sleeps. She knocks on the door, Mother calls out, "Entrare," and Ana proceeds inside. Mother, holding her smooth black prayer beads, stands by the open window, staring at the empty sky. Ana sets down the warm glass of milk on a table in the sitting area, then exits the room without saying a word. At that moment, Yusuf is escorting the two yellow-haired Swiss men with briefcases out of the house. He then rushes toward the hallway and tries to find a way to enter my room. But a chair blocks the door, and a long rope is strung between the doorknob and my pillow. Yusuf forces his way into the room, and the rope pulls forward, yanking my pillow off the bed. With fury, Yusuf moves forward and pins me down in the bed.

I scream "Mother!" as I struggle to pull him off me.

"Relax—be quiet!" Yusuf shouts.

"Mother!" I scream again. The Spanish folk music stops, and I scream again, calling for Mother. This time she might hear me, but instead of rushing in and stopping Yusuf's madness, Mother bends her head down in shame for selling my body. She holds the prayer beads tightly in her hands, and I hear them break off and crash to the floor.

"I'm sorry," Nigel said.

"Why didn't she hear me?"

I needed to continue releasing all the nasty feelings inside of me, expelling the poison. I blamed Mother for abandoning me with Yusuf.

"It will be too painful for me if I never see my family again, especially Father and my brother Asis." I spoke quietly, although

I was furious at them for being part of Mother's plan to force me to marry Yusuf. But I still loved them.

I told Nigel I remembered taking a few pills, not swallowing the whole bottle. Nigel suggested that I write down my thoughts and feelings daily, and each session he would teach me how to change those thoughts to something more hopeful. He said the more I talked about my past experiences and trauma, the stronger I would become.

"But no matter how many times I stand in the shower and try to peel off my skin to eliminate the filth, that scene always comes into my mind," I said and went on to explain that the most painful thing was not that Mother did not respond to my cry for help. What hurt most was that she took an early flight the next morning before I woke up. When I discovered Mother had gone back to Mogadishu, that I was abandoned in a strange country at age seventeen, left to my thirty-five-year-old cousin, I was overwhelmed with loss and confusion. The pain was the worst I ever felt; it took away whatever little sense of self I had.

Nigel explained the right way to deal with the wounded memories. He said I should not give her any power, that I was the only one responsible for my new life.

"If you could see just a glimpse of the person you can become, you would be very content, and you would use this therapy to help others who aren't lucky enough to be here," he said.

It was getting late, and Nigel offered to take me to the dormitory. I realized how much talking to Nigel was helping me and how lucky I was to have someone I could trust. And yet I was frightened by my emotional connection to Nigel. I knew we had a spiritual bond, but I wished, inappropriately, that Nigel would walk me through my exercises himself. I had told him this, and that's when I found out that he was gay and had a lover who had died not long ago. This man was married to the female hospital worker who had come into my room when I first met Nigel.

Despite my conflicted feelings, I reflected that Nigel's dry sense of humor, quirky attitude, and strange personality made it easier for me to forget about the past. He forced me to find laughter in the midst of fear.

†

Fear, however, was still with me. One day, on my way to the library, I noticed a black Mercedes parked by a building, and I thought Yusuf might be watching. I wanted to walk up to the car and get hysterical and fight with him, but I was calm and did not allow the fear to take over.

I watched as a young male student rushed toward the car and hurriedly got inside. Feeling relieved, I kept walking toward the library. But then I saw a man who looked like those yellow-haired, dark-suit-wearing men who worked for Yusuf walking toward me.

Suddenly I felt the sharp horns sticking out of my forehead, and, like a true wildebeest, I ran into the library. I couldn't stop when I saw Raj dressed in a suit addressing a group of female admirers. Chaos erupted when I crashed into him, but I didn't have time to say sorry, and I hurried up to the second floor. I opened the window and surveyed the area below to see if the yellow-haired man was following me into the library.

Raj rushed in. "You hit me!"

"Go away!"

Raj leaned over to see what I was looking at below. The yellow-haired man was walking toward the building. Raj waved and, when the man didn't see him, whistled. The man stopped and looked up at us.

Raj yelled out, "We're going in at three this afternoon!"

The man waved OK, opened the door, and walked into the library.

"You know him?"

"We're doing a mock trial together."

"What are you defending?

"Women's rights."

"What kind of rights?"

"Would you like to come and watch the trial?"

Mother in 1982.

Left to right: My brother Asis, sister Amal, me (at age one), and brother Malik.

Father in his Mogadishu, Somalia, office, 1975.

Passport photo, 1978, age seventeen.

Left to right: My cousin Jamila Ali, nephew Mohamed Mohayadin (Sakiya's son), a family friend, sister Raha, me, and sister Shams, 1978.

Grenoble, France, bus stop, 1980.

Left to right: Mother, me, my cousin Khalifa (behind me), her daughter Deeqa (in front), and a family friend, Washington, DC, 1982.

Above and right: In Grenoble with
some student friends, circa 1983.

Brother Malik and his best friend, Cabdulqadir Sheekhy.

Left to right: Shams, Jamila Ali, Raha, and our cousin Khadra Abshir (Yusuf's sister).

On a film set in 1992.

At a dinner reception I was invited to by the late Lloyd Bridges, an activist in several progressive causes, with his friends, 1996.

In some parts of Africa, after the "rite of passage" is performed on a girl, white clay is applied to her face, signifying that she is expected to recover and is now allowed into the circle of womanhood.

PHOTO BY BARBARA MICHELLS

Mother with her granddaughter Khadra, Shams's daughter, who is now sixteen and, thankfully, escaped the torture of FGM.

In Los Angeles in 2011. PHOTO BY LORI SHEPLER

"No. I'm busy preparing a long trial of my own."

"What are you defending?"

I told Raj that I was in the process of making up my mind to defend the human genitals and needed someone to help with the research.

He looked confused for a moment, then asked, "Can we first meet for coffee?"

I agreed, and we made a plan to meet downtown.

34

the courtesan

In my quest to understand human sexuality, I ventured into Grenoble's red-light district. I wanted to know if the prostitutes could reach orgasm by selling their bodies. As I made my way through the busy streets, I became so engrossed in my search that I lost all self-consciousness and inhibition.

Two women dressed in striking colors stood at a door and stared at me. I approached and addressed them in French. At first, they appeared to be confused; they didn't know whether I was a customer or a job seeker.

I told them about the Secret House in Mogadishu and how, as a child, I was curious to know what took place there. Just by the looks on their faces, I knew it was time that I told them what my assignment was.

"Could you define orgasm?" I asked.

"*Ça va être le bordel!*" one shouted as she ran inside the brothel. "It'll be chaos!"

The other female smiled and said I would accomplish a lot by going to the police department and asking the men there if their *lorettes* ("easy" women) have orgasms.

"Do you?" I asked.

"Do you want to come in?" she asked.

I told her about my first session with Nigel and how he needed to connect my head back to my body. I had seen my naked body for years, but now I had to take a mirror and carefully examine it. I listened as she talked about her male clients and the reason that she could not have an orgasm.

I had lost track of time, and suddenly I realized I was late to meet up with Raj at the coffee shop. I thanked her.

"I am coming back, and next time with my notebook," I told her.

⁂

I rushed into the coffee shop. Raj was not happy that I was late. I apologized and promised he would be excited once he knew about our research plan for that night.

First, I said, we should find out where the shocking films played.

"Horror?" Raj asked.

"Films about sex." I sat back and watched his reaction.

Surprised, Raj stared for a long moment, so long that I felt I needed to assure him that I wasn't really a freak.

"It's part of my research," I said, "but I understand if you can't help."

"Let's go!" Excitedly, he leaped up from the chair and rushed to the door. He stood there grinning.

Well, I knew the message I was sending, and it was too late for me to act innocent. He did not know about my mutilation, and this was not the time to tell him. I rose and followed Raj out of the coffee shop toward the movie theater.

⁂

Raj and I walked into the dark theater, and I heard those noises that had sounded so foreign to me when I had been captured by Yusuf. Raj and I sat at the back of the theater. Something was different about these sounds when they were attached to a person's facial expressions. I couldn't believe what I was seeing—I tried to make sense of it.

I missed noticing Raj's hand reaching out until it landed on my left breast. Raj wasn't Yusuf, and it wasn't fair to slap him, so I got up and walked out. Raj hurried after me and found me standing by the bus stop. He opened his ski jacket and put his hands on his hips. I could sense his frustration as he struggled to find the perfect words.

"I mean—what do you want?"

I calmly explained to Raj that this journey was not about him, and his hand landing on my breast was not part of the research plan. I apologized for not thinking clearly and suggesting the movie. I had been caught up in the excitement of my earlier discoveries.

I said, "The research—my assignment—is about biology. Sexuality."

"*Merde*—why didn't you say that?"

The bus arrived, and as we boarded, Raj took my hand and said, "I can help you with that."

I found an empty seat at the back while Raj helped an elderly lady stash her plastic bag under the seat.

⸭

Back in the dorm cafeteria, Raj and I continued our talk. Every few minutes, young female students would stop at our table to flirt with him. He seemed to love the attention, but I wasn't going to walk out. Earlier, he had said something in passing about photos from his parents. The comment had gotten my attention, and I wanted to get to the bottom of it. I sipped my hot tea and waited until the latest parade of breasts had ended.

"I help them with homework," Raj said with a smile.

"That's noble of you."

"Tell me about your research."

"Later," I said. "I'm curious about the photos your parents sent from the French Indies. What kinds of photos?"

"My parents like to hunt on my behalf."

"What kind of animal are they hunting?"

"Animal?" he repeated.

He raised his chin, tapping his fingers on the table. A blond approached our table, sliding her hand behind his neck.

"I'm going up," she said.

He looked up and nodded his head, and she walked away.

"It's not what you think," he said, referring to the blond.

"What happened with the hunting arrangements?" Knowing the Indian culture, I was aware he was talking about an arranged marriage. But I wasn't sure if he said yes.

Raj told me that he found my aggressive talk alluring. "I have the option not to agree with the woman my parents choose. They send me the pictures to get my opinion."

"Your marriage was arranged!"

"I'm not married!"

Raj could not understand why I was becoming so emotional and confrontational. I then realized he couldn't be part of my research. I thought it would be a change to go out with someone instead of obsessively thinking about the exercises and how to train my body for sexual understanding. When I had told Nigel how I jumped when Raj came over and put his hand on my shoulder, he said Raj might be awakening my sexuality, and I should look into ways to expand that experience further.

But now I saw that moving forward was not that simple. I realized, when I gazed into Raj's eyes, that I was creating trouble for myself. Raj was headed into an arrangement similar to the one I had just escaped.

"When will your wife be shipped?"

"No one is shipping me anything. OK?"

I wasn't OK, because I somehow knocked over my hot tea, and, thank goodness, Raj rushed to the counter to get napkins. I had a few minutes to breathe and reminded myself what it takes to walk the minefield alone. Everything that Nigel said could not be true, and I had to stop the nonsense. I would heal and find the joy of self-discovery. I watched Raj clean up the table and sit down again, glaring at me with those brown eyes.

"What was that multiple thing you were talking about?" he asked, referring to an earlier conversation we had had.

"Men can't have multiple orgasms like women."

"Really?"

"That's what my . . . teacher said."

"Only a feminist would say that!"

For hours, I sat there with Raj and took notes as he talked about a woman's body and orgasm. Totally fascinated, I would put my pen down and just watch his facial expressions and hand movements. He went on about the rhythm men make during the contractions right before ejaculation. Raj said he was an expert who liked to watch how fast the clitoris moved inward and waited until the girl shouted, "Grab me!"

"What if nothing was going inward, and you had nothing to grab?" I asked him.

He frowned, twisted his arms, then leaned back in his chair.

"What if the girl was a mutant?" I pressed.

"What do you mean?"

I decided to end the conversation and that dream about what could be between Raj and me if we went all the way with my assignment.

"Would you have lunch with me tomorrow?" he asked.

"I'll be in therapy."

"Acupuncture?"

"Psychotherapy."

35

squeezing the vaginal walls

After engrossing myself in classes and becoming much more comfortable in my new environment, I knew the time had come to look up at the full moon and have a talk with God. My intention was not to be angry and ask why he had forsaken me during the painful times of my life. I did not need to say how I felt as a woman, with a body caught in crosscurrents the moment I swam into the world; how, at thirteen, I felt like a lamb tied to a cotton tree, with my body dragged into the room where they burned my flesh and blood.

No, I didn't say all that. Rather I believed God needed to know why I bought the small TV, the videos, and the books that would stimulate my mind. He needed to know that the self-exploration exercises originated with Nigel, not me. Nigel said doing them would improve my health and spirituality and help me overcome the trauma my body had endured. But Nigel neglected to mention how long it would take for me to be able to reconnect the broken pieces within myself and learn trust and self-surrender.

God, these exercises are critical and have nothing to do with sex and orgasm. Setting up this sacred and quiet time with myself gives me a brief moment to step back from the pain and not focus on what has been removed from me. I want to know who I am and if I ever can love myself. I don't want to be stuck in the victim mode. I need to stop rewinding that image of my body on the fast, whirring sewing machine. I don't even care that these French women, with their sophistication and superb makeup, are never genitally mutilated. I just want to find myself and to be proud.

I breathed deeply and stood before the mirror. I began undressing, but I was stopped by a sudden wind that blew through the open window, covering me with shame and guilt. In my mind, what I was about to do could turn this tiny dorm room into a brothel. I mean, where would I begin? Should I ask God questions like *Is masturbation repulsive?* Or should I expect Mother to show up in my room with her seat cushion, as she did at the Plaza del Toros? Would doing this distract me from my new life and school?

God, am I committing a sin by trying to find out whether my vagina can expand, by digging deep to locate the clitoral tissue left behind?

I prayed the *dua*, an Islamic prayer of supplication, just in case the dormitory was burned to the ground as a result of my actions. I remember how easy it was for people to do the wrong things and then call out to God for forgiveness.

But why should I feel shame and guilt from standing naked in front of the mirror? How long could I torment myself by holding on to those old beliefs that say our bodies are the property of our husbands? We were told to never touch any delicate parts of our own bodies, from the chin down, in "funny ways." Only our husbands, our owners, could touch us. No one prepared us for the wedding night. Our parents and loved ones even forgot to mention our owners' forceful ways or how to deal with their weight crushing our bodies in the middle of the night. Our guardians made sure to entice us women into unwanted matches with those who liked to force obedience, not with love, but with ownership.

No, I said to myself, *I will not feel any shame.*

God should not be upset with me for wanting to learn about my body and peek at my vulva. He should be angry and shouting at those who said they heard him instructing them to chop off those delicate parts of our bodies and make the correction to his own creation.

I stopped my conversation with God and looked at those pictures taken during my reversal surgery. Those bloody pictures didn't make me sad but made me appreciate my body's endurance and strength.

Then I looked at those sketched pictures of a woman's normal anatomy that Nigel had given me. I stared at them for a long moment. The room got cold and my body trembled as I allowed fearful and negative thoughts to invade my mind and make me feel like I was a freak and could not face myself. That's when Nigel's words came to mind, telling me I could either remain in victim mode or become a survivor with a fierce voice, without shame. At that moment, I chose to become a survivor.

I am a woman who is not defined by what has been taken from me but by what I create with what I have. I am a woman who works tirelessly to find my place in this world. I am a woman who will heal and give back the gift with which I am entrusted. I will climb the highest mountain to find the truth that will help me claim my wholeness as a human and sexual being. Working from the inside out will guide me to the path of self-discovery, and, ultimately, I will be able to separate love and pain. Then I will learn how to fall in love with myself.

I walked to the open window and made sure the curtains were secured and no wondering eyes lurked outside. I placed a bright, soft bedsheet on the floor, took my clothes off, and stepped onto it. I sat down in front of the large mirror while holding the small one in my right hand. I am not going to tell you what happened next, except that I had a wonderful viewing position to examine the uncharted territory. I stared at myself, awed by that amazing place pulsing with life possibilities, then said to my vulva, *I promise no one will ever hurt or mistreat you as long as I remain conscious and awake.*

I continued with the exercise, squeezing my vaginal walls, and wrote in my mind those questions I would ask Nigel later. I heard whispering voices and thought someone was standing at my door. I stopped and listened. No one knocked. I went back to the exercise, facing the mirror.

Without warning, a bright light flashes. The door swings open, and a nurse rushes me into the emergency room. The room pulses with a strange energy, and I see myself as if from above, a lamb being readied for slaughter. What happened to her? says one of the shock-eyed, white-coated women staring down at me. . . .

I forced my mind back to my present reality; I was in my dorm room, doing the exercises my therapist prescribed, staring at myself in the large mirror. I tried to hold on tightly to the present, but before I had a chance to get up, another disturbing image overpowered my mind.

I am in Yusuf's house in Geneva, in my room, with the chair pushed against the door, my only protection against rape. Suddenly, there is pounding on my door. The chair is no barrier to my husband and his Saudi guests, who burst through the door and begin hitting me with hot sticks. . . .

I screamed at the top of my lungs, striking out so powerfully that my hand smashed the large mirror into pieces. My body was burning, burning so intensely that I wanted to peel my skin off and expose those raw nerves that Yusuf, fear, and my guardians had taken hold of. Crying hysterically, I struggled to stop scratching my skin and didn't notice the pieces of the broken mirror stuck into my hand.

Only after I saw fresh blood running down my hand did I realize it was impossible to cut off those nerves for good. I wanted to vomit all of that pain from inside, and I retched, but only water came out of me. I drank so much water that sometimes I forgot to eat because I didn't feel hungry. Now I envisioned myself as a burn victim who needed to walk back through the fire to get help. Sweating heavily, my body released water like a monsoon rain as the furious wind threw painful lashes all around. I was sucked into extreme emotional pain; I was grieving for myself. Crying from deep within made it difficult for my body to bend over and hold my aching abdomen.

Feeling dizzy, I began breathing rapidly. A soothing wind rushed in and calmed me momentarily. I closed my eyes and followed the rhythm of my breathing, but my mind continued to assault me with images, keeping me prisoner. I shouted at my mind, demanding it stop replaying those traumatic scenes. These were the images that loved to sneak in at night, that caused nightmares, threw me out of bed, and forced me to confront the haunting faces of my past. I would scream and watch those faces leaving but not without first showing me a preview of images for the next night, like the one when Mother and I walked into the shop of our tailor and the sound of nonstop sewing machines overwhelmed me.

I shouted at them, *No more! What you do is wrong, and I will not suffer silently! The world will know!*

The sound of knocking at my door broke the spell. I struggled to my feet, pulled on my robe, and went to the door. I heard Jane's voice calling out, "Are you OK?"

What was I supposed to say to her? My head was still full of the disturbing images of the past, of Sheikha, her four teeth, myself lying in the ring of fire while she showered me with dead chicken's blood. I took a deep breath.

"I was just having a nightmare," I said through the door.

"My boyfriend took the night off, and if you want, you can come stay in my room." She paused. "Just to be safe."

"I'll be fine. Thank you."

"Do you want me to stay over?"

"I think if my stomach was full, I wouldn't have nightmares." I opened the door.

"I've got some cheese and yogurt." She smiled. "I'll bring them over."

⚜

By the time Jane left, it was time to get into the shower and get ready for class. I got out of bed and had the urge to run toward

Nigel's home and swallow all the medicine from the bottles on his desk, without cleaning myself or picking up the broken mirror.

But I forced my breath deeper and deeper, until I began to feel relaxed, calmer. I managed to move back toward the bed, climbed in, got under the covers, and put my head down. Later, I woke up feeling much better and cleaned up the room and the broken mirror. I decided to get ready and visit Nigel even though he wasn't expecting me, so I was not sure he would be there.

While walking toward Nigel's house, I saw a woman sitting by a grave site. Lit candles, a music player, and a wine bottle sat by her side. She was talking to herself. Suddenly, she laughed, laughing until she broke down and cried.

36

flowers and footsteps

When I got back to the dormitory, I found roses on the floor outside my door. They were thorny so I picked them up carefully. I walked to Raj's dorm, convinced he had some explaining to do. How disrespectful of him not to put the roses in a vase! At least he could have left them with the concierge instead of putting them on the floor. I walked into his dorm, went straight upstairs to his room, and knocked. No one answered. A student passed by and said Raj was downstairs watching television.

I rushed downstairs, now feeling the nervous movement in my stomach. I entered the TV room where a few students were watching a comedy show. Raj sat at the back, flirting with a giggling girl. He looked up and saw me, and I walked out and waited for him at the door.

"Did you get my notes?" he asked.

"I got the roses with thorns."

Raj frowned and looked at me for a long moment. "Roses?"

"The ones you left at my door."

"Wait—do I look like a man who buys roses?"

My head was spinning. If it wasn't Raj, then who? Raj started venting his resentment about my not responding to his notes to me. He had even noticed that I stopped eating at the campus restaurant.

Suddenly, I sensed danger. Maybe Yusuf had found me.

"I have to go," I said and rushed back toward my dorm without saying another word.

When I got to the lobby, I asked the concierge, Jean-Pierre, if he had seen someone carrying roses upstairs. He said no, and that's when I felt angry for giving Yusuf the power to frighten me.

I went to the mail room, got inside the phone booth, and called my family's number collect. Sister Raha answered the phone, and, when she heard the operator say my name, she yelled "Si" over and over.

"Where are you?"

"I am in France."

I heard her shout to the family that I was in France and on the phone.

"Can I speak to Mother?"

"We found your movie!" she exclaimed.

"What movie?"

"Doris Day—have you met her yet?"

"I think she lives in America. . . ."

Mother took the phone from Raha and started crying. She said how scared they were when Yusuf told them about my disappearance. She said cousin Khalifa and the rest of the family were searching for me everywhere in Europe. "What have we done to you?"

"You left me with Yusuf, Mother."

In the background, I could hear the family talking and begging Mother to pass the phone. I told Mother I was in France, that Yusuf was after me, and that, if I died, she would be responsible.

Mother shouted, "*Allahu akbar!*" then screamed as she dropped the phone.

Father came to the phone and asked in a frantic voice if I was hurt.

"I will be if you don't stop Yusuf's madness."

After a long discussion about my state of mind, Father demanded that I give him my contact information so that one of them could come and rescue me. I agreed to give it only after explaining that France had laws and that I was over eighteen years old.

"Yusuf is your family!"

"I miss you, but I will never go back to him."

"What do you want?"

"A divorce."

Father got quiet for a moment, then told me not to fear Yusuf because he would never harm anyone. He said brother Asis was on his way to Brussels and that Khalifa would contact me. Khalifa and her family had lived in Brussels for a long time and brought Yusuf to Europe when he was a teenager.

I said OK and hung up. My knees were shaking, and I couldn't hold back the hot tears falling or the knot in my stomach. I had never spoken to my parents in that tone. I felt like a different person, removed from them. As I had spoken with them, Yusuf's face kept appearing in my mind's eye. I recalled calling them for help when I was held captive by him and their telling me to watch my hot temper. I left the phone booth and went upstairs, envisioning how I would face Yusuf.

I found myself staring into the darkness, lying in bed for hours, unable to sleep. I got up and checked the door, making sure it was locked. I walked over and opened the window, looking out into the silent night. Everything seemed calm and beautiful. In the hallway, I heard keys clattering and people laughing. Someone was at my door. Mortified, I grabbed the chair and stood in front of the door. A key was being forced into my door, and then I heard Jane's voice.

"Jane?"

"Yeah—why did you lock up?" She laughed while hitting the door with her hand.

"You're breaking into my room—"

"Fuck!"

I heard Jane and her boyfriend laughing as they moved away from the door.

At that moment, I heard another knock and flashed back to the night Yusuf broke into my room, but this time he was forcing himself into my dorm room in my mind's eye.

I slam the door in Yusuf's face and scream, "No!" Sick with fear, I vomit and shriek at the top of my lungs. Yusuf paces the dorm hallway outside my door, saying, "I am not here to harm you!" A policeman rushes into my room shouting, "Get down on the floor!"

It took a while for me to return to my senses. Feeling agitated, I looked around the room. Everything was calm and peaceful again. I got into bed, hoping to get a good night's sleep.

⁂

No more roses appeared at my door. Yusuf did not show up, and my family had not called back since we had spoken. Life returned to normal, except, on top of classes, I got a babysitting job and Nigel's health worsened. His body seemed to be fading away, but his mind was alert; he listened to me and guided me.

I decided the fear of Yusuf would not dictate how I lived my new life, but I could not pretend nothing had happened. I had to find ways to disengage from Yusuf and stop rewinding that image of him, in Geneva, wearing the white robe, walking toward me as he passed the bed. I knew it would take time to stop hearing the sound of the scissors cutting my body and the fast sewing machines. But I refused to become a scared lamb with sutured lips and an empty mind. The pain would stop, and I would get bold. I would work hard to get to know myself and continue on the healing path. I might weep or cringe when I faced the mirror and see the scar left on my body, but it would only remind me of my survival and the strength within me.

⁂

Eventually, after spending more quiet time with myself, I let go of the fear of pain and understood what personal power and freedom meant. The art of communicating with my body and learning the healing touch did not bring up the madness I had gone through with the first mirror exercise. Something had shifted; I did not feel shut down from within. I was not anxious, had no flashbacks and no physical discomfort. I was relaxed and present to the movements and changes that my mind and body were making.

I discovered that these exercises were far from being undignified, sinful, and plain nasty. I was learning about myself as a woman, more than by reading books and watching stimulating videos. I felt awake and very curious about the functions of the vaginal wall and the muscle contractions. I realized that talking to Nigel and having him in my life had built my confidence and emotional well-being.

⚜

After completing the hand-sliding body exercises (masturbation), I got quiet and glanced at the silver pen sitting on top of the notebook. Now I was wondering how to describe what just happened. I mean, how could I describe it? I sat with the pen in my hand, looking over the blank page in the notebook, then decided not to write anything until after I saw Nigel again.

I took a hot shower and was getting ready for a campus party when there was a knock at the door. I kept quiet and listened. The person knocked again, and I didn't speak.

"It's Raj—I know you're in there."

I relaxed a bit. "What do you want?" I called.

"I have a question."

I walked over and opened the door. In front of me stood Raj, dressed in black and surrounded with clouds of cologne.

"Are you a virgin?" he asked.

"Good question. . . ."

"Please, answer the question."

"Have you seen turtles having sex?" I replied.

He glared those brown eyes at me, then leaned his body back on the wall. I told Raj about my family visits to Hargeisa and that, while the others were getting to know our new home, I was in the garden, watching turtles making out by the fountain.

"And the point is?"

"The point is everything is slow and gradual."

"OK. . . ."

"I think, together, we should go to therapy," I said.

"Therapy? I have no psychological problems!"

I grabbed my jacket, locked the door, and walked to the elevator while Raj was still leaning on the wall. By the time Raj reached me, Elvis had come out of the bathroom. Ignoring me, he started singing Elvis's song "Trouble" as he walked down the hallway. His voice got louder and louder, and then we heard a door slam shut. The elevator came, and Raj and I entered.

"What's your religion?" he asked.

"I worship the full moon."

After we argued a bit more in the lobby, Raj decided to accompany me to the campus party. We walked in and found a band playing on the stage. The students gathered around and danced. The floor moved with the music, and everything pulsed with life energy. I saw a group of Somali men standing in the corner. With long heads and slender bodies, they looked like herdsmen standing tall with staffs in their hands. Their glowing dark eyes raced around the hall, and then they saw me. I went over to them and introduced myself.

Instead of polite greetings, the men moved their chins up, then wrinkled their foreheads, and looked at me for a moment.

"Are you really Somali?" a Somali man asked.

"Just look at my forehead!" I said.

"Are you Somali from Mogadishu or Somali from the North?" another man asked, trying to gauge my status in the tensions between the countries north and south.

"I'm Koreishite from Yemen!" I was never into tribe issues and was making a joke. To them I looked like Somalis from Yemen, which is just across the Gulf of Aden.

"*Masha Allah!*" one of the men exclaimed.

A female student walked in leading a group of African male peacocks. She appeared to be either Somali or Ethiopian. Hands up in the air, the peacocks smiled brightly while their feet danced as they greeted people. Their presence was intoxicating and joyful.

"The Calamitas are here!" a Somali man exclaimed.

"Calamitas?" I asked.

"Those men are sin-magnets—see the floor is tilting!"

I looked down at the floor and found it was not tilting. Then a strange thing happened. Most of the girls turned their backs on the band and stormed toward the peacocks. The girls formed a circle, started dancing with the peacocks, and the dance floor became a discotheque. The band was playing reggae music, but the African men started disco dancing to it, and the screaming girls appeared wild, as if they were seeing John Travolta and the other dancers from *Saturday Night Fever*.

"Who's that girl circling around the Calamitas?" a Somali man asked.

"She is *qaniisad*, a lesbian, from Mogadishu," a tall man with stooped shoulders answered.

"Somalis don't produce *qaniisad*!" another one said.

"We do. Just go and visit Torino," the stoop-shouldered man said.

"She is not . . ." another one said.

Stunned, the herdsmen looked at the stoop-shouldered man seriously.

Another man explained the girl could not be *qaniisad* because she wore an erect-penis necklace. While he described the necklace, the herdsmen couldn't stop laughing. The laughter stopped when they noticed the smiling Raj walking toward us with a beer in his hand.

"He's a friend of mine," I said.

"You mean boyfriend?" someone asked.

"Hello, I'm Raj. . . ."

"*Assalamu alaykum!*"

Startled by the tone of the greeting from the Somali men, Raj turned to me, appearing to hope I would say something.

I knew exactly what the herdsmen were thinking and what kind of questions I would be asked in regard to Raj. It was hurtful to the men to see me dating outside my ethnicity. To them, that marked me as easy, and they would question my integrity as a Somali woman. I did not want that discussion.

"Good-bye," I told the herdsmen. "Enjoy the party."

As Raj and I walked away, one of the men shouted the obscene word "*Vaffanculo!*" meaning "fuck you."

Curious about the erect-penis necklace, I dragged Raj toward the peacocks and their girl. Right away, Raj hit it off with the peacocks and started dancing like he was one of the Kikuyu dance performers.

I was busy chatting with their girl, trying desperately to find a way to see her necklace, but her white shirt covered her neck. Her name was Alem, and she was from Addis and lived with her Ghanaian boyfriend. Raj came over and pushed the two of us onto the dance floor. I found it joyful to dance among the wild group, but the sweat and the smell of beer made me run to a corner. Alem hurried after me as I tried to find an open window for fresh air.

"Are you OK?"

"I can't open it!"

"It doesn't open—let's stand by the door." She took my hand, and we hurried to the door.

It was wonderful to inhale the fresh air and be outside. Alem asked why Somali girls distance themselves from their African brothers and sisters. I told her I didn't notice it, only that most of us were busy with school and work.

"I heard you wear a bold necklace," I finally said.

Without hesitation, Alem pulled up the erect-penis necklace and showed me. At first, it looked like a shining, strong, dark fist. But as I got closer I realized it was really an erect penis. I stared at Alem not knowing what to say.

"What do you think?" she asked.

"What do I think?"

"I love penises. Don't you agree?"

"What's not to love!" I replied.

We broke into hysterical laughter until her Ghanaian boy-friend rushed up and cupped her face in his hands, and they locked lips. They returned to the dance floor and joined their friends. Raj came over and asked about the residual smile on my face. I told him about the erect-penis necklace, and, before I finished with the story, Raj was asking what Alem's tribe was.

"I guess she's Amhara—do you need a pen?" I asked sarcastically, feeling like he surely liked her and wanted her number.

Raj leaned forward and kissed me. My lips moved while I tried to angle my head, and I felt my heart skipping beats. Slowly, his tongue sneaked in and rubbed my teeth. I didn't know whether to push Raj away and laugh or let this experience be part of my learning process. I'm not sure of the duration of this kiss, but it's safe to say I got to the dorm very late.

I found a message taped to my door. Khalifa had called and asked that I call her back. It was too late to call, so I waited till the morning.

37

white sugar

When I called Khalifa, I had to wait until she stopped
weeping to hear what she had to say. She finally regained
control and told me not to be scared of Yusuf. He had bigger
problems.

She started apologizing and speaking on behalf of the family. "Whatever you wish will be granted," she said.

"What are Yusuf's problems?" I asked.

But she kept talking about how poorly the family thought
of the whole subject of arranged marriage.

"You were right, and I'm sorry we didn't believe you!" she
cried.

"It's too late."

"I said I'm sorry."

I reminded Khalifa about the frantic calls I used to make to
the family while living in Geneva and how I felt about living in
the Plaza del Toros.

"What are you talking about?"

"Yusuf turned my bedroom into the Plaza del Toros!"

"You're not making sense!"

"Did Mother get my bloody surgical pictures I mailed to
her?"

She ignored my question. "Yusuf was arrested."

"Arrested?"

Khalifa said Yusuf was trafficking drugs around Europe and was a wanted man. She and her husband planned to come to Geneva and help me get a divorce if that was really what I wanted.

"Was he handcuffed?"

"Handcuffed?"

"You said he was arrested—do you have photos?"

"He was trafficking drugs!"

"What kind of drugs?"

"Heroin. . . ."

"That white sugar was heroin?"

"Are you OK?"

"I'm in therapy, but it's too late for you to ask that."

"I'm flying in to see you."

I said OK, not really expecting that Khalifa would show up at my door.

But the news of Yusuf's arrest made me happy. Tears streamed down my face because I couldn't believe it was really over. Yusuf was in a place where he couldn't get to me. I was free.

When I got to my session with Nigel a little later, he seemed to be in a good mood. He asked about the notes and if I was still looking at those surgical pictures before the exercises.

"I sent them to Mother."

"What do you want her to say?"

"I want her to look at them—maybe then she can find herself."

Talking about this brought an uneasy feeling, and thinking how Mother would feel when she looked at those bloody pictures made me sad.

Nigel asked more questions about my thoughts and feelings about Mother. I said the wounds could be healed if my situation with Yusuf was resolved successfully and I could get a divorce.

"What happens after you get the divorce?"

"More work on myself—maybe explore intimacy with Raj."
I told Nigel that I learned almost everything about female anatomy but still had questions about the nerves, veins, and vaginal wall. I described the symptoms I had during the hand-sliding exercise and how I couldn't write anything in the notebook.

"You couldn't or you wouldn't?"

Nigel couldn't keep up with me; my words spilled out like rushing water, and I couldn't stop talking. I felt enormous courage now, while in his presence, to say what I didn't feel comfortable saying before.

"Hang on—were you dancing in your upper or inner world?"

"Inner world. . . ."

"Go on."

"Could you explain what those symptoms mean?"

"Were you thrilled, excited?"

"Thrilled? I was tickled!"

I told Nigel there were departments in my inner world that needed to be defined and understood. He talked about female anatomy, especially the sexual organs and their functions. But I really needed to know about the lower part of the anatomy, around the vaginal wall, where I felt waves of intensity. Nigel asked about those waves, and when I finished describing them, he looked at me as if I had accomplished an impossible task.

"That's absolutely fantastic!"

By the time he explained what those waves of excitement were, I started crying and couldn't stop. Nigel sat quietly and let the emotions pass through me. It is difficult to describe what I felt at that special moment. For the first time, my mind was intact and gently communicating with my tortured body. I was not disfigured or crippled for life!

"You're going through a transformational period."

Nigel talked about how I had been raised to suppress my feelings, both good and bad. Learning how I suppressed my own emotions made it easier to get in touch with my deeper self. I could open my heart and become whole again. He said I should go back into my body and feel what I truly felt and sit with that feeling for a moment.

I asked, "What if tomorrow my body reacts differently and nothing feels good?"

"Then keep opening up your heart until you connect with your feelings. Quiet your mind and learn how to balance yourself with good and positive energy. By surrendering to the process of healing, you can connect your old self to the new and find peace." He paused. "You will live your life with integrity, fully intact."

"This all sounds good, but what if others challenge my truth and keep me from shouting from the rooftops?"

"No one can silence your voice but you. What do you want?"

I said I would like the opportunity to meet with women survivors from home and tell them that they are not crippled for life. I wanted to share my experiences with them and make sure that they understood that healing the mind and body was possible.

"Will you be able to handle that responsibility?"

"I can."

Nigel suggested that I not begin a battle by bringing in others who might not agree with the journey of self-healing. "When you are strong enough and have made peace with the past, then your voice and knowledge will rise up for those women who are tortured and mutilated. They need a powerful voice, someone to whom they can express their feelings and tell their stories," he said. "First, become the woman you were destined to become."

Nigel's advice was to carry myself alone for a while, keep working on myself, healing and nurturing myself, until I came fully into my power. Only then would I find the strength to go into the world and do the work I came here to do. Nigel went on to say that if I kept the focus on myself, did the exercises, and became more gentle with my body and mind, then I would come to love myself fully.

"Tell yourself, daily, that you are lovable."

Suddenly, my nerves tingled, confirming something heart-rending was happening. "What's wrong?" I asked, feeling panicked.

"Nothing . . ." he replied.

I burst into tears.

"Whether I am here or not, remember you will always be looked after. In your journey, you will meet those who will listen and support you." He paused. "You will get into a habit of wearing the same shoes."

"Shoes?"

"Your feet are your base, and change is like shoes."

Nigel continued with the foot metaphor and said every point on a foot corresponds to a part of the body. "When you get new shoes, your feet will notice the change. You will feel better."

I shook my head. "I don't need new shoes, and I am not going to another therapist."

3⁸

the four breasts

It was face-off time with Yusuf, who was now out on bail. I landed in Geneva and followed Khalifa and her husband to their hotel. Nothing was going to stop me from getting my life back from Yusuf. I said to myself that anger would not get the best of me, and I began to breathe deeply over and over again. Somehow, I felt calm enough for the encounter.

It was Khalifa who called Yusuf and arranged the time for him to meet us. Within an hour, he showed up at the hotel room. I looked straight into his eyes and saw flashes of shame covering his face. Yusuf looked sharp in his suit, but he was a broken man.

"Everything was a big misunderstanding . . . ," Yusuf said.

"Good. Then let the *wadaad* touch your head and purify you," I replied.

"Soraya!" Khalifa shouted.

I was thinking maybe traveling to Geneva had not been wise. If anything went wrong, I would not know how to forgive myself for coming here.

The conversation was long and wasn't going anywhere. Khalifa handed Yusuf a note from my parents. After reading it, Yusuf, without looking up, nodded his head.

Khalifa wrapped her arms around him and let her fingers play with his goatee saying, "Let her go, please."

"Excuse me, don't speak for me," I said.

"Don't interrupt me!" Khalifa yelled.

"I'm sitting right here, not fenced in like a lamb!"

"Are you witnessing this? She has a sharp tongue!" Yusuf shouted.

Khalifa's husband got up and suggested that I leave the room and come back when I had cooled down. I refused, telling them I was no longer invisible and they had no right to control me or to kick me out of the room.

"I'll leave when Yusuf says the words to release me," I said.

Arguments broke out, and I felt as if I had returned to those old fearful ways with Yusuf. But after a while, Yusuf sat in front of me and repeated the word *talaq* three times, which meant that he was releasing me. This was strange, because Khalifa was specific when she said Yusuf should clearly say *Soraya, I divorce you* three times. But why would I care how he said it, as long as I was no longer attached to him?

Then Khalifa's husband started a long conversation about how Yusuf and I should remain peaceful toward each other. "You belong to each other."

"No. We don't," I countered.

"You're cousins and, therefore, family!" he said.

"Did you lose the baby?" Yusuf asked.

"Baby?"

"I thought you were pregnant—"

"Pregnant?" I interrupted.

In shock, we listened as Yusuf said he remembered my missing periods and how I looked pregnant before the escape. But missing my menses was normal for me, for up to six months at times. As the German doctors had explained to Mother, the horrible side effect of the mutilation was the retained blood that made my stomach blow up like a balloon and caused severe cramps.

I shuddered at the memory of the shots and painkillers, the only way for me to feel better and breathe like a human being.

"What happened?" Khalifa asked.

I was shocked that Khalifa and her husband appeared to believe the lies coming out of Yusuf's mouth as they insisted that I tell them the truth. What truth? I told them about the corrective surgery, how the doctors opened my scar, and how sorry I was for not having the doctors save a jar full of all the rubbish and blood that had been retained inside my stomach.

"I killed your perfect gift!"

"Calm down!" shouted Yusuf.

"You calm down!" I replied.

Yusuf stormed out of the room, and Khalifa's husband chased after him. I was beyond upset and refused to talk to Khalifa. I wanted nothing more than to leave, go back to the old private school, and perhaps see Sahir again if she was still there. But Khalifa insisted that we call Mother and talk things through.

Yusuf and Khalifa's husband returned. Yusuf sat in front of me and said three times he was divorcing me, as Khalifa had originally promised. She handed me a check for a substantial amount of money. She said the family would provide and take care of my needs as long as I remained in school and did well. But I had to promise to never say that I was forced to marry Yusuf.

"I should lie and say it never happened?"

"Anything that happened here stays here!"

This discussion brought me so much pain that I had to get out of the room, and I wanted to get out before Khalifa called my mother. I hurried down to the lobby and phoned the embassy. I told them I would visit in the morning before heading back to Grenoble. I went up to my room and thought about making time to go back to see Sahir.

After my visit to the embassy family, my childhood friend Shukri called and invited me to spend the weekend with her. She was going to a private college located at the most breathtaking place in Geneva and housing the wealthiest Saudi and Kuwaiti female students.

When I arrived at the dormitory, I met two other Somali students, Asma and Madoon. What I couldn't understand was how Shukri and the other two managed to mingle and live with those wealthy Arabs who were blessed with oil money. Watching the activities in the dorm, I realized I was witnessing girl power and the unity of women. The girls were well organized, and they listened to and respected one another.

After dinner Shukri and I went to bed. I'm not sure how long I slept, but I awoke feeling a body rubbing against mine. I flew out of the bed and screamed in the darkness. The light came on, and I saw Shukri wearing nothing but underwear, standing by the door.

"It's just me," she said.

I was frozen, not knowing what to say.

Shukri cried out, "Don't look at me like that!"

"What happened?"

"I feel like I am experiencing death itself!"

"I'm sorry. . . ."

"I love you—I have loved you since we were kids!"

"Don't say that!" I went over and held her until she stopped crying.

She put on a shirt, sat on the floor, and started talking and talking. I sat next to her and listened, but I was confused and still didn't want to ask more. When she completed her story, I told her that I wasn't judging her; I was just shocked and needed a moment to think.

She started crying again. "Please, just get out of my room."

I reminded her of all our childhood playtime and how close we were.

"I was never your sister," she said.

I told her that I hadn't even known what *qaniisad* was until I met the herdsmen just a few days ago, and I talked about Nigel.

"I'm not *qaniisad*—I just happen to love women!"

"A gay man is changing my life," I said.

"Stop!"

Wanting to understand more, I asked if she could tell me when she knew she liked women instead of men.

"Go and ask God why he made me this way!"

"But how can you play with four breasts?" I asked.

"Four breasts?" she shouted.

Shukri got up, dragged me out of the room, and went back inside, slamming the door behind her. While standing at the door, I flashed back to when Yusuf refused to let me visit this school. He said it was a place where girls played the "finger game." I knocked on the door, but Shukri would not respond. I walked down the hallway and knocked on Madoon's door.

She seemed surprised to see me. "What's wrong?" she asked.

"Can I sleep on your floor?"

I walked in and saw Asma lying under the covers. I said to Madoon that I couldn't stay with Shukri and didn't feel comfortable talking about it.

Asma got up and frowned. "I knew this was going to happen!"

"What?" I asked.

"I told Shukri to go easy on you."

"You knew?"

"What's wrong with that?"

"You and Madoon . . . ?"

"Yes. We're a couple," Asma said.

"I see—I'm happy for you."

There was a knock at the door, and Madoon got up to let in Shukri, carrying pillows and blankets. Without saying anything, she dropped the blankets and pillows on the floor and made a bed.

"You don't belong in this room," Shukri said to me.

"C'mon . . . ," I said.

"Did she tell you about the four breasts?"

Madoon and Asma shook their heads.

Shukri turned, grabbed the pillow, and smacked me over the head, over and over again. "We love playing with four breasts!" she shouted.

Laugher erupted, and the heaviness in the room evaporated.

"Madoon, how long have you been living in Switzerland?" I asked.

"Europe didn't make me who I am!" she replied.

"Do you have fantasies . . . ?" Madoon asked.

"Irish men. My fantasy is exclusive to Irish men," I said.

"But what do they know about the nomads?" Madoon asked, echoing the Somali sentiment that most foreigners think of them as nothing but nomads.

"I'm wondering about that too . . . ," I said.

They seemed taken aback when I told them how dizzy I'd felt when I met Nigel. My body was on fire, I told them, and to cover up what I was feeling inside I'd talked nonstop during the session. They were eager to know about the reversal surgery, but I said I couldn't show them the result; I just was not comfortable enough. I told them how good it was to talk about the healing process and, more important, how the physical exercises helped me and how my body could react to touch.

With lots of laughter, the four of us sat on the floor and talked until the sun came up. I promised to keep in touch, never judge, and always support their choices. It was time for me to get ready to head back to Grenoble.

39

going with the flow

Back in Grenoble, I focused on attending all my classes and working hard. Nigel was in Paris, and my thoughts were with him. I imagined him alone, lying in a hospital, dying. I had money, and during the school break, I wanted to be with him, but I had promised to honor his request to let him deal with his illness himself.

This was the time that many people began whispering about the disease that was killing gay men. At night, I would sit in my room and think about Nigel. In my mind's eye, I would envision my coming to support him, just as he had supported me.

I am sitting at Nigel's hospital bed, holding his hand. I read him my notes on how well I am doing with the exercises. Since he can't talk, I tell him all about the divorce and the four breasts. I tell him about Raj, and then I fall asleep, holding Nigel's hand. But the nurse comes in, wakes me up, and I panic, calling out Nigel's name. I turn and see his lifeless body lying in the hospital bed. I freeze, not knowing if I should cry or be happy that he is no longer in pain. I get up, kiss his forehead, and leave the room. Since he never talks about his family or his friends, I am the one who receives his remains. Not knowing anything about burial, I feel intense anxiety. Then I remember Nigel standing by the lake and smiling as he watched

*the calm water. Under the full moon, I go to the lake and spread his
ashes. I kneel down and watch the golden pot, carrying Nigel, sink
into the depths. I look up and call out to Grandmother, asking her
to make space for him in the full moon. Grandmother's face glows as
she says,* I have forgiven the Brits for blowing up the Kirrit in
Somaliland. Nigel has a place in the full moon next to me.

Within weeks of finding out about Nigel's passing, I was sitting across the table from a new therapist. I wanted to honor
Nigel's wishes and try the new shoes. But the problem was that
this therapist was French and reminded me of Father. He was
short, heavyset, with salt-and-pepper hair, and seemed to love
sweets. He had an expensive table dedicated to different kinds
of sweets, just like Father did at his office back in Mogadishu. While answering questions, I would watch the therapist's
thick fingers running over the table picking up candy. He would
chew and chew, looking straight at me. This was strange, and
I thought this man had an issue and needed to find his own
therapist. After a while, I said thank you, got up, walked out the
door, and never went back.

Soon after, I enrolled in a dance class and hung out with the
Somalis I had met at the campus party. But being with my fellow herdsmen was not productive; they were all convinced they
had something important to say. The talks would become fierce
arguments on the colonial era and how the North should never
have joined the South. Then those from Djibouti would start
shouting about the clans and how the Issa abused the Afars.
Leyla, a young woman who had become a good friend of mine,
would shout "That's a lie!" and defend her government's actions.
I wasn't sure if it was her father or her uncle who was part of
the government. Not wanting to take sides, I just listened. Then
Leyla would demand a reaction from me.

"I have something vital to take care of." I would get up and
hurry out of the room. Eventually, I decided to go in a new
direction and spend less time with my fellow herdsmen.

✢

Soon after, my tiny room became the meeting ground for girls inquiring about the process of reversal surgery. I found myself speaking like Nigel and discussing the groundbreaking exercises. It began with Leyla, who was dating a fellow Somali named Ahmed and needed help with intimacy. Other girls heard about my surgery from Leyla and wanted to talk with me. Egyptian and Moroccan girls began to seek me out like I was a healer. It gradually dawned on me that I was carrying out Nigel's wishes to help other women.

Leyla was the first to say she was willing to let the doctors open her scar. Excited, I planned to make an appointment for her with Dr. Omar. Leyla sipped tea and mumbled something.

"It's normal to be scared."

"What happens when I decide to return home?"

"You'll be healed within days, although your emotional healing from the mutilation will take much longer."

"But what will my future husband think of me?"

"You think your future husband will be a virgin? Maybe the man you will marry is unnerved by girls and right now is practicing celibacy." She didn't react, so I continued, "Since I have brothers and male cousins, it's safe to say that your man may well have dared to visit the dark alleys in Hamar Jajab and practiced brushing the vulva, many times over."

"Hamar Jajab? Where is that?"

"It's a district in Mogadishu."

"I'm from Djibouti!"

I begged Leyla to learn about her body and how it belonged to her, not to a man, her family, or her culture. I asked her to listen to the effects the horrible ritual mutilation had on her and how this surgery would help her heal from the complications. I understood where she was coming from, not feeling right to speak badly about our culture. She needed to hear more about how we had been brainwashed and manipulated and why others would call an uncut girl the Girl with Three Legs.

"Will the doctor be able to restitch the scar before I get married?" she asked.

"No. He will not."

"Wait. . . ."

I changed the subject. "I'm going downstairs to gorge myself on white chocolate!"

One of the girls followed me to the cafeteria and said her Somali boyfriend had an American woman on the side. My only advice to her was that she did not need any vagabonds in her life, but she insisted he wasn't a bad man, only frustrated because she refused to sleep with him.

"I want my scar opened," she said.

"Why? Will this gift be for him or for you?"

"What about you?"

"We're talking about you."

"After it was opened, was sex painful?"

"Not with myself, but I'll try it with someone and let you know."

Raj walked in, leading some friends. He stopped at our table and chatted pleasantly for a moment. I knew I had made the right decision in not getting involved with him. The bond between us was strong, but a love relationship could have made both of us miserable.

He asked why I was spending lots of time with his friends from Antilles, whom I had met at a campus party. After the party, they came to me for help because one of them was pregnant and needed money.

"Did you tell my friend to get an abortion?" he asked.

"The one from Martinique?" I had gone to the hospital with her, and after the abortion I took care of her needs. Raj was never happy that I was spending time with her. The girl had a boyfriend who knew about the pregnancy.

"Did you or did you not?" he demanded.

"Was she carrying your child?" I said sarcastically. I was tired of him controlling me and even telling me what kind of friends I should have.

Angry, Raj stormed out. I decided I did not want anything to do with him, ever, even though I knew staying away from him would not be easy.

Raj was right; I had made friends with the people he knew from the Antilles. One was a mature and respectable senior, Cedric, who was a member of a band. He was smart, politically oriented, and talked nonstop about the French Antilles. He was from Martinique and loved to put in my mind gorgeous pictures of the island's turquoise sea and beautiful forests. I found myself planning a trip during school break. Cedric and I spent lots of time together and loved hanging out with his Antillean friends.

During our private time, I tried not to scare him off with gruesome details about how my body and mind were transformed after the genital mutilation, but Cedric wanted to know. From then on, everything seemed to click, and I kept taking notes and noticing the changes in my body.

My classmates decided to rent a cabin in the mountains, and many of us would spend the whole weekend there. Cedric complained that I spent too much time with my classmates, but when I invited him, he said he had a show. This created friction and didn't help our relationship.

One night, we sat talking about what we would do during the school break. I expressed my desire to travel to new places and meet people, but Cedric was not supportive. Something shifted that night, and we drifted apart but with open hearts. Cedric and I were not willing to commit to a relationship that didn't have a strong foundation. At times I would feel suffocated and refused to be put in a cage, no matter how much I loved him.

Needing to get away, I planned a trip to Greece, and one of my classmates insisted that I stay in her family home. Armed with the family phone number, I landed in Athens and took a taxi to her home. At the door, I was greeted by my classmate's cousins, and when they took me upstairs, I realized the family had organized a huge party. I was overwhelmed with their warmth, and all I could do was hand them gifts and say "*Merci.*" They hugged me, shouting, "*C'est avec plaisir!*"

The ninety-year-old grandmother took my hand, sat me down on the couch, and forced me to eat. Kindness and love poured from her soul, and I didn't have the heart to ask whether the thick soup was cooked with meat. I just prayed I wouldn't get sick and vomit all over the colorful rug.

The family was planning a wedding for one of the cousins, and I was dragged to the groom's home for another big party. Within the hour, an earthquake rocked the city, and I found myself hiding by the kitchen door. Nobody was hurt, so the party continued.

At night, while the family was busy with wedding plans, I would go to a restaurant and have a meal. Sometimes others would join me at my table, and I would ask which island was the best to visit. I could see that they were proud that a tiny African girl traveled a long distance and was eager to see their country. I would pick up a fork and hit the water glass, trying to find a moment to speak and explain that I did not travel from Africa but lived in France. But they were so gregarious that my words fell beneath the table, and all I could do was cover my dinner plate, to protect it from flying human saliva. Then they would fight for my attention and ask the strangest questions about Africa, about things like tribal masks and voodoo.

"I've seen how they put the masks on. . . ."

"No—first they wear the distinct style of clothing. . . ."

"They are charming people!"

"They love to laugh and dance!"

One night, without warning, the conversation turned philosophical, and Socrates dominated. Inspired, they jumped up, insisting on taking me to the Acropolis, and they headed for the door.

Overwhelmed, I stared and asked them to wait while I finished my dinner. Later, I left the restaurant with my new friends and went toward the Acropolis. I was awed, lucky enough to stand in this historical place.

After a few days in Athens, I felt I needed to travel alone to different islands. The family helped me plan my trip, and I spent the rest of my vacation going to different places and meeting more people. This trip was magical and helped me heal many of my fears as I got to know myself and my strengths and learned the value of my independence.

I returned to Grenoble feeling refreshed, and several weeks later my brother Asis and Khalifa's son Khalid visited me. Khalifa was moving her family to Libreville, Gabon, East Africa, while Asis remained in Brussels. I found peace with Asis. I had moved off-campus to an apartment because the Somali herdsmen were asking questions about Father, and I didn't want to get involved with the north and south politics in Somalia. Back in Mogadishu, our parents had never allowed any of us to focus on anything relating to tribal conflicts, and we were told we were all Somalis.

Not long after they left, I got a call from my friend Mahad. He was now married and had brought his wife to Paris after she developed complications from genital mutilation. He asked if I would come to Paris on the weekend to help her. He would pay my travel expenses and lodging, and I could translate for his wife during the doctor's visit.

I agreed and traveled that weekend to Paris and met his wife, Asmara, and Mahad's brother Guleed. They had rented a very comfortable apartment, so I didn't understand why Mahad had gone out of his way to put me up at the George V Hotel.

I took Asmara to her doctor's appointment. Her complications were severe, and she might never have children. This was very difficult, and I wished I didn't have to share this troubling news with Mahad and Asmara. I asked if they wanted to talk to another doctor, but they said no and continued with the same doctor. Asmara said it was up to God whether or not she had a child.

I returned the following week to help again, and I found Mahad distracted and Guleed acting oddly. Asmara's health was improving after treatment, and she was following the doctor's instructions to remain in bed. But while Mahad was out of the house, I found Asmara in the living room, watching her grown brother-in-law playing with himself. Horrified, I knocked his feet off the couch.

"What are you doing?" I shouted.

"My soldier needs some attention!"

"You have no shame!"

Asmara laughed and laughed while her brother-in-law held up his soldier and started bouncing it left and right. I could not believe it myself, standing there, watching this grown man play with his soldier, as if it were a banana and he was tormenting a distraught monkey. I didn't know whether to cry or remove my shoe and hit him over the head.

"He loves playing this game!" Asmara exclaimed with a smile.

"You're sick!"

I grabbed my purse and headed for the door as she shouted, "My husband doesn't need to know this!"

Later, when I was back at my hotel, Mahad showed up without calling. He sat staring at the phone.

"What's wrong?" I asked.

"I'm going to the Netherlands to visit my friend."

I felt it wasn't my place to say anything about his sick brother and wife, but I needed to extricate myself from this unhealthy situation. I told Mahad that I was not going to be able to continue traveling back and forth and suggested he call the embassy to get someone else to translate.

He looked down at his hands. "I know about what she's doing with my brother."

I had to let Mahad know how important Asmara's treatment was, and under no circumstances should she have sex. But after listening to him, I understood how unhappy he was and how his brother was taking his place.

Mahad would not answer all my questions and started talking about his childhood. I remembered how my sisters and
others spread mocking gossip about him letting boys slap his
behind. I was only too aware of the issues of the culture we grew
up in and how complicated his life had become.

In silence, I took his hand and sat on the couch with him.

40

the dark hole

Jamila, a friend I had met through the Somali herdsmen, called and said that she might consider having the corrective surgery, if only the doctor would restitch her before she went back home. I told her not to waste my time until she figured out to whom her body belonged.

After hearing about my little workshops with African women and about how much the doctors helped me, the men requested a meeting with me. I agreed and told them to meet me at a downtown coffee shop. Jamila's boyfriend, Bashir, whom I had once slapped after he put his hand on my butt, walked in with the other Somali men. We moved to a booth, and they started talking about the damage I was creating in the men's relationships with Somali women. Their whole argument was based on the fact that they thought I was opening the women's eyes and, therefore, polluting them.

"Have you seen a woman giving birth?" I asked.

"What for?" Bashir asked in response.

"To appreciate women," I said.

"I have a problem with you, not women," Bashir said.

I explained to them, as Nigel had once told me, the birth canal is unsterilized, yet it is capable of handling a child's birth. Only a very small portion at the back of the vagina responds in an orgasmic way. Therefore, the clitoris is the explicit site for triggering orgasm. The clitoris is the woman's sexual organ. Its glans and shaft have erectile tissue, just like the erectile tissue of the penis. The lips (specifically the labia minora) move against the clitoris to stimulate orgasm. Our rite of passage castrates a woman by cutting this tissue off. The brain of a young girl is not mature enough to understand the horror of cutting her healthy organs.

"She thinks this is something the grown-ups must have good reason for doing," I said, "but she's scared. She is so terrified that something inside of her shuts off. No one is there to hear her silent screams. She is 'made clean' and becomes the property of one of your sons."

A man named Salad broke in and explained that they might not smear their bodies with millet and run around villages like the Bagishu men, a Ugandan tribe, but knives touch them, too. "Our foreskin is chopped off in order to remove our femaleness," he said in a scoffing way.

"Have you heard of the eunuchs?" I asked.

"Who?" Bashir asked.

"A eunuch is a castrated man. He has a duty, just like us, to be your bed keeper," I told them. "A eunuch has his penis, testes, and scrotum removed and kept in a jar. For years, the body parts swim in a jar of alcohol. A man gets them back when he dies, in case he wanted to return as a complete man."

"They are living?" the herdsman Omar asked, in bewilderment.

"Just like we mutilated women are living. . . ."

"Would you stop!" Bashir yelled.

"Except our clitorises are not kept in a jar. They feed them to the diseased-looking dogs on the sidewalks."

Omar met my eyes for the first time.

"Do you think God made a mistake?" I asked.

"Enough!" Bashir said.

Confused, the men looked at me suspiciously. It was obvious they did not want this conversation to continue. The waiter approached our table, and I ordered more hot tea.

"Do you know the function of the pubic bone?" I asked.

"What?" Bashir asked.

"It's supposed to be stimulated, even if the vulva is cut," I said.

"You mean by me?" herdsman Abshir asked.

I told them that they missed getting to know the leftover nerves by focusing too much on hitting their target, the vagina. The waiter brought my tea, and I felt warmed by sipping it.

"You're one of those who count the glowing stars on the dark ceiling while the bed rocks!" Bashir said.

Omar shot a look at Bashir to stop him from talking. Bashir again explained the reason that I was asked to come. "You're a bad influence on the Somali women students," he said, "and you need to stop talking about genital cutting altogether. We didn't call you here to have an anatomy lesson—we are telling you to stop those workshops!"

"It's really me who should decide that, not you."

"Well—"

"Well, it's my vagina."

I told these men that Leyla helped me spread my healing message to others, and that's how the weekly tea gatherings had started. I explained that my doctor had taught me how to trust myself and others. I was learning about other cultures and adopting what was good in order to heal. Learning about the oppression of women throughout history empowers women. Learning how not to feel crippled in the eyes of those who think you are, and making peace with the past, can only further greater understanding and healing. It leads to finding oneself.

"I'm not polluting anyone but am showing how much rubbish fills our minds with fear of being who we are meant to be," I said. "Women could be more 'woman' if they could participate more fully in the orgasmic experience. If you take away her sexual organs, then the act of coming together to make love physically, or to create a baby, is badly damaged. If God realized that he made mistake, he would order the universe to correct it; he would not order man to correct it."

"Interesting," Bashir admitted reluctantly.

"No bride would fear her groom assaulting her on the wedding night, and there would be no more smoke rising from the woman's ears," I said.

Bashir talked about "the dark hole," meaning the vagina, and said that I should be focusing on helping the Issaq clan overthrow the oppressive regime of Siad Barre.

"Why call the vagina a black hole?" I asked him.

"It sucks your brain out!" Bashir shouted. The others laughed.

"How?" I asked.

"You just have to hit it. The rest is whatever," Abshir responded.

"Do you actually know what you're hitting?" I asked.

Abshir shot me an angry look. I told him it sounded just like having an oil change. To hit it, you have to crawl underneath the car to find the dark bottom of the oil pan.

Omar threw his hands in the air and stormed off while others stared at me in silence. They tried to change the subject back to my workshops. But I had been holding everything in for so long that I couldn't stop. The coffee shop was full of students, and I had nothing to fear.

"A good hard fuck will shut your mouth!" Bashir yelled out in French.

"I'll feed your skinny bones to the police," I said.

"I suggest you meet us daily after class and read the Quran," said the herdsman Salad, who got up and walked out of the coffee shop. The others followed.

41

father's illness

Our university had a program whereby groups of students were chosen to travel to different countries to learn their culture and politics. On my first trip with the student group in 1983 we went to Britain for three months. We were scheduled to stay in London for a month and then spend two months in Oxford. But some of us were young and stubborn (I was twenty-two) and decided to go to Portsmouth for the whole three months.

Our teachers found families who would host us. Our mission was purely to have fun and to forget about school and political debates. It was a much-needed break, away from my workshops and counseling sessions with the other female students. I soon moved in with a young single mother. She had a seven-year-old son and a very hot temper. I called Asis in Brussels to let him know that I was doing well.

Shortly after, I got a surprise call from Sakiya. I found out she was in Munich finishing up another degree, and she offered to send me money. A few days later, I received the money along with photographs of Sakiya in her apartment looking happy. It was at this moment that I decided to use Sakiya's money to apply for a trip with the students to Los Angeles the next year.

✵

Back in Grenoble, I realized I needed more funding for the Los Angeles summer program, and I decided to call Father in Mogadishu for help. I asked if he would send me the money. He did not ask anything and said that it would be wired from Brussels. A few days later, I got the money and paid the Los Angeles summer program in full.

But then I received an unexpected call from Sakiya.

"Father is on his way to a Paris hospital," she said. "You need to come now."

My heart pounded as I dialed Asis's number as soon as I hung up with Sakiya. He said he was taking the next flight out and would meet me in Paris. Khalifa and her husband were already at the airport.

I rushed to the airport, and on the hourlong flight I replayed childhood memories of my close relationship with Father and how I had always felt I was his favorite until I discovered I had been sold. Father had taken up smoking after the Ogaden War, and he had become a chain-smoker. He also had high blood pressure. Mother quit smoking with the hope that he would do the same, but he didn't. When I landed in Paris, I got information about my father from the embassy and took a taxi straight to the hospital.

As I hurried through the hospital door, I noticed a group of Somali people standing by the entrance. A Somali woman, dressed in a suit, hurried to hug me.

"Your father is in good hands," she said. I picked up my suitcase and thanked the people for coming. She said her name was Fatima and she worked at the Somali embassy in Paris. Fatima put her hand on my back and rushed me inside the hospital. We got to the waiting room, where Khalifa was sitting with her husband and surrounded by men. Looking at the faces, I recognized General Ali and other army officers.

Khalifa got up and rushed to hug me. "I'm so glad you're here," she said.

"What's wrong with Father?" I asked. Sakiya had not mentioned Father's illness on the phone.

"He was having numbness in his arms and chest pain."

I greeted the men and sat down, hoping to hear good news from the doctors.

"Your father is getting old." Khalifa laughed as she patted my back. I forced a smile, feeling uncomfortable. I couldn't help but hear, in my mind, Ali moaning *Allah!* back in Mother's *asilo*, followed by heavy breathing. The image of him and Khalifa making love disturbed my mind, and I wanted to flee from the hospital waiting room. Khalifa's husband wrapped his arms around me and pulled my head onto his chest. I didn't dare to look up or say anything.

"Everything is going to be fine," he said.

I nodded my head, unconvinced. "Where is Asis?" I asked, but I couldn't say any more, and slowly I freed myself from him and hurried down the hallway, where I broke down and cried. I felt fingers running through my hair. I looked up and saw Khalifa had followed me.

"Your father feels responsible for what happened to you," she said.

"Are you blaming me?"

"No—I was thinking about your aunt, my mother." Suddenly, I noticed Khalifa holding back tears, as she told the story of how my mother became her mother. My muscles were tense, and my heart beat rapidly. I had heard this story before, and I did not want to hear it again.

"As a woman, you do whatever you can to keep your family together," Khalifa said.

"Sakiya and Asra are my sisters," I said, choking back tears.

"But they have a different father. . . ."

I walked away, not knowing how to deal with my emotions. Khalifa hurried after me again and took my hand. "Like Mother, I remarried and had children."

"Stop, please," I said.

"Stop looking at me like I'm a prostitute!"

I was overcome by a huge sob, thinking how, at a young age, Mother also was forced into marriage, but she survived and became the woman she was today. Khalifa pinched my cheek and walked back to the waiting room.

We were never allowed to say that Sakiya and Asra had a different father and were not fully our sisters. But, somehow, they kept their father's name as Khalifa had. I looked over and saw two doctors walking toward the waiting room.

I rushed to them. "How is my father?"

"Your father is stable," one of the doctors said, "and we are monitoring him. His high blood pressure has caused damage to his blood vessels and heart. We're going to keep him here for a few days. You can see him now."

He led me to Father's room, and as I entered, the dark spot on his forehead shone. Watching him closely, I realized how much I resembled him—his full lips, round face, wide forehead, and soft skin. When angry, Mother said I was switched at birth. But the truth was that, when I looked in the mirror, I saw her, too.

A few days later, Father was released from the hospital and was taken to the embassy house in Saint-Cloud, where I was staying. So many visitors came that Father could not rest. So I booked him a hotel room and moved him there without telling anybody.

Khalifa and her husband stayed with Father in Saint-Cloud, and I flew back to Grenoble. The phone rang as I walked into my apartment. It was Khalifa, telling me that Father had not stopped crying since I had left him. He feared he would never see me again.

"It would be a good idea for you to take him back to Mogadishu," she said.

An intense fear overcame me. "I'm not sure if I can," I said.

Khalifa was upset. "If you keep using 'I,' soon you will be a foreign entity in our family. You'll prove your father right in thinking the family will never see you again—"

I hung up and walked to the kitchen. The phone rang, but I refused to answer it.

⊹

I couldn't sleep that night. Early the next morning, I went to see my favorite teacher to discuss some concerns about school. She thought I was not doing well in her literature class and suggested working with me during the Christmas break. If not, she urged me to cancel my trip to Los Angeles. We agreed to meet twice a week after school for one hour.

When I got home, I called Father. He told me he was doing well and said he had asked Khalifa to transfer money to me.

"Father, I'm OK with money—you don't need to do that," I responded.

But later, I checked my account, and I could not believe the amount in it. I called Father immediately.

"Father, what is all that money for?"

"I just don't want you to worry about money anymore."

"Thank you, Father."

The next day, after class, I flew back to Paris to see Father. I got to the hotel and I could see Father was in good health. During our dinner, Father handed me a plane ticket.

"Wandering too long around in the snow will make you rootless."

"I won't forget my roots, Father."

"Visiting home will strengthen your roots."

"There is a part of my life that I don't want to revisit."

He put his fork down and stared at me. My heart raced, and I felt my tongue dancing between my cheeks. I felt the hot waves building inside of me, as heavy emotions surged.

"Whatever happened in Geneva will remain there." Father said that my future was bright, and all I had to do was complete my studies.

"Did Mother show you my surgery photos?"

His face tensed, and he went back to eating.

I told him how my body was reconstructed by the doctors and that my period was back and flowed easily. I was off the pills and had not had any pain or panic attacks since the surgery and therapy.

Father was quiet, and in our silence all I heard was chatter and forks on plates. I picked up my fork and started eating.

"I have a plan, Father."

He looked up at me and smiled. "Are you doing your daily prayers?"

I wanted to say yes, but there was no point in lying. Too much had happened, and I didn't want to carry another unnecessary load.

"Father, my plan is to speak against what happened to me at thirteen. I've been reading a lot, and I realize that it is wrong and must stop."

"Your focus should be on getting your degree."

In the end I acquiesced, and during the Christmas break Father and I left for Mogadishu. The fear in my gut disappeared when I saw the faces of Shams and Raha. They had grown so much, and I noticed the fire in their eyes.

I asked if Mother had given them their "gifts." Raha bent her head down and walked out of the room. Shams told me that she visited the same doctor. She said she felt no pain, and she looked forward to going to college.

Mother found out about my plan to speak against female genital mutilation. Questioning this ritual would mean digging into the graveyard of our ancestors. Nothing good would come out it, and it would only turn people against me. If I didn't obey the family request, then I would be ostracized and all of my support would be cut off.

"Don't worry, Mother. I would never do anything against your wishes." I would have said anything to save myself and to get safely back to Grenoble.

But things got better. I reconnected with Fadwa and neighborhood friends. The city was growing so fast and abundantly, and it was alive.

I told Father that I would like to visit Halgaan, and I found out he was in prison. He was known to hate the government, but I didn't know what had happened. Father became upset at my request, and he made it clear that I was not allowed to see Halgaan or go near the prison.

But just as in my childhood, chatting with the workers brought a great idea about how I could get into the prison. I gave them cartons of cigarettes and bottles of perfume. Later that same day, our night guard took me to see Halgaan. I brought along his favorite cigarettes.

Getting into the central prison in Mogadishu is easy, but witnessing the harsh reality of prison life is unbearable. It was crowded, and while waiting for Halgaan, I was told that the government was using other facilities, such as military headquarters and schools, to jail those opposing the regime.

Halgaan was brought into a room to meet me, but the man standing before me was not the Halgaan that I used to know. Before me was a man with a broken spirit and deadened eyes. I wanted to wrap my arms around him and hear his heart beat. I wanted to feel his pain, but I could not.

He sat down and stared at the cartons of Benson & Hedges. I slid them to his side.

"How can I help?" I asked.

"Tell your father to leave the glass house," he said.

"What do you mean?" I asked.

He looked up and met my eyes. "Did you see any dark clouds?" he asked.

"No. The sky is clear," I said.

"I mean the clouds in people's eyes," he said.

Halgaan was from north Hargeisa, known to suffer under the army regime. But I still didn't understand his message.

"People's eyes are smiling," I said.

"Soon, smoke will rise, and Mogadishu will burn to the ground," he said.

I realized that only those who were angry with the Red Berets talked about burning buildings. "Is that why you want Father to leave the glass house?" I asked.

Halgaan grabbed his cigarettes, rose, and left the room, following the guard.

When I got back home, I went straight to Father. I had no choice but to tell him I had once again gone against his wishes and visited Halgaan. But I had to tell him what Halgaan had said. I knew it was a warning.

Father overlooked my disobedience, as he had so often in my childhood. Understanding Halgaan's message, Father said a group from the north had formed the Somali National Movement against the single ruling party.

"The 'glass house' means I must be vigilant," he said. "There is nothing to fear. We are prepared in case dark clouds come."

I thought now was perhaps the time to ask him about rumors of his affair with another woman with whom he had a daughter. But he wouldn't say anything about it, and I didn't press. One day, I knew, I would find out, and I hoped the knowledge would not destroy me.

Later that evening, I overheard Mother and Sakiya talking about withholding my passport. Amal, who was sitting in the living room with them, suggested having a talk with me. I ran to my room, got my passport and plane ticket, and hid them. I decided to walk back into the living room and act as if nothing were wrong.

When I entered, Mother asked, "Are you enjoying your stay?"

I assured her that I was. "Are you still helping at the orphanage?" I asked.

She shook her head. "No, my schedule has just been far too busy."

I nodded. Everything seemed OK, and no one asked me anything about my return to Grenoble.

That night we had one of our best family dinners as laughter and jokes rang throughout the night.

⚜

The next day, I decided to go back to Grenoble immediately.
The earth began to shake when Mother was told I was carrying
my suitcase to the car.

"Mother, I need to get ready for school."

She stared at me for a moment as Raha and Shams held
each of my arms.

"Your mind has a mind of its own," Mother said. Father
walked into the courtyard. I went to him with Shams and Raha
clinging to my arms.

"I'm leaving, Father."

"Why so soon?" he asked.

"I need to work with my teacher, or I might not make it."

"It's either your family or your plan!" Mother said.

"I don't care what you say, but you can't use our family name!"
a tearful Sakiya said, and walked away.

"I will be back," I said.

"Go, fly away, and see if you can live without our support!"
Mother said.

Father wrapped his arms around me and said, "Is this what
you want?"

I nodded.

In anger, Mother went into the house. Raha and Shams ran
toward the car and waited. I went inside to see Mother. She
untied my hair and spread it across my chest.

"Remember, I gave you birth."

"I know, Mother."

"Then you won't raise your voice to me," she said. She was
withholding tears and said it quietly.

"Did you see my surgical photos?"

"I burnt them," she said.

I took my hair clip from her and squeezed her hand tightly.
I left the room and did not look back.

❖

The only thing on my mind, when I landed in Paris, was to
call home. I needed to break the chains that were holding me

emotionally and still causing pain. Mother answered the phone. She clearly was not pleased. I asked why she refused to look at my surgical photos.

"Looking at them would have healed both of us."

"You must choose."

She meant I must choose either my family or an activist path. I could not have both. Parents in my culture believe they have the right to control you and discard you if you follow your own path.

I told her that I chose to climb to the rooftops and shout so that the world would know the abuse of girls must stop.

Mother hung up.

I called Asis and told him what I had done.

"Why would you do that?" he yelled.

"It's my desire to speak about my vagina and let everyone know how young girls are tortured!"

"I didn't think your hot-tempered tongue would do that."

"What do you mean?"

"Get smart, and check your bank account!"

Fear took hold of me. "They wouldn't do that."

"Let me know when you get to Grenoble." He hung up the phone, and I rushed to catch my flight.

That phone call was the last time Mother and I would speak for a few years.

42

the crushing weight

I had only one thousand francs. I could feel the cold chill on my back and my feet sinking into the floor as I asked the teller to check again. The same results came back. My family wanted to teach me a lesson about how to live without any money.

Something came over me as I remembered how I escaped from Yusuf, and I realized this was another turning point. I left the bank and went to some Iranian friends I had met and asked them to help me find a roommate. Within a week, Lillian showed up and moved in. I had six months before I left to go to Los Angeles, and nothing would stop me. My teacher helped me find a new babysitting job. My apartment became like a UN feeding place because Lillian loved to show off her delicious cooking for friends from all over the world.

I listened to stories about the petit bourgeoisie and how the shah led Iran with help from the West. Others cut in and started arguing about the war on the mujahideen and the anti-Khomeini sentiments. My new soft-spoken Saudi friend's lips released sounds that shook my little apartment and had neighbors angrily knocking on my door. It was rumored that one of our Iranian friends was sleeping with his own younger sister, so perhaps that's why he felt so strongly about the subject. I opened the door and apologized to my neighbors and promised to send everyone home. But how could I? It was Friday night, and no one wanted to sleep.

A Moroccan friend changed the course of the conversation by talking about religion and sex and anything in the pharaohs' time when women ruled. She argued that prostitution began when the patriarchal family came to be. This was the perfect time to educate myself and learn more about the subject that affected me, genital mutilation. Although my family had cut me off, fresh air had come into my life, and I had a new start.

⸕

At the cafeteria, I met up with Ahmed, who told me that I should have watchful eyes with regard to Bashir; he was still very angry about my discussions with Jamila and my opinions on women. Bashir might hurt me. I told him I would change the locks at home because Jamila used to housesit while I was traveling, so Bashir might have had access to my keys. Lillian was away, and I was home alone.

The students had organized a Friday night party that we called Boom. The dancing was continual, with a DJ playing records when the live band took a break. That Friday I decided to go to the party. But when I saw Raj, I decided to take the next taxi and go back home. Raj hurried after me, and I stopped to wait for him. In silence, we walked together until we reached the outskirts of the campus. We waited for any sign of a taxi, but there was none. The freezing cold made it impossible to stand still, so we kept walking until a car stopped in front of us. Raj's friends from Martinique were inside.

"Are you going to a concert?" they asked Raj.

"No. Can you give a lift to my girlfriend?"

I wasn't prepared to hear that word again, and Raj saw the shock on my face.

"I'll see you in the morning," Raj said, then locked his lips onto mine.

I got into the car and didn't look back. The guys were reminiscing about the last Bob Marley concert at the Palais de Sports in Grenoble. They took me to my apartment, and I thanked them.

I had settled in to watch TV when there was a knock on the door. I lowered the volume and kept watching my movie. My neighbor had a bad habit of knocking on the door at odd hours. Struggling with insomnia, she would bring tiny cups filled with Turkish coffee and offer to read my future.

But the knocking persisted. I pushed myself up from the couch and went to the door. "Please, I'm tired tonight," I said through the door.

I heard nothing and went back to my movie, forgetting all about it until I heard another knock. Irritated, I got up and, without caution, I opened the door. Bashir stood before me.

Fear paralyzed my body, and I froze. He grabbed my neck and pushed me back into the hallway inside my apartment and slapped me. I screamed as I began to find the power of my legs. His hand covered my mouth, and I bit, feeling my teeth rip through his skin. He threw me to the ground and jumped on top of me. His heartbeat was strong, and his eyes were on fire.

My screaming and fighting made him more violent. His skinny legs became an iron pole forcing mine apart. My fingers aimed for his eyes, and the blood from his eye flooded my face. Suddenly, I felt Bashir force himself into me as fast as a bullet going through a wall. The pain was unbearable, and this was the last thing I remember. I awoke lying on the ground with two paramedics kneeling before me. I was surrounded by distraught neighbors, but I didn't see Bashir.

My Turkish neighbor was missing, too. I was wheeled out of my apartment and into the ambulance. I was trying to grasp what led to this horrific violence. I had vigilant giraffe eyes while living under Yusuf's constant abuse. Those eyes were all I had. They allowed me to watch my enemies on all sides, without moving my head. I was ready when Yusuf, like a lion, would charge toward me. Lying in the back of the ambulance I shouted, "You will not destroy me!"

Why did I become full of myself and let my guard down? I asked myself. I was rushed to the emergency room and examined. The doctor's touch opened the wound I had tried so hard to heal. My body was again not my own. I was reminded of Edna, back in Mogadishu, who suffered a horrific beating by her husband after giving birth to her fourth baby girl, not a boy. Furious, her husband, Jamaal, shouted a quote from the Prophet, and the words spilled like blood: "When one of you inflicts a beating, he should avoid striking the face."

Like Edna, I felt powerless. Words like these ripped my heart by striking at my humanity, integrity, and womanhood. I saw a big wall rise before me, and I was scared to face it. Nigel was not here to dismantle it and remind me that I was not a lamb kept in a fence. But I could see myself crawling and finding a dark corner in the fence. I questioned my actions and self-worth as I pressed charges against Bashir.

Did I do the right thing by challenging him at the coffee shop?

Will the others do what Bashir did?

Did I deserve to have my mouth shut with a "good hard fuck," his words that day?

I heard a loud voice, echoing inside of me, *Don't go there!*

Once again, I was a cloth that could be stitched and reopened for someone else's pleasure. My branded scar defined my worth as a woman. But what Bashir did was worse than hearing the sound of the scissors cutting my flesh.

⁂

I had to move back to the dormitory to try my best to forget the rape. But I could not sleep or eat, and I would find myself in the shower taking my skin off with a bar of soap.

Finally, I began taking Valium again, and I could function, study, go to work and to school. But I could not stop throwing up. I refused to go back to the doctor, but I received a call from the hospital asking me to come in to talk with a doctor with the results of postrape tests they had done. I went to the hospital only to be told I was facing another nightmare: the doctor said

I was pregnant, and I had to make a decision. I was stunned and did not know what to feel.

I asked for time. My whole body shook with fear about such a decision.

When I got back to the dorm, I called Mahad in Paris and, sobbing, told him what had happened. He said he would support any decision and would help me with it.

⁂

The next day I came downstairs and found Mahad chatting with the concierge.

"Mahad!" I exclaimed and ran to embrace him. I could not believe he was here.

"Are you hungry?" he asked.

"No," I said. "But I'll come with you to a restaurant so we can talk."

At the restaurant, I told him that I had decided to have an abortion.

"That is the right thing to do," he agreed. "The pregnancy would just be a painful remainder of that horrible night. I will come with you to the hospital."

"No, Mahad." I took a deep breath. "Please, I want to do this alone." I knew he cared about me very much, but I needed to be alone.

"Of course," he said. "I just want you to know I am always here for you."

We spent the rest of the day together, and then he returned to Paris. I called the hospital to tell them my decision.

The night before my scheduled abortion, I awoke bleeding. I was rushed to the hospital, and my pregnancy was terminated. Other than the medical personnel, the only person who knew this was Mahad, and he promised to never tell anyone.

I prepared my body and mind to commit to my mission of speaking out to end the abuse of girls. Soon, I would be going to America. After much thinking and many discussions, I had decided I would make a documentary on female genital mutilation.

PART THREE

a nation of bards

1984–2011

Nothing can dim the light which shines from within.
—Maya Angelou

43

the angelinos

The most amazing thing to me was landing in Los Angeles during the 1984 Summer Olympics with my fellow students on Grenoble's exchange program. At the airport, we felt the electric excitement and found the Angelinos to be very welcoming and friendly. Our guardians loaded us up into a huge bus, and we were off to UCLA. It was a very hot day, and while the rest of the students toured the campus, some of us sneaked out to buy T-shirts. We watched one another's backs as we tried on the T-shirts, feeling the cool wind calming our heads, but it was our first mistake, and we got a warning from one of the guardians. She held our passports and tickets back to Grenoble, and she never smiled.

After some sightseeing, a female student from Morocco and I were dropped in Duarte, California, at the home of our hosting family, a young couple from Bengal, India, with a daughter. I felt right at home.

I called brother Asis in Brussels to let him know that I had arrived safely. Asis was worried about me coming to America with three hundred dollars and a dream to make a documentary on female genital mutilation. He said he would call the Somali embassy in Washington, DC, and help me find the Somali community in Los Angeles.

He called back with the phone number of Elias, the brother of the Somali supermodel Iman. He lived in Los Angeles with his wife. Asis had arranged it so that when the program ended, I would move in with them.

None of the guardians, students, teachers, and friends on the trip or back at college knew of my plan to not return to Grenoble. But this was my only chance to find a way to speak against this personal issue that faces so many women around the world. The day before we were supposed to return to Grenoble, I told the guardians my plan. They were shocked, and the one who never smiled crossed her legs and said she would not give me back my passport and ticket.

"Why are you ruining your education?" she asked.

"I'm not—I will continue it here."

"But you didn't complete your classes," she countered.

"What about your diploma?" said the other.

"Three years are enough," I said. I was twenty-three and beginning my fourth year.

I knew they had sincere intentions in wanting me to return to Grenoble and complete college, but I had made the decision to follow my life mission and end FGM. The guardians called Grenoble, and after a long discussion I was given back my passport and ticket.

The following day, Elias and his wife took me from Duarte to their Los Angeles home. We called Asis to let him know that I was in good hands and shouldn't worry, but he was worried and asked Elias to enroll me in language school while I still had the visa. I could hear Asis's voice breaking as if he were trying hard not to cry.

"Did I make a mistake by coming here?" I asked him.

"No—I want you to be happy," he said. "Fadwa and her brothers are coming to school in New Jersey, but when she heard you are in California, she said she would show up there."

"You don't need to worry, Asis. My mind is focused, and the only dream I have is to continue healing and making the documentary."

"Please do not say anything about your dream to the community, and be careful. Many will not want you to discuss this tradition. And do not get into political issues, and never talk about Father and the government. It is too dangerous."

"I promise to follow your advice," I assured him. "And I will call you every Friday to tell you how my life is progressing." I appreciated Asis's concern.

Elias and his wife were generous and welcoming people. I shared a room with another Somali female who was in transit to a different part of the country. The apartment was very comfortable, but it soon became a hanging place for the herdsmen, and the flow of visitors turned the apartment into a refugee camp. All day people came and went. Feeling nostalgic, I would listen to their stories, which made me think about my family and our home in the army camp back in Mogadishu. In the living room, the herdsmen would warn me about America and give me instructions on how to survive in Los Angeles.

A man who always wore polyester suits said America poisoned its people with too much freedom. "There is this freedom," he went on to say, "to be who you want to be. You can even camp in the streets!"

"Yeah, and your ass will be put into a siren-blasting car!" another man said.

"Don't let me start talking about the police!" Polyester Man was visibly upset when the police conversation came up.

I listened as a herdsman described an incident when the police stopped him as he walked around the Westside area. He told the police his car had died, and he wanted to get to another herdsmen's apartment nearby. But the police were curious about his bloodshot eyes and thought he was high on something.

Polyester Man explained that he didn't drink alcohol or smoke pot, but the police did not buy it. He went on to tell them that he inherited the red eyes because most Somali people chewed qat for the past millennium. The herdsmen laughed and clapped their hands as they finished telling the police story.

Polyester Man got up, stood by the open door, and lit a cigarette. My mind was busy trying to figure out why he wore 1970s clothes.

"When did you come to America?" I asked him.

"Many Americans think they have freedom—but they don't." He didn't answer my question.

"Who is going to get the doughnuts?" someone shouted.

Suddenly, the herdsmen were arguing among themselves about who should pick up the doughnuts and who would secure some qat. Since they couldn't decide and argued more, some, feeling hungry, ventured into the kitchen, returning with full plates.

We heard Elias's wife shout, "Enough!"

Those holding the full plates looked up, shook their heads, and said Elias was crazy to fill that woman's stomach.

Polyester Man dropped his cigarette on the ground and stepped on it. He walked back into the living room and took one of the herdsmen's full plates, set it on the table, and started playing with his beard. He talked about how many Americans believe they have freedom and say they can do or be whatever they want. But in other parts of the world people were raised not to push things, and, therefore, they could not do something big and different. Most just did their best, went along with the program, and hoped to stay out of trouble.

I listened as others described this subtropical city where people behaved differently than in any other part of the country, and, to prove it, I was taken to Venice Beach. On the way to the beach, I heard more great stories about the Angelinos. I was told that if one of them invited me to dinner, I must grab an apple before heading out of the apartment.

"Why?" I asked. They laughed as they shouted out answers to my question.

"Because they have their own system of ordering," one man said.

"They even have a system for the stop sign!" said another.

"They roll over it and do not stop at all."

"Those are the ones driving Lamborghinis!"

"They own the streets!"

I couldn't help but laugh with the herdsmen, feeling they were the best people in the world. They warned me about the neighborhoods in Los Angeles and places to stay away from and never visit. They said it had something to do with tribal issues in America.

"America has tribal issues?" I asked.

"Worse than us!" a man exclaimed.

Then someone yelled out, "I'm from Boston!"

"What are you talking about? I'm from the Bronx!"

"That pizza tribe has a stronghold in Philadelphia. . . ."

"There are millions of tribes here. . . ."

"So far I heard only the Italians—the pizza tribe."

I listened as the city of Los Angeles was divided from west, east, south, and north. Westwood, they said, was where I would find the intellectuals; Beverly Hills housed many wealthy Iranians, who cleaned out their own country; Hollywood had its own hills, which housed the dreamers and the entertainers. The South Central area was blessed with liquor stores and hosts the blacks; and East Los Angeles, with its vibrant tradition, was home for the Latinos. I was surprised when I was told that even the streets names have tribal connotation, like Rodeo Drive in Beverly Hills versus the Rodeo in the South Central area. One was pronounced with ease, while the other with clenched teeth.

We arrived at Venice Beach, and immediately I was blown away by the spectacular activities around the area. I watched as the half-naked women roller-skated with their dogs on leashes while drunkards fought for the last bottle. The orange glow of the sun shone down on the Angelinos, and they appeared to be the most beautiful people in the world. I played the role of a tourist, walking into the shops and looking at the merchandise, feeling the need to spend a few dollars, but my new friends rushed me out of the store and into the area where men were weightlifting. I could not believe what I was seeing.

One of the men waved and started walking toward us. I was frightened; he looked like a gorilla moving away from his troop. I didn't know whether to cry or run away. I had never seen any human being with a body like his. His muscles were so huge that his upper body was pushed up, choking his neck, as if his head was sinking into his enormous chest. I wouldn't know how to describe those huge veins covering his arms. My eyes would not let me look past his arms, and I was grateful. He approached and started chatting with the herdsmen while he glanced at me.

"Would you like to take pictures?" he asked.

"How long would it take to develop muscles like yours?" a Somali man asked.

"Like drinking alcohol, the Somali body is not fit to develop muscles!" another said.

The Gorilla Man smiled when he took a good look at the herdsman's skinny features. While the herdsmen laughed and talked with the Gorilla Man, I was in a state of shock, thinking about the nightmares I was going to have that night.

⁂

Soon after, once I had gotten a feel for my new city, I regained my focus and stopped hanging out with the herdsmen. I found a church where they taught foreign students English without pushing religion. Asian and Mexican students dominated the place.

I met a Japanese student, a young man named Yuki, and we pledged to each other that we would find jobs no matter what. Our plan was to do well in school and to watch TV for one hour each night and write down new words. But I would find myself laughing as I "studied" at night, watching cartoons. And now and then I would be struck by the wonder of my journey—the daughter of a Somali general, a survivor of female genital mutilation, a survivor of an abusive arranged marriage to a relative, now an activist for African girls and women, sitting before a television in Los Angeles, watching *Tom and Jerry* to learn English so I could take my message out into the world.

⚜

After a month, Yuki and I agreed that we were ready to find a job. We went to shop after shop, asking for a job. Yuki found a Japanese store, and a Japanese woman with dark lips and short hair approached us. She bowed and said, "*Konnichiwa.*" I followed suit and bowed, feeling a little proud that I knew that the word meant "good afternoon." The woman and Yuki talked for a moment, and I couldn't help but watch her lips. Those dark lips of hers reminded me of the Sheikha back in Mogadishu. She went to the back office. Another woman and two men emerged from the office and talked to her. I found all eyes on me, and Yuki said they would like to hire me.

"Me?"

"They want to put your face on their merchandise boxes."

"Boxes?"

The woman led me into the office and showed me boxes with gifts and souvenirs that they sold. I found the faces on the boxes to be professional models, but I could not see my face among them. I said no. Then the woman asked if I would like to fill out an application just in case something opened up in the store. A few days later, I was hired as a cashier. I was excited and started work the following week.

At home, I continued to watch cartoons to improve my English, but I found the herdsmen's tales more enticing, distracting me. I also discovered American country music, and one day my fellow herdsmen found me listening to Dolly Parton. One after another they began to chastise me.

"Are you losing your mind?" one man shouted.

"You never pray—we have not seen you pray even once. Instead you laugh at cartoons and now listen to this!" said another.

"You need guidance!"

Polyester Man stepped forward, talking about the benefits of prayers and the sin of leaving the Islamic faith. He picked up a Bavarian cream doughnut and looked at it for a while before putting it into his mouth. "Are you a Hindu?" he asked with his mouth full.

I watched quietly, wanting to ask how the doughnut was cooked. I remembered being warned after arriving that many US restaurants fry their food in lard because of the good taste. From then on, I had no choice but to carry fruit and carrots all the time. I was scared to eat in restaurants for fear of getting sick. I couldn't even go to that Scandinavian all-you-can-eat restaurant with crepe-like pancakes on Sepulveda Boulevard.

"You're committing a crime by leaving your faith," Polyester Man said, taking another bite.

"I'm not the one eating the pig fat."

"Pig fat? What do you mean?"

"Doughnuts and Muslims do not mix."

The herdsmen were in an uproar, not really understanding my point.

"Pig fat?" a man shouted.

"You insult us and accuse us!" yelled another.

A cool wind slapped my back, and fear began to take over my heart. I stood up and moved away from the herdsmen but looked straight into their eyes as I said, "In this town, everything is fried with lard, and that includes the doughnuts you continually eat."

"*Bismillah*—I'm *fasiq!*"

"We are all sinners!"

"You fed us worms!" one man shouted at the one who had brought the doughnuts that day.

Some men jumped up and rushed into other rooms, looking for Elias's wife. She worked at one of those large hotels by the airport and must have known how the food was cooked.

I'm not sure if they were successful finding anything, but in the living room the conversation about pig fat was heating up. Polyester Man wanted to walk back to the doughnut shop on La Cienega Boulevard and witness how they were making the Bavarian cream doughnuts.

In our culture, although pork was forbidden, an animal's waste materials, such as the lamb's or goat's tongue, brain, liver, intestines, heart, head, and nose, were considered delicacies. Meat eaters and cooks wouldn't leave anything out and would even suck the bones. They knew I ate no meat, much less animal organs.

"Have you ever eaten a lamb's testicles?" I asked.

"Please tie me to the couch!"

"She is *shaitan*!"

Whether I was the devil or not, I had made my point.

Polyester Man was upset. "Give me your parents' phone number. I am going to talk to them about your mouth!"

"I grew up in an Islamic family, but my spirit belongs somewhere else," I replied. I was always on the outside looking in. As an individual spirit, I respected their faith because it worked for them. Grandmother's spirit guided me. "This is the path God set for me, and I will continue to walk it, even if it is not a popular road for my countrymen to travel. It is what it is." And I left the room.

I knew it was time to move on. I would find a second job so I could have my own apartment.

44

the ecclesiastical path

Even though two jobs plus classes would be a challenge, I was determined. I found out about a place downtown that was hiring hostesses in a dance club. I did not understand what that meant, but I went to the club. A young woman with raccoon eyes, wearing all black and high heels, walked over to me.

"I'm looking for a job," I said.

"Awesome!"

"Excuse me?"

"A girl like you can make six hundred dollars a night!" she exclaimed.

I listened as she talked about how the hostesses entertained rich Japanese businessmen. She walked me to the back, to dark rooms where the hostesses listened in private about the businessmen's busy days at work. She took me into the boss's office.

The boss looked me up and down, focused on my outfit. "Are you going to church?" she asked sarcastically.

A gorgeous young man, dressed elegantly in a sky-blue shirt and jeans, walked up, and the boss's face flashed hot red.

"Who is she?" the handsome man asked.

"What is he doing here?" the boss said to the young woman with raccoon eyes.

"You don't belong here," said the man. He took my hand, led me toward the bar, and up to the dance floor. Horrified, I saw a long, bright-red couch, and chills passed over my body. I was reminded of the house in the red-light district in Grenoble where I met the prostitutes. Their couch was classier than this, but I knew what it represented.

"Who are you?" I asked.

His name was Carlos, and his job was to throw out any man who mistreated the hostesses. He showed me where the Japanese businessmen would take their chosen hostesses to do private touching. The longer the hostess kept the businessman satisfied, the more money she would make.

"You don't belong here," he repeated.

I called Yuki and asked him to pick me up, and he came with a friend and drove me home. On the way, Yuki asked what I was doing in a club at this hour. I didn't know what to say and kept looking out the window. Yuki was upset and wouldn't talk to me for days.

Soon after, my Japanese boss was ready to throw me out of the store because I wouldn't sell a female customer a gift she wanted to buy. When the woman came into the store, I was aware that she attracted many onlookers, but I didn't know why. I was seriously trying to show her other items, better than the one she wanted and for less money. But she wanted the roller coaster, which had a tiny silver ball that circled around. It was really expensive.

The dark-lipped Japanese woman took the roller coaster box from me and sold it to the woman. The woman smiled at her and left, and some of the other customers followed her out.

"I was trying to be helpful and save her money," I said.

"She's got more money than you and I!"

"Who is she?"

"She is famous!" She said the woman was an actress who had a new film out. She wouldn't say the woman's name.

My homework, she said, was to get to know the faces and films of famous people living in Los Angeles because many were her customers. For starters, the dark-lipped Japanese woman suggested I go watch the customer's new movie, *The Color Purple*. I went to see it, and when I saw Whoopi Goldberg on the screen, I jumped up, shouting, "She was my customer!"

⚜

The man the Somalis called the Godfather informed me that cousin Fadwa and her brothers were on their way to Los Angeles. I was happy to hear he had found them an apartment in Inglewood while looking for the perfect college for them.

But they got off to a rocky start in the United States. The Godfather picked them up from the airport and took them to the bank to help them open an account. They were asked to wait, and soon the FBI showed up. The agents asked Fadwa and her brothers why they had arrived in L.A. with loads of cash. The mistake was that they had not declared the money when landing at the airport. The Godfather explained that Fadwa's father was a powerful man back in Mogadishu and this was their education money. The agents did not believe him, so the Godfather called the Somali embassy in Washington, DC, and the matter was cleared up. Fadwa and her brother were allowed to open up their account and were free to go.

Xadiyo was in Europe and trusted that the Godfather would find the best schools for Fadwa and her brothers. But they had different ideas than their mother. They wanted to party and burn up the money as soon as possible.

I moved in with them, and, within weeks, the apartment became the feeding center for the partygoers. Herdsmen and herdswomen from my childhood would fly from parts of the United States, land in Los Angeles, and would not leave. It was the norm to find intoxicated herdsmen lying on the living room floor or sleeping on the couches. Sharing a bedroom with Fadwa was difficult because she would enter without knocking, often leading in a shirtless herdsman wanting to take a shower.

I would get out of bed and walk out of the apartment, still wearing the satin pajamas Fadwa brought me from home. I would walk around the neighborhood until it seemed enough time had passed for me to return home.

On one such occasion, I found myself standing in front of the Jehovah's Witness Kingdom Hall on Centinela Avenue, thinking. I realized I had to change my situation once again. I believed if I focused on faith and God, my plan of making my documentary on genital mutilation, which I had decided to title *Fire Eyes*, would come together. I must have looked like someone who needed help, because two female Jehovah's Witnesses approached, and, quickly, I told them I wasn't crazy.

⁜

Religious people began showing up in my life, and I found myself agreeing with everything they said and even visiting their churches. Every Sunday, an elderly couple would pick me up in their Cadillac and take me to their Baptist church. The place would be packed with people wearing their latest fashions, and some women would go overboard and wear the strangest hats. I would smile and nod while they talked, and then the church would turn into a dance hall as people acted out their emotions. Some would lift up their hands and scream while others became possessed and started speaking a language I didn't understand.

On my first visit, thinking this was an American tribal language that I would learn, I asked the woman next to me to translate.

"She's speaking in tongues," she said.

"But what is she saying?"

The woman's bulge-eyed expression and intake of breath told me I had said the wrong thing. The woman sitting behind us leaned forward and explained that the woman was being possessed by the Holy Spirit and therefore she spoke in "tongues." It was not a language.

On one Sunday during the service, the couple with the Cadillac walked over to me, leading a woman who stood beside me. She asked, "Are you ready?"

"Ready?"

The couple leaned over and said the ceremony was coming up and everyone was eager to welcome me into their faith. I got up and followed the woman to the back of the church. We walked into a room where two women were waiting for me with a white robe. They told me to take my clothes off and change into a white robe.

A change came over me the day I found myself standing before the Jehovah's Witness Kingdom Hall on Centinela Avenue. Since that day, I smiled at people on the street, and I stopped saying no. I wouldn't interrupt if I didn't understand what someone was saying; I simply nodded and said yes. Now that acceptance had brought me to where I stood, wearing a white robe and ready to be baptized. I didn't complain or resist but simply followed the women's instruction. As I walked toward the podium, I saw a pool of water and heard the thundering praises from the congregation. The pastor walked over and, when he saw me staring at the pool, asked how I was feeling. I was worried about whether the water was clean or who else took a bath before me, but I didn't mention that. As my body was lowered into the water, people yelled out praises, excited about my desire to convert into their faith.

Later, I was taken back to the room, took the white robe off, and changed into my dry clothes. One of the women handed me a certificate that proved my baptism. Walking into the hall, I was surrounded by people who rushed over and gave me many warm and wonderful hugs.

The couple with the Cadillac took me home, but that was the last time they ever saw me. I moved away from Fadwa's and found my own apartment near downtown.

⊹

I found a second job; at night, I would work at a fancy restaurant in Beverly Hills as a hostess, making reservations, welcoming the guests with a smile, and taking them to their seats. One night, a young man approached me and asked if I would like to model. I laughed because I couldn't imagine my feet allowing me to wear those high heels or my face smeared with heavy makeup.

The man was insistent, and finally I agreed, deciding that this path might lead to more connections to those people who would want to know my mission. On the weekends, I did petite fashion shows for prizes and money. To my amazement, one night I won first place, with three different prizes from which to choose: a trip to Hawaii, a backstage pass to the DeBarge concert, and a scholarship to Van Mar Academy for acting.

I chose the scholarship and enrolled in the acting classes, which changed my life.

45

bold moves

Through the acting classes, I met many new people, including Michael Jackson's family. Mother loved their music, and I told them that, but I did not call to tell her about my new friendship. Soon enough, I found myself sitting in the office of Michael's father, Joseph Jackson, in the Motown Building in Hollywood, talking to him about the horror of female genital mutilation. He suggested that I would be better off working in films and with music videos, which would expose me to more people who would be able to help with *Fire Eyes*. I listened to Joseph, but deep down I knew that was not my path. But he became a father figure to me. His assistant would call and invite me to a family gathering after the baseball game, or I would get tickets to their concerts with backstage passes.

In Brentwood, while visiting one of the Jackson brothers' homes, we were taken to O. J. Simpson's home nearby. He met us with a smile and introduced us to his wife and baby. Many years later, I was shocked when his wife and her friend were found dead.

⸭

My next lucky break in film came from an unlikely source, my friend Jerry Mosley, a firefighter. He told me that the UCLA extension was looking for someone to film lectures and workshops, and although I did not know how to work cameras, at his insistence I applied for the job.

Afterward, I dragged him to the school's technical office so I could see the cameras. I boldly approached the man working there.

"How long would it take me to learn how to operate a camera?" I asked him.

He frowned and stared at us. I told him the reason I came to America and how important it was for me to get this job and learn everything about filmmaking. He suggested I take classes in the film department.

For days, I found myself obsessing about the job and finally returned to the technical office and asked the man if I could watch him at work. He agreed, and after following him, I became an assistant and soon got the job. My intention was to learn filmmaking, not earn a diploma, and I was allowed to visit the film department to learn as much as I could.

And there I met Professor Teshome Gabriel, who specialized in third-world cinema. He became my mentor, and through him I met more film people, including visiting African professors and students. The word spread like wildfire when we found out that Belgian documentarian and anthropologist Douchan Gersi was coming to teach at UCLA. He knew Africa better than I did, and I become his assistant and the camera operator in his classes. He was so amazingly smart and wildly funny that a group of students formed who followed him everywhere. He was a truly gifted human being, filmmaker, and teacher.

One night, Douchan asked me to speak to the class about my African heritage. I started talking about the practice of female genital mutilation, and I was pleasantly surprised by how the students opened their minds and hearts to listen instead of shutting down as so many people did. After the questions and answers, I asked if they would support a documentary depicting the torture of this practice. All of them said yes.

I was so encouraged that I decided to quit my job, buy a tape recorder, and venture to Orange County, south of Los Angeles, where the Somali community lived.

⁕

I sought out any Somali willing to talk about FGM. This path was not an easy one, and almost everyone I met was opposed to my investigation of our culture and its taboo subject.

But after many dead ends, I met a few herdsmen willing to discuss how they felt about mutilation. They promised to introduce me to the elderly women in the community, and eventually I would have an opportunity to interview them.

I needed to live closer to the community so that I would be ready when the opportunity presented itself, instead of having to drive from Los Angeles. The herdsmen offered me a room in their apartment, on one condition: I must not criticize their choices of movie rentals. I said I did not care what kind of movies they rented, but what were they renting that they thought I would criticize? They hemmed and hawed, but finally I figured out they liked gathering in front of the television with friends and watching X-rated films.

I asked if women were included at their get-togethers. They said women were not allowed to watch those films; therefore, I should plan an activity during their movie night. I agreed and moved in.

My fellow herdsmen were instrumental in my finding women who agreed to open up their homes and talk about their experiences with genital mutilation. On the weekends, I traveled to Oakland and San Jose to interview more women and some men. When my Fiat broke down from all my traveling, one of the herdsmen, Ibrahim, helped me buy a Nissan.

Ibrahim's fiancée was helpful as well. She would cook a feast, invite the young herdswomen in the community, and allow the open discussion in her home. She was so giving that I did whatever she needed during their wedding ceremony. The only thing she asked was to be part of *Fire Eyes*, and I told her she would be sitting in the sacred circle of women in the movie.

But her and Ibrahim's reaction was an exception. Once people realized how serious I was about making *Fire Eyes*, they expressed their anger and tried to shut me down. I persisted and continued traveling, now with Ibrahim, who escorted me to interviews.

Then my father's work with the government became an issue, and people believed I was spying on them. They thought that talking to me put their families back in Somalia at risk. I was shocked. I explained how my family cut me off for deciding to become a voice against genital mutilation. None of them believed me, and they shut their doors in my face.

On my last trip to Oakland, I met Farah, who took me under his wing and helped me find the right people with whom to connect. Through him, I met people willing to be part of *Fire Eyes*. I was extremely grateful for finding their voices.

Farah traveled to Los Angeles, and we spent the weekend visiting his friends who lived in the San Fernando Valley. After spending long hours together, Farah and I became a couple, against his sister's wishes. She said I would not fit in with their family because I was making a documentary about women's private parts. But I had learned not to care what anyone thought about me. I could not change their perception of me, and I wouldn't even try. I knew I was a God-loving soul, and I woke up every morning wanting to do good, the best I could. If someone had a problem with me, there was nothing I could do about that. My goal was to share my story with women, to help them stand up against this painful cultural act, and to stop the mutilation. They must resist, no matter what anyone said about them. The trouble was that we Somali women were taught to hide our pain. We believed we had no right to offend anyone by saying what was in our hearts, that speaking out was not polite. We did not want to get angry and tell the truth for fear of being cut off from the family and ostracized by the community.

But how long could we go through life dealing with everyone else's fears? We had our own fears to work through, but everyone else put theirs on top of ours, and the weight alone kept us locked in a box. My focus was to let people know there were women who were suffering, who could not hold their bodily fluids due to the genital mutilation, and how degrading and inhumane this could be. Although I had been mutilated, I had escaped the torture of fistula, but I knew pain and understood what those women were going through. I spoke for them, at a cost.

Destroying the interview tapes, spitting on me, breaking a chair on my back as I got up to leave, threatening to take my life, and looking down on me—all of which happened to me—would not make me disappear. I only became more determined to accomplish the mission that brought me to this blessed country, America. I remember saying to my fellow herdsmen that "Africa gave me birth, Europe raised me, and America gave me a voice." I was proud to be in America, not just because here I found my voice but because the country made me the woman I am today, a woman with a fierce voice, a woman without shame. I grew up hearing that I was stubborn, a troublemaker, hardheaded, and not good enough. But I had been wise enough to look in the mirror. I liked what I saw, and I said to myself, *I am worthy, lovable, and good enough.* Branded like a lamb, horrendously scarred, I knew we women must share our stories, not as victims but as survivors. Talking about FGM and knowing that we were not alone would help us heal. We would find a way to educate the mutilators and make them put down their knives. For me, this was not just a personal mission but a humanitarian one, for the rest of my life.

I had dealt with my own family and learned that battle meant "hanging in there" and being courageous enough to say *I love you—but I'm going to tell you what I think and how I feel. I am not backing down. Your act of cutting me off and ostracizing me will not make me hate you, even though you might withhold your love from me.*

The difficult thing is when your family knows how much you love them, your community, and your life, but they look at you and say, *We don't want your love!*

Having to relive that experience through my dealings with the community was humbling but did not make me despair. To know the depth of my love, and to have my love rejected, kept me on task. I had a second chance to evaluate my life and see the beauty that surrounded me, no matter what. Knowing this beauty made it easy to run with the love that shines inside and to shout, *My love is beautiful!* even if I heard negative people saying, *Get away!* Instead of shutting down and feeling defeated, I realized I was not here just for my family and those people. I was here for something bigger, something empowering, which gave me peace of mind so I could sleep at night.

I had no time to concern myself with who did not support or appreciate me.

46

the relinquishment

I moved away from the herdsmen in Orange County and found my own place back in the central Los Angeles area. I was seriously dating Farah and getting used to us commuting between Los Angeles and Oakland. Farah lived with his young sister, and she continued to have difficulty with our relationship.

On weekends, I traveled to see Farah and stay at their home, then drive to San Jose and interview those Somalis willing to be part of *Fire Eyes*. Farah's sister would say how much her brother had changed since we'd been together, and she asked me to stop talking about genitalia.

"Your behavior shows you are not a proper Somali woman," she said. "As a people, we have our ways of courtship, and you should not be alone with a man without a guardian." She said I was loose and had become too Americanized, and she asked me not to leave my shoes at the door of Farah's bedroom.

"What's the problem with my shoes?" I asked.

"Your shoes make me very uncomfortable."

"Why?"

"It's a sign that you're sleeping with my brother."

"You know that by looking at them?"

"Once our guests see those shoes, the whole community will know."

When she said this, an image flashed through my mind of a recent night during Farah's and my private time. He said, "Shhh," and I angrily asked if he wanted to put the pillow over my face to silence my moaning. And during meals, when Farah, his sister, and friends would gather around the dining room table, I watched as he became someone else. He sat rigidly and talked about nothing but religion and arranged marriages. This tense conversation with his sister was helping me understand why Farah behaved the way he did when surrounded by his family.

Later that night, while I was in the bathroom, Farah walked in. When I saw his hand opening the shower curtain, I found myself frozen. I was remembering how Yusuf would rush into the bathroom and terrorize me.

"Were you really infibulated?" he asked.

"Fuck you!"

"That's exactly what you did. . . ."

I flew out of the bathroom and into the bedroom and began to pack my clothes. Farah rushed in, acted as if nothing had happened, and asked where I was going. The only thing I wanted to do was slam the door in his face and head for the airport. I don't remember how I found a taxi to take me safely to the terminal. I was so angry that I wanted to slap any herdsmen who stood in front of me.

Did Farah expect me to become a rock? Should I be punished for experiencing a sense of joy and celebration for healing and working hard on myself? I wondered what happened to other women who experienced pleasure. Do their partners ask if their genitals were chopped off? Do they go back and ask the doctor or midwife to shave off more down there to eliminate any residual pleasure?

Would they at least tell her that sex is both pleasurable and procreative, and ultimately she has the right to choose one or both? Or would she find herself being ostracized for moaning, with a pillow over her face?

Clearly, sexuality was threatening and had to be silenced, controlled, abused, and regulated. If you were to feel the sensation of blood flowing through your body and, God forbid, your muscles tightening during the peak of climax, you would have to shut it down.

I thought this would be the perfect time to make flyers that said, I HAVE MASTERED MY OWN GENITALIA, AND I CAN HELP YOU BECOME THE OWNER OF YOUR GENITALIA, TOO.

The incident with Farah was a huge lesson and showed me that I was worthy of something greater. It helped me remember back in Grenoble, when I said to my vulva, *I promise no one will ever hurt or mistreat you as long as I remain conscious and awake.*

I felt strong, and the fire within was igniting once again, telling me about the best of who I am, and it was "here and now." That was the last time I shared my gifts with any herdsmen or any man who did not deserve me. I would no longer be available; my body, mind, and sexuality would not be available.

⁜

I returned to Los Angeles and found a message from brother Asis saying he was on his way to America. Soon after, Asis and his Belgian girlfriend arrived, and all they wanted to do was party. Fadwa and her friends took over and made sure they enjoyed being in Los Angeles.

Without my knowledge, Asis called our parents and said how well I was doing and that they should open up communication. They said I had made the choice, and if I needed to talk to them, I should pick up the phone and call them.

Within days, Mother called and said she was on her way to America, telling Asis and me to take a plane to Washington, DC. I couldn't understand why she wouldn't come to Los Angeles, but Asis insisted that we go and find out. Asis's girlfriend went back to Brussels while we traveled to DC. Asis and I were picked up at the airport and taken to Mother's hotel. Mother wasn't there. She was visiting the children of our Mogadishu neighbor, Vice President Kulmie, who were living in Virginia. When we arrived there, it was packed with people. I was overwhelmed to see those I had grown up with, who were now married with children. It looked as if the town was housing all the children of Mogadishu. Most of the girls and herdsmen, who used to circle around the dark alleys back in Mogadishu, now wore suits, spoke like Americans, and drove expensive cars.

When she arrived, instead of hugging me, Mother took one look at me and asked when I last had any food. She said I looked frail and too skinny. The peace sign kept flashing in my mind, and I didn't want to wage war with Mother. I smiled and sat beside her. Mother untied my hair and started advertising to everyone how she used make it shine by soaking it in henna mixed with lemon and olive oil. I watched and listened to how Mother's girlfriends talked over my head and tried to match me to their educated and soon-to-be-professional unmarried sons.

I knew what I had to do to stop this nonsense. I got up, made my plate before the men had a chance, sat on a high chair, and crossed my legs. Burning looks of disapproval stared up at me, and, to cover their frustration, Mother's girlfriends fixed their colorful scarves over their heads. The nonsense about marriage stopped. That was all I cared about. At the hotel, Mother and I had a chance to talk about superficial things. She then expressed how much the family disapproved of my making the documentary and talking about the cultural practice of genital cutting. She said if I remained stubborn and continued with my plan, then I was not allowed to use the family full name.

"But Miré is part of me and can't be cut off."

"What have we done to you?"

I was going to bring up those bloody photos, but, instead, I talked about how I saw Mother, like me, being tied to the surgical table. Every time I wanted to get angry and lash out at Mother, I remembered how she gave birth to all of us. I couldn't imagine the pain she went through and how, for each birth, her body was cut open and then closed like a curtain. I told her the reason women would find their dead baby's head stuck in their vaginas during birth, and how fistulas developed. Mother sat on the edge of the bed and dropped her shoulders.

"Forgive me, Mother."

"Go to your room!"

"Not this time."

"You have lost your mind!"

Mother got up and walked into the bathroom, shutting the door.

Trapped in the silence and feeling shut out, I decided to say good-bye to Mother and Asis and boarded a plane to Los Angeles. This was not the first time I was shut out and cut off from my family, but now I felt the unbearable pain of never seeing them again. On my way back to Los Angeles, I thought about the role of parents and how difficult it was for their children to blame them, because they were products of their own culture. They were doing the best they could, and I knew that no parents wanted to hurt their children.

That day in DC marked the beginning of another long silence between me and Mother.

47

the path to *fire eyes*

I heard about a production company called Cenex that hired extras for film and television shows. I ventured to their Burbank office and signed up. I quit the Japanese store and began my first infomercial job. During a break, I chatted with the head wardrobe person, Norma. She asked about my goals in this business and if I liked being on the set and working as an extra. I told her the only reason I became an extra was to have a chance to one day meet Debbie Allen. She was surprised and asked why. After watching the television show *Fame*, I felt the need to have Debbie, in her *Fame* role as Lydia, look at me as she did the other students and ask, *You've got big dreams?* I would look up and say, *Yeah—would you help me end the cry of the dark vulva?* Norma laughed nervously as she played with her African cuff bracelet. I expressed my vision of making my *Fire Eyes* documentary and trying to gather strong women's voices behind my effort. Norma said she would look out for me.

Norma expressed her desire to assist me with the project and to gather crew support when I needed it. Soon after, I was called to assist the wardrobe department on a film in which Kevin Bacon was playing the lead. Not knowing anything about the wardrobe job, I called Norma and asked her advice.

Armed with new insights, I showed up early on the set and had my first cup of coffee. That was a mistake, since I was already wired up and didn't need the caffeine. My stress hormones were on overdrive, with my hands shaking, heart racing, and my blood pressure rising. I met my boss and her assistant, to whom I became an assistant.

This job was short-lived, but I was soon sent to other sets around Hollywood, which brought new people and connections into my world. I would get calls from new friends who insisted I get an agent and pursue acting jobs. Finally, I decided to put my acting training at the Van Mar Academy to good use, and I went out on auditions. I hated going out for commercials and prayed to God to help me mess up so that my manager would erase me from the client list.

Through my new connections, I was able to hang around different sets, until fate brought me face-to-face with Debbie Allen. I found that Debbie was directing an episode of a sci-fi series called *Quantum Leap*.

I showed up at the set and watched how her talent guided the scene. She would be at ease while focused on the work at hand and stared when she felt under pressure, as if she were communicating with an invisible force. During the break, I went up to Debbie and introduced myself. She was so normal and wonderful that we sat down and talked about Africa. I told her all about my dream of making *Fire Eyes* and how much I would love her to direct it. She seemed uncomfortable getting into cultural rituals, especially the issue of genital mutilation. She felt audiences would be horrified and wouldn't come out to support a film on such a painful subject. I said it would be a success if two people showed up because those two would tell two more. Our talk ended on a good note, with warm hugs.

On the weekends, I would listen to the interview tapes and, while transcribing them, envision the whole documentary in my head.

❖

I learned about how the Red Berets were massacring masses in Mogadishu and about the death of the beloved Catholic bishop Salvatore Colombo, who had been critical of President Siad Barre's regime. The news coming from Mogadishu wasn't good because the government was targeting those from the North, making their blood wash into the turquoise water of Jasira Beach.

In panic, I picked up the phone and called my family home. Father answered, and immediately I knew something was wrong. A chill ran down my spine as Halgaan's words came to mind: "Tell your father to leave the glass house."

"It's me, Father. . . ."

"What's wrong?"

"I heard about the massacre."

Father coughed badly and acted as if all were well. "Did you speak to your brother?"

"Asis?"

"Something is wrong with him."

Of course something was wrong with Asis, with Mother interfering with his personal life and making him miserable. He believed love was a choice, forgetting that Mother was the one who would find us a match. On the other hand, brother Malik was fine with her meddling and allowed everything, accepting a big house with accessories and a new wife. The only problem was that Mother kept showing up and interfering with the honeymoon. The new wife was a firecracker, and she refused to let Mother into the house after her daily unannounced visits. The honeymoon was over, Malik was upset, and he divorced his wife for disrespecting Mother.

"Father, remember what Halgaan said about the glass house?"

"Everything is fine."

Father was not willing to speak about the chaos in Mogadishu, and I decided not to force the issue. I asked if I could speak to Mother, but Father said it wasn't a good idea. I hung up and began running in circles around my apartment, trying to shake off the pain in my heart.

⁑

Soon afterward, I was struggling to hide from a repo man who was hired by the car dealer because I was behind on payments. I begged him not to take away my car. After work, I tricked the man by parking blocks and blocks away from my apartment. When I got home, I would drop my body on the couch and stare at the wall. Begging for a new path, I would have a serious conversation with God.

Luck showed up when I was hired to work on a volleyball movie called *Side Out*, and an American car dealer was giving away a car during the making of the film. I put my name on the raffle ticket and hoped for the best. The repo man had caught up with me, and I had no choice but to tell him where the car was parked.

The day of the raffle, I walked around the shore where we were shooting and prayed. I saw a flash of insight about how the lead actor, C. Thomas Howell, would be calling my name as the winner of a new car. As the flash of insight disappeared, I heard my name blasting from the stage. Stunned, I stood there and couldn't move my body. I wasn't sure if I was hearing voices in my head and needed therapy again. The actor was really calling my name, over and over. The crowd shouted with excitement that a fellow extra had won a new car. I was guided toward the stage, where the actor was waiting. Realizing my confusion, he walked over and took my hand, lifted my arm in the air, and said, "She is the winner!"

God moved the mountain, and the only thing I wanted to do was pick up my new car and drive to Chicago to beg my sister Oprah for help. Although she did not know I existed, I felt Oprah Winfrey was my sister and the only one who could fund *Fire Eyes*.

I went to the set of *L.A. Law*, where I was a regular, and talked to Anna Maria Horsford, who played a judge. She listened to my crazy idea about how I was going to quit my job, get the money from Oprah, and shoot the documentary. She glared her big eyes at me, picked up the script page, wrote something, and handed the page to me.

"Here are the directions to my house," she said.

"Your house . . . ?"

"Listen, it's time for me to have a motherly talk with you."

Anna felt my energy was being drained by running around the film sets and not focusing on a long-term plan. She said I needed a base, a support system, and she wanted to offer me hot meals and a place to call home. I was so touched by her love and compassion that I couldn't hold back the tears. She got up, hugged me, and walked away to shoot her scene.

In the meantime, I went around the set, asking if anyone had friends or family near Chicago whom I could stay with, and a friend gave me the address and phone number of his sister in Kalamazoo, Michigan, and said his visit to his sister's would overlap with my visit, so he would see me there and we could drive back to L.A. together. The next day, I went to city hall, registered my production company, and planned my Oprah trip.

⊰⊱

I called her studio, wanting to speak to her assistant or maybe the producers because I was sure they would listen. They would want to support the making of *Fire Eyes* and to have a show about genital mutilation. After all, I said to myself, Oprah loved to empower women, and I was no different than any other woman. But the woman on the phone was not forthcoming and thought something was wrong with me.

I thanked her and hung up, but I did not change my mind about my trip. Everyone had warned me how dangerous it would be, and some went so far as to mark up a map with areas I should avoid because of rednecks. Before their fears stopped me, I packed my car with survival stuff, filled the gas tank, and placed the map on my lap. I drove down the freeway, headed toward Kalamazoo.

⚜

I felt fearless and drove all night, watching the star-filled sky and thinking about the structure for *Fire Eyes*.

I smiled when truck drivers flicked their lights to greet me. During the day, I would fill up the tank, eat something, and sleep in the car. I didn't want to go into motels and use up my money, just in case something happened. But, after a while, I had to get a motel to take a shower, rest for a while, and wash clothes. Before getting back on the interstate, I looked for a police officer to make sure I was on the right path to Kalamazoo.

I always had deep respect for anyone wearing a uniform and felt safe with them. During my trip, the police officers I encountered were helpful but worried for my safety. I listened to their advice and stopped traveling at night.

I was pleasantly surprised when entering the redneck areas that I was warned about. The people I met seemed eager to get to know me. At gas stations, young men would approach and ask if they could pump gas. At the mini-store, the man at the register gave me directions, then before I left, handed me snacks and milk. While a group of young men were discussing washing my dirty car, I was thinking about where the name *redneck* came from. When I asked them about it suddenly, the cigarettes fell from their mouths, and they laughed hard. One of them stood in front of me, then turned, took off his hat, and showed me his sunburned red neck.

"I see—the sun was hitting your neck!" I was enlightened as the men talked about the racial use of the term *redneck* and asked if I considered myself an African American.

"I'm an African."

But the men were more interested to know how I signed an application paper. Did I circle "African American," "black," or "other"?

I worried about getting into a conversation on a subject I didn't know much about. I felt I was wasting time and should have been on the highway by now.

"I sign myself as black," I said.

"What was your country name?"

"Somalia."

"Then Somali American fits you well!"

I said from now on I would be signing applications as a Somali American and gave them the snacks and the milk. With kindness, the men directed me toward the interstate.

✢

After three days I arrived safely at the Kalamazoo house and met my friend's family. I had a warm meal, went up to my room, and took a long, hot shower. My plan was to rest for a day before heading to Chicago and then be the first person to arrive at Oprah's production office.

Early the next morning, I got lost driving around Chicago trying to find a coffee shop where I could use a bathroom. I was lucky enough to find a McDonald's. The day had started well, and nothing would stop me from talking to Oprah.

Before leaving McDonald's, I asked the customers to direct me toward Harpo Studios. Some gave me strange looks; others smiled and asked if I was a guest on the show. I was trying to think of what to say when a couple rose and walked out with me, then directed me toward Harpo.

When I found it, I drove the car around the building and parked in the lot, then walked to the entrance and rang the bell. A man's voice blasted from the intercom, asking my intentions.

I leaned toward the speaker. "I'm here to meet Oprah and talk about a very important health issue facing African women."

The man said nothing, and the silence was unbearable.

I rang the bell again, and suddenly the door swung open and I was looking up at a tall man standing in front of me. His face was serious, and his body like one of those sports players. I did not care; even with those muscles, he would not block me from meeting Oprah. "Do you have an appointment?" he asked.

"No—but I drove from L.A. to meet Oprah."

He smiled, then crossed his arms over his chest and stared at me. He listened as I explained my journey and that ending the practice of female genital mutilation was my personal mission. But the man wasn't having it and said I was making the whole thing up.

"You need to get your car out of the private parking lot," he said, not smiling this time.

To prove I wasn't lying, I asked him to follow me to the parking lot to see the California plates on my car. He did, and when he saw the blankets and leftover snacks in the back of my car, the man cracked. I begged him to at least let me talk to Oprah's assistant so that I could hand her the outline and budget of *Fire Eyes*. Reluctantly, the man walked me back to the entrance and into the building. "Wait here," he said.

A few moments later, a woman walked over and introduced herself as Lisa.

"I'm a producer. So, is it true that you drove all the way from Los Angeles to meet Oprah?"

"Yes," I said, "and, if you have a heart, you will not send me back on the road without meeting Oprah." I explained my mission, and I could see her struggle, trying to understand and make sense of my irrational way of doing things. Lisa wouldn't look at the *Fire Eyes* outline and budget, but a young woman showed up and stood next to Lisa, listening to our conversation.

Lisa said I was going to be in the audience and after the show would be able to shake Oprah's hand. She warned me not to force anything on Oprah or hand her my *Fire Eyes* papers. The assistant walked me to the back of the building, where a crowd of women had gathered. I was quiet, following the assistant and the crowd into the studio.

After I took my seat, the assistant said she would return when the taping of the show ended. I don't remember what the show was about because I was going over what I wanted to say to Oprah. She walked onto the stage and greeted all of us with a great smile and a few jokes. After the show ended, and while the audience was getting ready to shake Oprah's hand, the assistant rushed in and stood behind me. Slowly, I put the outline papers back into my bag and moved forward, following the line. When only two people remained standing between Oprah and me, I felt fear rise in my throat.

With a smile, Oprah extended her hand. I shook her hand, moving my body up to the stage and ignoring what Lisa said earlier. Quickly, the assistant's hand was on my back, and she was telling me it was the time to move out of the line to let the others step up. But Oprah kept holding my hand as I began talking. I talked like one of those desert trees when they saw the blessing of God's rain; the words poured out.

"You drove from L.A.?" Oprah asked when I paused to take a breath.

"Yes, and I was sleeping in the car, and please—"

"Please, you're holding up the line," the assistant said.

"Let her finish," said Oprah.

"I'm so happy to meet you—"

"I'm very happy to meet you. Thank you for coming."

The assistant successfully managed to push me out of the line and toward the door. I told her I wanted to speak to Lisa before leaving the building, but she said to follow the crowd out. I would not leave, and she had no choice but to take me back to Lisa.

I thanked her for helping me to have the quick meeting with Oprah, and I asked if she could help me raise fifty thousand dollars for *Fire Eyes*.

"I'm sorry, that's not possible," she said. "But I wish you the best of luck, and have a safe trip back to L.A."

I returned to my car and cried and cried until I had no more tears.

48

bloodshed

The phone was ringing when I got back to the apartment. I picked it up and heard Asis yelling and crying, but nothing made sense.

"Stop yelling and tell me what is wrong!"

As the story poured out, a sense of urgency and alarm rose in my stomach. Asis said Siad Barre could not recover from last year's "Mogadishu Manifesto" calling for his resignation, and civil war was imminent.

"Father is not listening," he exclaimed, "and he is taking too long getting the family out of Mogadishu. Call Father—find out more. The violence has gotten out of hand. . . ."

I hung up immediately and attempted to reach my family, but I could not get a clear line to our home.

I called Asis back, my hands shaking as I dialed.

"It's too late!" he shouted. "Barre's government collapsed, and he is already out of Mogadishu." He paused, trying to regain control of his speech, and I could hear his sobs. "Our family was taken out of Mogadishu, but the helicopter crashed in Kismayo. . . ."

How do you respond to such news? I dropped the phone and wailed like a tortured animal. In my mind's eye, all I could see was the glass house breaking as my parents, sisters, brothers, and the workers escaped without shoes.

I thought about the lamb tied to the cotton tree at the house, the Fiats, the German cars, and, with all that wealth, my family escaping only with the clothes on their backs.

In a complete panic, I called Gabon and talked to Khalifa, who was on her way to Nairobi. "Do not believe any news!" she ordered. "Wait for my call—rumors are flying everywhere."

I hung up, but calls continued to come in with disturbing news about the death of my family.

After rescuing and sending his wife and children back from Hargeisa to Mogadishu, our cousin Shuke, Yusuf's brother, was killed by a car bomb planted in his car. Supporters of General Mohamed Farah Aideed, who had helped overthrow Barre, caught, tortured, and mutilated Uncle Hussein alive when he couldn't say where Father was. Our only aunt died after hearing what happened to Uncle Hussein, and Aideed's men killed my two other uncles as well, wiping out Father's family.

Khalifa never called back. Looking for answers, I went to the Red Cross and the Doctors Without Borders offices in L.A., but they had no news. I repeatedly called Khalifa's family home in Libreville, and when they finally tired of me, they said to await her call.

I could not understand the need to withhold the whereabouts of my family and information about their safety. I was reminded of when the family cut me off because I chose to become an activist.

Crying all day and feeling miserable were not getting me anywhere, so I decided to be of service when the Somali refugees started landing in California.

I went around the community to find out about any refugees who needed help with housing, translation, or doctor visits. I was asked to find a place for a family of four. I found an apartment near Baldwin Hills in South Los Angeles, and quickly the family settled into their new place. The couple's fifteen-year-old daughter seemed frail and would often throw up.

I suggested that we take her to the hospital for a checkup. I had heard horror stories about rape in the refugee camps in Kenya, and she brought back memories of myself after my rape. The more insistent I became, the more the father refused to speak to me.

I was taken aside by other refugee workers, asked to stop talking about the war, and told not bring up the subject of post-traumatic stress. Like most of the refugees, this family fled torture, hunger, and the unimaginable pain of war. To keep me silent, they sent me on errands to buy groceries and other supplies the family needed.

A few days later, I happened to walk into the bathroom and find the fifteen-year-old daughter throwing up. She burst into tears the moment she saw my face. I just knew she was pregnant. Cold chills ran down my spine.

As I started to move closer to the young girl, her mother walked in and asked me to leave the bathroom. Within a moment, the mother walked into the dining room and told me to get out of the apartment and never come back.

I said OK and walked out. One of the Somali women who had brought me followed and caught up with me. "What happened?" she asked.

"The girl is pregnant."

"What do you mean?"

"That man is not her father, unless incest became part of this war!"

A few weeks later, we found out the fifteen-year-old was the man's second wife in this very tight-knit family.

I next was assigned to help the refugees in San Diego, and on my way there, I was warned not to discuss anything about how men brought several wives into the country, claiming they were daughters, cousins, or other relatives. I had been speaking about it because I was concerned about the health and the mind of the pregnant fifteen-year-old wife.

In San Diego, I didn't witness anyone struggling with pain or flashbacks of the violent civil war. Instead, I saw elderly men showing off their new style of henna-colored hair and beards. The women didn't look anything like the women I remembered seeing in Mogadishu. These new Somali women wore dark colors and hid their faces and bodies with *hijabs*. It was time to prepare the *salaat*, an Islamic prayer, and I followed the women toward the courtyard where a water hose was running. I remembered how my family used to prepare for the prayer. Three times, I repeated the act of washing of my hands, rinsing my mouth, washing my face, cleaning my nose, ears, arms from wrist up to the elbows, starting with the right one, then the left, rubbing the water over my head, and finally washing my feet and cleaning between my toes.

After the washing, I walked out, thinking that I had probably missed something important, but I was too scared to ask. I followed the woman into one of the neighbor's apartments and saw women wearing huge brown and black *hijabs*, sitting in front of a black curtain. On the other side of the curtain, I heard a young *wadaad* calling for the prayer. This empty living room was their mosque, with the black curtain dividing men and women.

I stood behind the women and followed their lead, loudly saying, "*Allahu akhbar*." That was the only thing that came out of my mouth because I couldn't recite past the first line. As the prayer rose around me, I thought back to when I was nine and my parents were getting notes from teachers, neighborhood mothers, wives, and even my playmates filled with complaints and accusations about my spying. Instead of learning how to pray, I was circling around the neighborhood, investigating anything I heard that I felt needed answers. I recalled early one morning I was up as Father prepared for the prayer. He knew I was following along simply to impress him, but he was kind enough to let me stand next to him. I made sure my feet were straight, hands to my side, and head tilted down toward the prayer rug. Since Father traveled a lot and was busy, I thought he wouldn't know that I didn't know how to pray. He said sternly he wanted to put me out of my misery when he found out that Allah had given him a lying daughter. In order to pray, your heart had to be in it. That was the last time I tried to pray the *salaat*.

⁜

Those who had urban life experience and were well educated back in Somalia said adapting to the American way of life would not be difficult. The other women preferred not to mix too much with the community and were frightened when they met aggressive American women. They said most did not honor their womanhood, walked around half naked, and would practically grab any man walking down the street to have sex on the sidewalks. These mothers feared that their children would be badly influenced by outside forces, and they thought it best to keep their daughters in the house, away from schooling.

I told them not to reject the American way of life and not to cling rigidly to our own cultural thinking. How beneficial it would be for them to exchange thoughts with their neighbors and community, showing that Somalis are warm, friendly, and easygoing people. I said this would be the perfect way to show how grateful we were for the Americans' assistance. Some were worried that their teenage boys were hanging around the neighborhood and organizing gang activities. Some of their children had become hostile and disrespected their parents and their elders. After a while, the conversation turned toward marriage and the issue of female circumcision, as they liked to call it.

In order to lead gradually into the discussion of FGM and not scare them off, I explained how a wealthy American woman sometimes chooses to go to a doctor to change her body—make her breasts bigger, shrink her waist, or make her lips fuller. The woman does this because the American culture's standard of beauty makes her feel ugly. In Somalia, the mother cuts the clitoris off her young daughter because of cultural ideas. But the daughter has no choice.

I expected hot hands to fly at my face. But the women dismissed the clitoris issue and asked me to tell them more about American women and their bigger breasts. I said that what took place in plastic surgery clinics was like an automobile accident but controlled. My friend who worked at a plastic surgeon's office told me horror stories, and I passed them along to my fellow herdswomen.

More hot tea and sweet dates were served, and the women were eager to hear that 98 percent of American women did not want to know anything about the risks of plastic surgery; they just wanted to look pretty. I told them that a knife might be taken to a woman's breast, around the nipple, under the breast, or perhaps entered through the arm, to put in a water- or silicone-filled bag to enlarge the breast. For tummy tucks, the doctor cut from hip bone to hip bone to remove fat. Most women ignored the fact that they would have scars. They didn't care because they had given permission to the doctor to cut them and they were adults. These were not children who had no choice, and such unnecessary surgery done to a child would be considered child abuse and illegal in the United States. In our culture, our mothers watched as our bodies were dragged into dark hallways and mutilated. Both plastic surgery and FGM are done to please men; both are done to be liked, adored, and accepted by men.

"In the United States, circumcision is called female genital mutilation," I said as I sipped my tea.

"Mutilation?" one woman said.

"I was mutilated at thirteen—" I said.

"What do you mean? My aunt did not mutilate me!" another woman exclaimed.

"I'm sorry—I mean that's how the girls are purified." I caught myself and realized that this conversation came too soon. The women were very uncomfortable.

To change the subject, one woman started talking about how she escaped on foot from Mogadishu without her family and found angels who helped her cross the Kenyan border.

But some women continued to argue about my use of the word *mutilation*.

"You've been infected with Western culture," said a small woman in a black *hijab*.

But the woman helped by the angels spoke up. "You aren't willing to hear my story about how I was caught in the crossfire and saved!"

Others joined in and talked about witnessing the outbreak of torture and violence and watching as Mogadishu was destroyed.

It was fine for the women to hear the plastic surgery tale, but they did not want to hear that something was wrong with our culture. But I understood their fear and rejection of the challenge such new thoughts would bring. How could a woman deal with a family or a society that did this to her? How gentle could my message be, when I told them that our families and society made us victims of our own culture and that we should see ourselves as survivors? How could one stand up and say *no*?

"Go on being like the Americans!" one woman said.

"The breasts make women beautiful?" another asked.

"No. It's the light from the heart that makes women beautiful," I said.

"What is the reason for the woman wanting to have big breasts?" she asked again.

"She wants to please her man and also protect herself," I answered.

"How can she do that?" another woman asked.

Looking for ways to make them laugh, I said if the woman's husband or boyfriend was hurting her physically she would be able to lift up her big breast and give him a black eye. Those who were not laughing got up and walked out. I continued with the plastic surgery conversation, making sure that my fellow herdswomen understood American women didn't have much of a choice, either. Having a choice means being informed of options, alternatives, and risks, and then making the choice.

Here in America, a woman's choice was based on advertising and what you think the cultural model is for how you should be. In Somalia, women were forced into the ritual of initiation, where a scar would be formed to mark our womanhood. That was not a choice, and, like the American women who are sucked into surgery by the ads, we, too, were forced to make the men become our mirror. It became the norm to accept looking a certain way. Some women did not want to hear the medical, problematic effect of FGM, and I noticed dark clouds invading the apartment. Several women left, and a woman stood up and leaned forward, whispering into my ear, "You talk too much, and that's a bad quality for an unmarried girl." She walked off, taking two more women out of the living room circle. They stopped in the dining room and talked among themselves.

My heart was heavy. I was to help mothers go grocery shopping and take their children to the hospital for checkups and help with anything they needed. Now I worried they would not trust me.

A hand landed on my lap, as a woman with a bright smile sat down next to me on the couch. "No one can stop me ensuring my daughter's chastity."

49

tailing the dream

I returned to Los Angeles and dedicated my time to getting funding for *Fire Eyes*, giving up my other work in TV and film.

My first goal at this time was to find a way to contact Iman, the Somali American supermodel I'd come to know. She was shooting a video with Michael Jackson, and I arranged to meet her on the set. When I arrived I waited until Iman completed the scene she was working on. She knew I was waiting for her, and when she saw me, she rushed to me and gave me the warmest hug. We went to her trailer and laughed about her lines in the video and her upcoming wedding. She asked if I knew how to apply Somali herbs on the body. Usually turmeric paste and other herbs mixed with special oil are applied to a bride's body. It was believed that these herbs give the skin a healthy glow. I told her how I had watched Aunt Ubax applying those herbs and, later, emerging from the room glowing like the sun.

I also talked about my vision of having another Somali woman help me end the horrendous pain of genital mutilation. I asked if she would lend her voice to *Fire Eyes* and support my work. I know no Somali girl can escape the ritual, but Iman never talked about it and seemed uncomfortable every time I mentioned the subject. She was hesitant, thinking it was not the right time to speak about this issue when there was so much suffering in Somalia. While respecting her decision, I told her about my need to talk about those women and girls whose suffering had gone on for centuries. We were like the scared lambs tied to the cotton trees. My intention was not to drag Somalia's mindless political clan wars and the mess they had created into the light but to bring light to the cultural act that mutilates women and girls in the midst of the chaos. I explained that my life mission was to end violence against women and children, and opening up the dialogue was the first step, and that was my reason for coming to Los Angeles and for making *Fire Eyes*. Through education, we might be strong enough to get the world to join us, holding our hands and helping us implement laws globally that would criminalize the practice of female genital mutilation.

Iman was kind enough to sit and listen instead of throwing me out of the trailer. I said that I knew the fear of opening up and talking about our deepest and most private pain, but we never had any choice in the matter. Now, not only did we have choices, but we had the opportunity to help others and to make a difference.

She was quiet, holding my hand, then she spoke about her own mission, helping Somalia during the civil war, and that was her focus at this moment. We hugged, exchanged phone numbers, and promised to keep in touch. A few days later, I called her, gave her information about those herbs, and wished her well with her wedding.

I kept hustling to meet more new people who possibly could be supportive. In the meantime, I met a man named Bill at a jazz club in L.A. He became my boyfriend and we moved in together. Bill understood my purpose in life, which made my mission easier. But sometimes he would complain, saying I was taking him for granted, that I chose to live out of a suitcase, chasing stories about mutilated vulvas. During one of our heated arguments around Thanksgiving, I reminded him that the door would always be open because I knew how hard it was to be involved with a crusader.

Early one morning, the phone rang, and Bill answered. He couldn't understand who was calling, so he handed the phone to me. It was Father calling me from Libreville, Gabon. I burst into tears, crying so hard that Bill panicked, not knowing what to do.

"Father . . . ," I sobbed.

"Did I hear a man's voice?"

"I heard your helicopter crashed in Kismayo. Then it wasn't true!"

"Are you married?"

"No, I have a man sleeping in bed—" The words slipped out before I realized it, and I clamped my hand over my mouth. Bill gave me a worried look.

"Is he a Muslim?"

"Father, you're alive—"

"Let me speak to him!"

I didn't know how Catholic Bill and Muslim Father would find common ground. I passed the phone to him and watched him struggle, each man speaking a different language. Quickly, I got a notebook and wrote a message, telling Bill to say his intention was to marry me. I thought that would end the conversation and calm Father's nerves. Bill froze, covered the phone with hand, and stared. After a moment, he said, "But you're anti-marriage!"

I took the phone and changed the conversation by asking Father about their escape and if I could talk to Mother and the rest of the family. But Father was insistent and wanted to know everything about the man who was in my bed. I told Father not to worry because I was once married, and Bill wasn't Yusuf. That ended Father's questions, and he passed the phone to my siblings, but not to Mother, who would not talk to me.

Talking to my brothers and sisters one by one made me realize that, whatever happened, Father had known one day war would erupt in Somalia. I remembered how he had gotten tutors to teach nine children different languages, just in case. Some of my siblings had traveled to Europe, and I was happy to hear the family was safe and living with Khalifa, who was now living in Gabon. I told them it would be better if the family came to live in America and how easy it would be to get their papers. It was the perfect time because the United States was sponsoring thousands of Somali refugees. But Father said America was not the right place to raise children. He was heading to an unknown destination, but for security reasons, he wouldn't say where.

Many years later, I found out the details about Black Sunday, the day of the uprising, and how my family escaped Somalia's civil war. On December 31, 1990, my family woke up hearing the bombs exploding in Mogadishu. The sound of tanks and marching artillery from the old port toward the other side of town filled the air.

What is it? the family wondered.

A call went to Rome, where sister Sakiya and brother Adaax had gone for a business trip. They were told to remain where they were, and the rest of the family was told to leave Mogadishu immediately. Father made calls to the family and extended family asking them to gather at the main house by the old port. Eighty-four people showed up at Father's house. While walking to what they hoped would be safety, they had been stripped of their savings by soldiers for the warlord-general Mohamed Farah Aideed.

The family storage room full of food and water couldn't feed eighty-four people for long. Bullets were showering the family house from the sandy hill above, and one relative was already wounded. Father put the family in five cars, and they drove to another family house that was being rented by the Saudi Arabian ambassador. The ambassador had already abandoned the house, taking an American ship or plane to safety. For the next three days, my family took refuge in the house. They decided to stay together, but danger drew nearer with each breath.

A cousin of ours named Taka owned construction trucks and had worked with the government before the fall. Another cousin owned an import business. The family decided to load up the trucks with supplies, along with the eighty-four people. In this way, they escaped and arrived safely in Kismayo. There, they found relatives who owned restaurants and hotels, and everyone settled at the hotel and opened up a restaurant to help the war refugees. But they were not able to escape the country to safety.

Cousin Khalifa left Gabon and landed in Nairobi with the goal of removing the family from Kismayo. She had shipped tons of medicine to Kismayo, hoping to help the wounded, but when the plane landed there, the rebels took everything by force. In addition, war broke out in Gaalkacyo, claiming five hundred lives. The only way to get out was by plane.

Khalifa rented a plane and sent it to rescue the family. But instead of flying to get the family in Kismayo, the pilots landed in Garowee, taking the wounded and refugees to Kenya. At the Nairobi airport, Khalifa was notified about the situation, and when she couldn't get her money back she took charge, hiring Kenyan officers as bodyguards and insisting the pilots follow through. They had no choice but to let her board the plane and fly with them to Kismayo to rescue the family.

In the midst of chaos and war, men tried to inject law and order by giving protection to planes landing in Kismayo. They helped Khalifa's plane land safely under protection of the army. In addition, trucks circulated in the neighborhoods announcing names of people whose relatives had sent help from abroad to remove them. Khalifa provided a list of family members' names, and suddenly, a voice blasted from the loudspeaker of a truck, "General Mohamed Ali Miré, your plane is waiting at the airport."

Nineteen members of the family, including Father, were rescued to Nairobi. The rest of the family stayed behind, finding ways to reach to Kenya, Yemen, and beyond. In Nairobi, Khalifa rented a hotel for the family and worked to get visas to take them to Libreville, Gabon. In peacetime, the family had gazed at the lights shining across Nairobi. They expressed their gratitude for Khalifa's selfless service to them. The family received their visas and boarded a plane to Libreville. Everyone settled peacefully and planned for the future. Khalifa even helped Father get his back pay from working in Italian Somaliland as a commanding officer.

In the meantime, the family had received visas to emigrate from Africa to either the United States or Canada. Father decided to move the family to Toronto. Sisters Raha and Shams headed there via New York. At the same time, my family was notified that the rebels had surrounded Uncle Hussein and the rest of the family in Kismayo. They gathered the men and cut their throats and body parts while leaving women and children behind. Soon after, these mad rebels began raping the women and children.

The time had come to ask, *What has happened to our beloved Somalia?*

50

rockefeller

A lice Walker's book on FGM, *Possessing the Secret of Joy*, had
been published the year before, and she was planning to
shoot a documentary in Africa. We had been helping each other
find ways to end the practice.

Not long after I spoke with my father, Alice Walker called
and said ABC was doing a show with Dr. Dean Edell, the host
of a radio talk show, that would focus on the practice of female
genital mutilation. She had talked to them about my being a
guest on the show, telling me this was a good opportunity and
people would be very receptive to my message. So I flew to San
Francisco and met the other guests.

An American woman who was raving about the genital
surgery that her East Coast doctor performed, called the love
surgery, said sex got better once the hood of her clitoris was
removed. She was grateful to the doctor and talked about how
he enhanced her sexuality. The other guest was an amazing soul,
Marilyn Milos, who is the founder and director of the National
Organization of Circumcision Information Resource Centers
(NOCIRC). Marilyn leaned over to me and said to focus on
my issue and not give the other woman a chance to argue. The

306

show went well, and Dr. Edell had prepared himself very well on the issue of female and male genital mutilation.

After the show, the news came that I would get funding for *Fire Eyes*, and Marilyn said someone would call me. At the time I did not know that Marilyn had asked a close friend of a donor to tune into the show. The other guest's son walked over to me and said he was sorry and embarrassed about his mother's love surgery. I could see how distraught he was, and I didn't have the heart to say what I really thought of her. I gave him a hug and thanked him for speaking with me.

I returned to Los Angeles, and the miracles started happening so quickly that I forgot to call Alice to tell her how well the show had gone. A woman named Hanny Lightfoot-Klein contacted me to say a donor was interested in funding my documentary. She first sent me to San Francisco to meet with Marilyn Milos and other powerful women who were doing great work for humanity. Then Marilyn and I flew to New York to meet with the mysterious donor, whose name had not yet been revealed to me.

When we walked into the Rockefeller Center in New York, I was still clueless about my donor. The only thing that mattered to me was that I would be bringing my message to the world.

When the elevator door opened, I saw the classic carpets, and I knew where I was even before I saw the picture of the Rockefellers. The office staff greeted us like royalty and directed us toward a conference room. I handed Marilyn my proposal packages and fled the room, then locked myself in the bathroom. Overwhelmed, I found myself wanting to shout joyfully, but I couldn't. I held a towel over my mouth as I stood in front of the mirror and tried to release the energy by remembering the Method techniques I had learned at the acting school. I let myself feel every emotion without screaming or crying. Afterward, I felt better. I washed my face, put on makeup, and walked out.

Back in the conference room, we met with George Lamb, Laurance Rockefeller, and two women. Laurance asked me to talk about the practice of female genital mutilation and how *Fire Eyes* would make a difference in stopping it. I knew the meeting was only for an hour and Marilyn needed time to speak about her proposal, but I couldn't stop detailing the horror of FGM. Once the questions and answers ended, Laurance said many people had presented in his office, but I was the first one who gave him weak knees. The funding was granted.

※

Before flying back to Los Angeles, I decided to find the Somali community in New York and shoot interviews. I found a cameraman, and we set out to find herdsmen and herdswomen.

While walking down to get breakfast, an idea flashed into my mind. I told Barry Ellsworth, the cameraman, that there must be herdsmen walking around the streets just like everyone else. We could find them by searching for people who looked and spoke like me. Stunned, Barry stared, then looked around at the New Yorkers taking over the street like waves. He thought I was close to losing my mind.

As we argued about our different approaches on how to find interviewees, I heard someone speaking the Somali language. I stopped and listened, and, to my amazement, two young Somali men were moving through the crowd of pedestrians.

I took Barry's hand and dragged him through the crowd, chasing after the herdsmen, shouting, "*Salaama—joogso!*" Hello—stop!

"*Subax wanaagsan.*" Good morning.

"*Iska waran.*" Hello.

The herdsmen couldn't figure out what a Somali woman was doing with a blond, blue-eyed American chasing them down on New York's streets. I explained that Barry was a cameraman and associate producer helping with a documentary about the practice of female genital mutilation. The herdsmen grinned, turned their backs on us, and started walking away.

We followed the herdsmen and asked if they could help us
find any refugee male who would like to be interviewed.

"*Qaxooti*—refugee?"

"Yes—do you know any? What about you?"

The talkative herdsman chastised me and said that I must
have a death wish to make a movie about this topic.

But the other said in Harlem there were herdsmen who
came to America in the sixties, still chewed qat, and wore loose-
fitting sarongs.

"Would you take us?" I asked.

"*Khatar!*"

"Why will I be in danger?"

The talkative one walked away without saying a word. But
the quiet one took the phone number where I was staying and
said he would find people.

Within the hour, the young man called with the information
I needed. I called Barry and told him to bring everything and
meet me at the hardware store in Manhattan where the herdsmen usually met for chatting and qat chewing.

As Barry and I approached the hardware store with our equip-
ment, two herdsmen stood at the door and watched. I told
Barry to free his right hand and shake their hands. They smiled
and greeted him, then looked at me for a long moment.

"What do you need?" one of them asked.

I told my fellow herdsmen we were there to bring their message to the world. The men assumed they would be interviewed
about the chaos in Somalia.

They simply said, "*Sogal,*" or "Come in."

The store owner, also a herdsman, sat among six others, sipping hot tea. With a large smile, I greeted them, forgetting to
introduce Barry because I was so nervous.

To my surprise, the owner got up and walked to the back
room, shouting for me to follow. "Come—*kalama!*" With bulg-
ing cheeks and alert eyes, three more herdsmen emerged and

stood before us. I didn't dare to ask how long they had been chewing and if the New York police had made qat illegal.

I was very glad when my fellow herdsmen agreed to the interview, but they refused to answer some of the questions. And often they would listen for a moment, then interrupt, and everyone would begin talking over one another. But I sat calmly in front of them, asking my questions.

"Why do you want women to be circumcised?" I asked.

"It's a tradition."

The owner moved his body forward as if I couldn't hear him. "In the morning, when you leave your apartment, would you leave your door opened or locked?"

"You can't compare the body to a door," I replied.

"You trust your woman when she's stitched!"

"She is like a door?" I asked.

"She's a property of someone!"

"She is your property?"

"Yes, she is. And, while she's my property, she is private."

"She is your private property?"

"I don't want to share her with anybody!"

Then the other herdsmen joined in and started talking at one another and wouldn't listen to me. My body began trembling, and fear choked my throat. But I tried to listen and find a way to continue my questions.

The owner jumped in and said, "Circumcision has been with us for such a long time. What amazes me is that women, like you, have begun to complain and refuse the continuation of this practice."

"Why?"

"Our mothers and grandmothers had it done, too, and never talked or complained about this practice. What makes you want to change this practice now?"

Before I had a chance to respond, the young and glowing herdsman shyly looked down at the floor and said, "I only want a woman who's stitched."

"Why?"

"I like her to be shut and keep the custom."

"You want her to be sealed while you go around having fun?" I asked.

"I want this pain and suffering of women to continue!"

⁂

The interviews with the herdsmen left me with profound pain and confusion. I had not known my people to speak so cruelly.

A few days later, I interviewed Asha Samad, a powerful woman who taught at one of the colleges. She talked about her Somali organization and how it helped survivors of FGM. Seven herdsmen were there as well. Before the shoot, they expressed a wish for me to make a documentary that would highlight the beauty and wonderfulness of Somalia. I listened, and, after a while, the interview began with a herdsman who reminded me of Polyester Man.

"It's social control, not just physical, what happens to women," he said. "Clinically or otherwise, it's not supposed to happen. To bring a change, you must change the mindset of the society and how they look at a particular cause. Educate them."

Another man spoke up. "After giving birth, women are recircumcised, over and over again. This is an economic question also. I think women who're involved in this need to be retrained for a new way of making a living."

"There is no connection between circumcision and marriage," said another.

"You mean in Somalia?" I asked.

"In Somalia, virginity is something people value," the herdsman went on. "But to say that because the dowry system exists in Somalia, Africa, and parts of the Middle East, the more the woman is disfigured, the more the dowry is—that is totally absurd. I don't think any man would want to find out if this woman is circumcised or not."

"Circumcision is one of the unfortunate Somali customs," another man chimed in. "Hopefully, in the near future, our people will give it up. Personally, it is one of those things I disapprove of in Somali culture."

"What's the reason?" I asked.

"The reason is it represents a mutilation of a human being, causing lifelong pain. It causes a lot of pain for women. We relate to women as sisters, mothers, and wives, so, as such, whatever causes pain to them also causes pain to us. It will not happen to my daughters."

"Would you marry an uncircumcised woman?"

"Because of my age, I would probably marry a woman who was circumcised."

He went on to say that I should look at the larger picture in the social structure and the social position women had in society at large without focusing on circumcision itself. Until the position of women changed in the Somali mind-set and the cultural thinking, changing this cultural practice would be very difficult.

"This is a pharaonic custom," he said. "It was started, as far as we know, in ancient Egypt. It's practiced not only in the Horn of Africa and East Africa but from Senegal all the way across the Saharan region into Malaysia and into some parts of India. This is a custom that we have to look at within context."

Asha talked about the frustration the women survivors faced, dealing with the medical establishment and clashing with the American culture. She said, "In New York, we have members of our community who are circumcised. The American medical establishment is not aware of the practice and are mistreating these women and stereotyping them. They are no more freaks than women in America who have operations to increase this or decrease that or wear corsets to make themselves sexually attractive. Every culture, not only the Somali culture, has ways of mutilating and distorting women's natural bodies."

"Would it be possible to end circumcision?" I asked her.

"The best way to stop circumcision in Somalia is for the community to start speaking out. Every member in our generation should start, and everyone should be prepared to start with their own family and with themselves."

51

achieving the impossible

After the New York shoot, I returned to L.A. My wonderful Somali herdswomen in Orange County agreed to be part of a long weekend shoot. Everything seemed to be working smoothly, but it became clear that traveling to Mogadishu and shooting an actual mutilation, as I had planned, was impossible.

Many said I would be killed before walking out of the Mogadishu airport. But even more, I felt the sharp pain between my legs and could not believe I was unconscious enough to think I could go back to Somalia to film the torture and mutilation of a young child. What was I thinking? How could I have lived with myself? Often, people would hear me say, "I speak for those who have no voice. With artistic truth, I bring their stories to life."

I decided to follow the refugees and shoot *Fire Eyes* in the United States. While struggling with insomnia, I saw how *Fire Eyes* would be structured, beginning with a wonderful midwife and dancer, Arisika Razak, whom I had met at a gathering of powerful women in San Francisco. She would make a sacred circle for the Somali women survivors, and she would talk about childbirth. After seeing the process, the women survivors would realize we are not the weaker sex. I wanted them to understand that, besides having babies, our bodies also have a place for our own sexual pleasure.

Arisika would end her monologue by saying, "Every human being who has been on the planet has passed through the body of a woman. We transform blood into milk, and we feed the world." What followed would be the enactment of a young girl who was about to undergo genital mutilation. I wanted the audience to feel the pain and hear her unthinkable cry. By re-creating this horrible act of violence in film, I did not need to convince anyone or explain why I referred to the practice of the genital mutilation as the "ultimate child abuse."

I drove to San Diego to pick up one of the refugees, the one I called Bright Smile, and, when I got there, I found that she was pregnant. I thought the drive and shoot might be too difficult for her, but she insisted on coming.

Despite a few difficulties early in the day, everyone's commitment, hard work, and talent allowed us to find common ground and complete the day's shoot. After the mutilation scene, Bright Smile wanted to speak out and say what was on her mind.

"It's our ancient custom," she said. "It happened to our mothers, grandmothers, and was followed by the next generation. We have to circumcise them—it's our tradition, and, if we don't do it, our men won't marry us. It's a problem, but no man would have married me."

We wrapped up and rushed to interview Dr. Michael Scott, a urologist who worked closely with women survivors in the Los Angeles area.

While going over the questions to ask the doctor, one of the crew turned to me and said, "Why don't you speak about your own journey and how you felt when the male doctor circumcised you? We can interview you, and the documentary will be more powerful because you will be standing up as a survivor, not a victim."

When Dr. Scott came in, he told how his involvement with female circumcision began when he was an intern and was called to the emergency room because a young Sudanese woman couldn't urinate and the nurse couldn't find the opening to insert the catheter. He had to separate and open the labia to allow catheterization.

He said, "Because of my action and, in some way, my ignorance, I opened the whole thing up. I thought that was what was necessary. She went back to Sudan and wrote, telling me that she had to have reinfibulation or reclosure before she got married. There is a personal sensitivity to the whole process of female circumcision."

After the interview with Dr. Scott was successfully completed, it was my turn to speak. One assistant played with my hairstyles while another assistant applied makeup to my face. While sitting on the chair being interviewed, I wasn't even sure who was asking the questions. I left my body, forgetting how to speak correct English. I was resisting any flashback that would take me back to the ER in Grenoble. I did not want to see myself lying on the exam table, but I heard myself saying, "One day, I got sick, and they took me to the hospital. I woke up, and there were twenty doctors surrounding my bed. They were looking at me, but not just looking at me the way I look at you. They looked like they were watching a horror movie. . . ."

In my head, I heard the voices of the women survivors who sat around my apartment and talked about their personal anguish. I heard them clearly, some saying how much they would like, for the first time, to visit a gynecologist. I would tell them how possible that was, that there are great American doctors who know how to correct bodies like ours. One woman didn't feel the need to visit a doctor, but she asked if I would coach her and talk to her American boyfriend about alternative sex. She did not want to lose him, but she was scared of the pain associated with sexual intercourse.

As I sat in front of the camera to speak about my own journey, pain, and empowerment, I became blank and unable to speak any further about myself. When I opened my mouth again, the words coming out weren't mine. They were the words of the women survivors during our private gatherings. I said to the camera, "I know I'm a woman, but I feel like there is something wrong with me. I want you to help me. I want you to listen to my pain because I can't go to a psychiatrist because the psychiatrist won't understand me. I'm afraid to be involved in an intimate relationship with a man, yet people keep saying, 'You're so beautiful—so exotic.' But deep down, I know I'm not beautiful because I'm not whole. I'm not complete. . . ."

⁂

For the Orange County shoot, most of the Somali women survivors showed up and cooked an amazing meal. I showed the women my questions and asked if anything was offensive. When they shook their heads, we began the interview with my asking them to talk about the day they were mutilated.

"They did not give me an anesthetic," began one woman. "They grabbed me and sat me down in the middle of the circle. I was surrounded by women. Then a big woman came and sat on my chest. All the women had to hold me down."

"My mother ran away when I screamed with pain," recalled another.

"Four women held me down. One put me between her legs while two other women held my legs. Then my aunt sat on my chest."

"I was afraid. I saw blood and heard the screams of the girl who was circumcised before me," one herdswoman said.

"All I remember about the midwife who did the circumcision is that she was blind and old," said another.

"I was happy. . . . Before then everyone called me names and said I was not a grown woman. The ones who were circumcised had more honor."

"You feel alone and ashamed if you're not circumcised."

"Once they remove that piece of flesh from you, then you feel like a grown woman. Everyone loves you—so you feel accepted."

"In the US, when you tell your male friends that you have been circumcised, they seem to avoid you. They feel uneasy with you, thinking that something is wrong with you. It's difficult to make them understand. It's difficult to talk about."

"I will not stitch my daughter the way they did it to me," said one of the women. "I will do the mild circumcision, the *sunna*, to her, bleeding her clitoris, cutting off the tip."

"I will do the mild circumcision," echoed another herd-woman. "It's not as brutal as the infibulations."

After Orange County, we drove to San Jose to interview the community, and I decided not to prepare any questions. All I wanted to do was show the women survivors the segment of the New York hardware store interview, when the herdsmen compared a woman's body to a door.

Wearing Somali clothing, I sat with the survivors and we watched the clip. With frowns and silent stares, the women stared in disbelief, and when the tape stopped, they turned to me.

"I did not write those words," I said.

One woman said, "Well, he answered the way you would expect a man to answer. He is not a woman. If he'd been castrated like us, he wouldn't be talking the same way. Men do not have to deal with the pain of circumcision for most of their lives. They have no right to tell us that it is wrong to give up this part of our Somali culture. They have never experienced the pain of excision, of having a razor cut off healthy flesh. I will never forget the pain of my wedding night or my screams at the time of birth. My two daughters will never suffer as I did."

"What kind of a man is he, comparing us to doors?" another woman said. "Unfortunately, many men think the same way. They think that women are there to be locked and opened at their command and for their pleasure. This shows the insecurity of men."

"He is right, saying that our mothers and grandmothers never talked about the pain. They were told by their mothers that every woman on this earth was infibulated. I thought that this was true before I traveled around. I was shocked to find that this was not so."

⚜

I was lucky enough to find a religious man who was willing to be interviewed. He requested that I cover my head, not make eye contact, and not interrupt, even if he was taking time making his point clear. I agreed, which I knew would be difficult for me to do. I went to his house, bringing hot tea and snacks, then showed him the questions. He said the circumcision question should be the last and not to ask him to discuss anything to do with the vulva.

Thank God the camera was rolling when he began reading the Quran. We could begin by talking about something completely different.

"Men have more power and strength than women," he said.

"Because of his power, then, a man is allowed four wives?" I asked.

"Well, that's true. But, as you know, men have more physical need than women."

"If it's true that women have less physical need, why does the Quran say to circumcise her?"

"The Quran does not tell us to circumcise. But it is a tradition."

When the short interview was complete and we were heading out, a call came that women were gathering in a grandmother's backyard for prayer. I asked if we could come and ask a few questions. The answer was yes.

The women made a beautiful circle around the grandmother. They passed one another incense burners and candles. They put the incense burner under their headscarves and perfumed their hair. I told the women we were recording and, if they felt uncomfortable, to let me know, and we would stop.

The regal grandmother spoke about how grateful we should be to the Americans who helped our country. How safely they brought the refugees into the States and gave them a second chance. We listened as she prayed for Somalia to heal itself and allow us to return and touch our holy land.

I asked the women sitting in the circle to lift up their hands and pray. I don't know why I did it, but it felt right. After the prayer ended, I began with the questions. "My generation wants to stop the practice of female genital mutilation. Can you advise us what to do?" I asked.

"It is beautiful when a woman is stitched," the regal grandmother replied. "After infibulation, the area around the scar becomes smooth and clean. I know that a lot of women do have problems as the result of this," she admitted. "Every month, during their period, at the time of marriage, and during childbirth—but because of these things we should stop."

"The women are continuing to circumcise their daughters," I said.

"It is hard to change tradition. But it can be done," said the regal grandmother.

Silence broke in. I watched how beautifully one of the women picked up the incense burner and put it under her shawl to let it perfume her hair.

I had dispatched many of my friends to find any American women who had experienced clitoridectomy or visited the East Coast doctor known to perform the love surgery. One day after I interviewed the religious man, my phone rang, and a woman with soft voice said she was calling from San Francisco. She identified herself as a white American who had experienced genital mutilation.

The next day, I flew to San Francisco to meet her in person at her home. I found a woman who possessed calmness, warmth, and smarts. She was born with a large clitoris, and her parents had decided to cut it off. Now she was an activist working passionately to improve the lives of intersex people born with ambiguous genitalia. She talked about how it felt to walk through the pain of genital mutilation and what she was doing to heal the wounds. Later, I watched her sex therapy session, which brought back the memory of Grenoble and Nigel's guiding words.

After she agreed to be interviewed for *Fire Eyes*, I asked if she would fly to Los Angeles and meet Dr. Groesbeck Parham at the Martin Luther King Hospital for a checkup. It was necessary to let Dr. Parham examine her before the interview to make sure that everything was as it was said to be. She agreed and passed the examination.

For more than a year, with the help of Dr. Parham, I sat in hospital offices and asked doctors to offer the reversal surgery to women survivors. Dr. Parham knew how to perform not only reversal surgery for mutilated patients but also fistula repair.

A Sudanese woman was brought to the hospital, and Dr. Parham was going to perform her surgery. He said the patient requested that I talk to her.

I spent time talking with the patient the day before her operation. She asked many questions about the surgery and the healing process but said she would not need therapy. I told her that I would guide her during the healing process and not to worry. She said she would feel better if I was holding her hand during the surgery. I assured that I would be holding her hand, and, together, we would hold the light for the others to do the same.

The procedure went well, and Dr. Parham described it for use in my documentary.

"The surgery has to do with making an incision in between the two lips around the opening of her vagina, which had been sewn together," he said. "The form of circumcision she had entailed taking a stitching material and sewing the lips of her vagina together on the midline, so that her vagina was almost completely closed and you could barely get a Q-tip into her vaginal opening. I took a scalpel and made an incision on the midline, in between those lips that had been sewn together, and then sewed them back on themselves. After the operation was complete, the vagina was back to its normal size. Fortunately for her, her clitoris was not damaged at all. Her biggest problem before the surgery was difficulty urinating, and she had had severe pain during her menses. Now that a slit has been cut open around her vagina, she should be urinating without difficulty and having blood flow from her vagina without it causing severe pain. The operation will result in a normal life in terms of sexual functions and functions of her urinary tract."

He described how, after FGM, the vagina becomes so small and so rigid that a woman can have difficulty getting pregnant because the opening is too small for her to have sexual intercourse. The other problem after infibulation is childbirth. When the woman goes into labor, the head of the baby becomes impacted in the vagina. The scar tissue around the vagina is so thick and the vaginal opening so small, the woman cannot push the baby out. Often the baby dies with its head stuck in the vagina. With the head in the vagina, pressure is put on the bladder and the rectum. After these babies are delivered, sometimes dead, seven or eight days after delivery, the tissue between the bladder and the vagina or the tissue between the rectum and the vagina ruptures, creating a fistula. The woman is left with urine flowing from her vagina or feces from her rectum flowing through her vagina or both.

He went on to say, "In America, with that kind of situation, what we often do is take muscles and skin flaps from the thigh or around the vagina and actually transport them up into the vagina to close those openings. In other countries, this type of procedure is difficult to perform because funds or the high-level technology and medicine are lacking. Some women with these types of problems cannot be surgically repaired. In Khartoum, Dr. Abbo opened a house in which these women live because they were ostracized by the society, by their husbands, and by their families."

He paused, then said, "These women have no place to go."

52

beating you to the punch

I called Teshome, my mentor at UCLA, to ask if I could use their postproduction facilities to work on *Fire Eyes*. He said yes, and I was given the best room to work in and was able to shoot the still photos for the narration sequence. An early screening of the movie at the New York Independent Film Market had piqued the interest of representatives from the Sundance Film Festival. Daily I would get calls from the festival's team, asking about the postproduction progress. I would assure them that everything was on schedule and I wouldn't miss the deadline to send the print. That was a very big lie because we were way behind schedule and I was running out of money. I was too pigheaded to call Laurance's office and ask for help.

A writer from the *Los Angeles Times* showed up at my apartment after getting my calls. She wanted to watch a clip of *Fire Eyes*, then write an article about the issue of mutilation. She wanted to write down everything I needed to complete the documentary for the article. The funding from Laurance Rockefeller wasn't enough to cover the expenses on postproduction and everything else that was coming in daily. I wasn't willing to pick up the phone and call George Lamb to ask for help. I wanted to see if I could get help from the film community when they knew I might miss the chance of going to Sundance. To my great surprise, the article came out and offers poured in from all directions. I was given a full postproduction house with offices, kitchen, and even an extra bathroom with a shower. We moved in and began working with an editor who I wasn't really crazy about. Cutting the film was hard enough, but he wouldn't listen or honor my vision on how the piece should be put together.

After he would leave, I would lock myself in the editing room and recut the whole piece, forgetting to eat or listen to my tired body. I was obsessed because the whole documentary was already cut in my mind and I wanted to match it to that vision. The next morning, the assistant would find me lying on the floor after collapsing from hunger and exhaustion. After getting breakfast and a hot shower one morning, I returned to the editing room and found the editor pacing the room in frustration.

"She beat you to the punch!" he said.

"Who's beating me?"

"Alice Walker!"

"How?"

"Her documentary is already coming out." The editor stopped pacing, tilted his head down onto his chest, then picked up his black leather bag and walked out. I moved over to the flatbed machine and looked at his edited piece. Suddenly, the door opened, and the editor peeked his head through.

"I'm sorry—it shouldn't end like this," he said.

"Good-bye," I replied.

He closed the door as I sank my body into the chair, feeling the weight of my worries all over my body.

While looking for another editor, I called my fellow filmmakers, production staff, friends, and others to watch *Fire Eyes*. I was looking for how each person reacted to the film, without worrying about fancy music or cuts.

"That white woman was really mutilated?" asked one of my fellow filmmakers, a woman.

"Yes."

"Did you talk about plastic surgery?" another filmmaker asked.

"That's not my focus," I said. "Those women are like the drug addict who chases the tail of the dragon."

"Wait, what's wrong with enhancing your appearance or that of your child?" another asked.

"You mean your daughter? You can't live through your daughter," I said.

"What about those mothers who want more opportunity for their children?" another filmmaker asked.

"They should leave their daughters' breasts alone," said a friend of mine. "I'm for keeping clean—keeping your body neat and enhancing naturally what you have and adding a little lipstick or nice hairstyle—anything that is noninvasive, anything that's pleasant to your eyes."

"Many don't have time to listen to a guru or want to hear that shit about going inside oneself!" said a fellow filmmaker.

"Good for them," I replied. "But many of us want to go deep inside, which will help develop the natural beauty that lies within. Now, going back to *Fire Eyes*, please understand that the young girls don't ask for body-enhancing surgery. Most didn't know what was going to happen to them."

"Why would they cut the women's sexuality?" one man asked.

"They are threatened by it," I told him.

"Soraya, I know your story, but I didn't hear you talk about how your family ostracized you," said my friend.

"This is not about me," I said.

"I know but still . . ."

"Anyway, talking about my family and telling the truth will not magically open communication. I know how motherhood is idealized in my culture," I said, "but, in this world, only a small percentage of people have a kind and virtuous mother. The rest of us are suffering under some woman who is complex: good and bad, right and wrong, beautiful and ugly, just like my mother."

"OK, say that!"

The phone rang. It was Joan Muira, calling from Alice Walker's office, inviting me to the screening of *Warrior Marks* at the Academy of Motion Picture Arts and Sciences. Joan is a very special soul, with a full heart, and always ready to lift my spirit. Sometimes, she would call and ask about my emotions during the process of making *Fire Eyes*. She was my guiding light who, during our friendship, became the go-between person for Alice and me. I thanked Joan and promised not to miss the screening.

One of my assistants hurried into the room and informed me that he had found an editor. He said she was on her way to the office. I felt relieved and thought maybe it was time to thank the viewing group and end the conversation. But, no, it was just the beginning for them.

"As a young girl, did you have a secret?" a fellow filmmaker asked.

"Secret? What kind?" I asked.

"A sexual kind of secret."

"I didn't know anything about pleasure until my playmates talked about sitting on top of the bidet!" I laughed. "But, in Europe, while healing and learning how to communicate with my body and mind, I realized then that sexuality was an essential part of life."

"Aren't you angry that they chopped off a healthy organ from you?" someone asked.

"That's rude!" a friend interjected.

"It's not," I contradicted. "She asked a good question. In my culture, this was their way of subjugating us, but our minds are fully intact. Now we're learning the power of sexual energy, which is linked to our freedom, creativity, evolution, and, hopefully, equality."

"In America," said one filmmaker, "sexuality is something that was experienced early in life but hidden. It's dirty and something you don't talk about. Many young girls have experienced sexual abuse at the hands of men in their families."

The conversation went on for some time. I listened to their questions, advice, and suggestions and promised to make changes and to meet again for more dialogue after the post-production of *Fire Eyes*.

⊹

Not long after this, a call came informing me that someone had seen my younger sisters, Shams and Raha, in Buffalo, New York, waiting to cross to Canada. Shams and Raha were refugees, living in a convent with nuns near the unused high school where the Somali refugees were held. In my mind's eye, all I could see was my sisters, walking through the frozen snow among the sea of the refugees, crossing the Canadian border. There was no time to let the pain settle in my body. I picked up the phone and called Marianne. I met Marianne through Norma, and we became good friends. I remember when she would visit her father in Buffalo. Marianne was already in Buffalo taking care of her father. I told her I was on my way to Buffalo and asked if she could help me search for my sisters. Marianne was worried, and she promised to head to the high school where the refugees were held to find my sisters.

While packing, she called back and said there were no refugees living in the high school. It seemed like they had already crossed to Canada, but I believed my sisters might be still living in the convent, and I had to look for them. Marianne picked me up at the airport, and we went straight to find the convent. When we couldn't find it, we stopped at the high school. The organizers gave us a tour of the classrooms, which had been turned into dormitory-style rooms and a dining room. While walking down the long wall full of photos of refugees who crossed to different states, I felt painful emotions and couldn't continue. Marianne found the directions to the convent where we might get lucky and find Shams and Raha in good hands. We thanked the staff and rushed to the convent.

When we got there, we couldn't get any information with regard to my sisters. But while the nun was describing the

Somali women who stayed there, I felt Shams and Raha were among those women. Marianne and I got back into the car and found ourselves stuck sitting and sadly staring at the convent's closed door. She was kind enough to let me release whatever emotions I needed to let go and said, "Your sisters are safe."

53

tremor and the indie
pilgrimage

My apartment was in North Hollywood, far from any ocean, but it was moving like the waves, and I was terrified. A boat seemed to be carrying the building through the darkness, and my fear of water made me imagine my death. Suddenly, the earth shook so violently that I jumped and, with my cat Damita under my arm, stood in the hallway door.

Earthquakes are part of life when you live in Los Angeles, but, to this day, this was the worst in my experience. My landlord and next-door neighbor were at my door, yelling out my name and knocking, but I could not speak, Flashlights shone through my window. The earth kept shaking, and I was dizzy.

After a moment, I went to the door and opened it. My neighbor dragged me and Damita out into the pool area, where all the tenants had gathered. Hearing the sirens and screams from the neighborhood, we realized we were the lucky ones, blessed with no injury or damage to our building. Our landlord and his wife called out everyone's name, as if they were taking roll call, and made sure no one was missing.

When I was allowed to return to my apartment, the phone rang, and it was Tim, my sound mixer. He said the studio was hit badly, and *Fire Eyes* was damaged. It would take weeks to fix the problems. We didn't have weeks; to be exact, we had to show up at Park City, Utah, with a print of *Fire Eyes* in four days. The Sundance Film Festival would begin on January 21.

"Are you OK?" I asked.

"No—my guys are on their way to the studio."

"Tim—"

"We'll try to find a corner in the studio to fix the film."

"Did you get hurt?"

"I'll call you back." He hung up.

A sharp pain pierced my abdomen. At that moment I wasn't really thinking about the earthquake's devastation. I was feeling bad for those people who had already bought tickets to the *Fire Eyes* premier at Sundance. I thought about how Geoffrey Gilmore, the festival director, would stare when I told him I didn't have a print. I felt dead inside, and that was when the cold flood of blood rushed between my legs. I realized I had gotten my period early, but I felt I was giving birth to a dead baby, my damaged film.

But Tim and his team worked nonstop and somehow managed to put *Fire Eyes* together as best they could. Then at the last minute, money became an issue because we had to process the final print at a different studio. I went over budget and couldn't take the print out of the lab until I came up with big money. I had a late flight scheduled to Sundance, and I did not know where to turn. Finally, I had no choice but to call Alice Walker. She gladly stepped in and paid the lab in full.

My plane landed in Salt Lake City in the middle of the night, and the whirlwind began. I was met by the Sundance Festival staff, boarded a van to Park City, and arrived at the theater where *Fire Eyes* would premiere the next morning. The projectionist took the print from me and spliced it together with the other films that would be shown along with *Fire Eyes*. The staff person then dropped me off at the condo where I was staying and said someone would fetch me in the morning for the showing and suggested I get a little sleep.

I had only four hours before the first screening of *Fire Eyes*, which was sold out. After the earthquake and the problem with the film, my mind and body were on the brink of collapse. I decided to sleep in and skip the audience question-and-answer session.

But in the morning, I woke to see a tall man hovering over me while I was still in bed. "The van is here waiting—"

"Who are you? How did you get in here?"

"I'm Randy, your roommate—you're late for your screening."

"I need a shower—"

"No time. Get up!"

Randy Holland was a filmmaker, and his documentary *The Fire This Time*, about the Los Angeles riot, was being screened. I rushed out of bed and into the white car, which sped toward the theater. It was beautiful to see the blanket of snow covering every corner in town, reminding me of the beauty of Grenoble.

Nothing had prepared me for the crowds at Sundance and their love for films. The car stopped in front of a packed theater. After struggling to pass through the crowd at the door, I was rushed into the theater where *Fire Eyes* was already in progress. We sneaked into the darkness and stood at the back. The staff and people around us shouted, "Shhhh!" when someone in the audience screamed, "Stop holding her down!"

Another shouted, "Barbaric!"

Then someone began screaming for help because a young woman had fainted. She was taken into the lobby, and I rushed after her. She said the words of Dr. Parham had pained her and asked about the mutilation scene, and I explained the young girl wasn't really mutilated. I was hurried back into the theater for questions and answers.

The day had begun on a positive note, and I stayed on the harsh schedule. I attended the other screenings of *Fire Eyes*, was followed and interviewed by a crew from Black Entertainment Television, met with the press, and met the other filmmakers at the Sundance headquarters. But instead of feeling proud and joyful as I was introduced to the other filmmakers, I felt woefully out of place. They were well prepared and relaxed, as if they had just come from weeks at a spa. They smiled a lot and pitched their current film and future projects to distributors and producers.

But once I met with the two women distributors, Linda and Sue, whom I had met during the New York Independent Film Market, and sold the domestic rights to the Filmmaker's Library, I relaxed. I did not have another project in the pipeline and could not write a screenplay on the spot. My goal was to talk to the audiences and help them understand the importance of ending this practice, which was already invading America.

I was shocked to find that I could not walk down the streets of Park City without being pulled over suddenly and hugged by strangers. People were genuinely crying and asking what they could do to stop genital mutilation. They realized the severity of the situation when I revealed the practice was happening in America.

I would say emphatically, "We must send a message to the refugees arriving in America!"

Some men would stare at my long hair and comment on my eyes, saying, "But you look like a normal woman!" as if I weren't normal at all.

How painful, I would say to myself and keep walking and remain focused on the issue.

At the restaurant, others were eager to pay for my soup and salad in exchange for a cultural lesson about the strange things the African people do.

⸸

Sundance was a beautiful event, and the townspeople were warm and welcoming. There were great films to see, and parties went late into the night. It was so exciting that I didn't feel the need to get back to the condo to rest.

Attending the social events also allowed me to avoid the filmmakers who would knock at my door, begging to sleep on the couch. Many loved drinking while sitting naked in the hot tub and had no worries about the freezing temperature or the snow falling over their heads.

On the awards night, as all the filmmakers prayed their film would win, I turned to look at a man who had sneaked in and sat down next to me. It was Samuel L. Jackson, and he leaned over and said, "The fact that you're sitting right here means you're already a winner!" He smiled, and I watched him walk away as the ceremony began.

That night at Sundance, the award went to another documentary, but *Fire Eyes* went on to other international film festivals, including the Berlin Film Festival. But I had already internalized Samuel Jackson's words: I had already won by facing my private pain and making *Fire Eyes* to stop other girls from mutilation at the hands of their culture.

54

breakaway

Speaking and screening requests for *Fire Eyes* were coming in from around the globe. I had already been helping Lydia, a Nigerian-born refugee whose lawyers were asking the judge to suspend her deportation process on grounds of female genital mutilation. Lydia had two American-born daughters and feared they would be mutilated if they returned to Nigeria. The lawyers needed permission to let the judge review *Fire Eyes*, which I granted.

In 1995, during the court process, the *Nightline* crew followed Lydia and her lawyers, then they showed up at my apartment for an interview. Later, the phone rang, and it was the *Nightline* producer, saying that Ted Koppel wanted to interview me live, that night! The car showed up at my door, and I was rushed to the ABC studio.

Colorado congresswoman Patricia Schroeder, who had cosponsored a legislative bill to make female genital mutilation a felony in the United States, would also be on the program. I was waiting nervously for the questions via satellite when I heard the commanding voice of Mr. Koppel say, "There are few topics that we tangled over on this program more important than the one we address tonight. Tens of millions of girls and young women are affected. . . ."

Talk about being hit by flying bricks of fear! My knees shook as my eyes looked at the camera lens and my ears waited to hear the questions he might ask about Mother. Mr. Koppel directed a question to the congresswoman, asking if the practice of female genital mutilation falls under child abuse law.

Ms. Schroeder wasn't sure but made her position clear by saying, "We want to be able to tell people coming into this country that certainly this issue would be considered child abuse. They have to be prepared to understand that, if they are coming into our culture, we don't accept this—this is how the European countries and different places deal with it. It's very important to put people on notice as they come in."

Koppel talked a few moments about *Fire Eyes* and asked if I had a chance to talk to Mother. I told him that I spoke with Mother a year before while she was living in Gabon. We cried and laughed, and I was getting to know her better.

"I couldn't be mad at her," I said. "This happened to her, her mother, grandmother, and great-grandmother. Our talk helped me understand Mother better, and I still love her."

Mr. Koppel asked if I knew any children in the States who had been mutilated.

I said, "There are thousands and thousands who are at risk, but it is difficult to give data on how many young girls have been genitally mutilated in America."

After the influx of refugees and the publicizing of the issue, many people were willing to stand up and fight against this harmful practice being performed here. The fear was very real, since the Somali doctors, midwives, and nurses now were living within the community in different states as refugees. Many were highly respected, and we, the activists, realized that they were likely performing the genital surgery in their own homes. The United Kingdom and its social service agencies successfully enforced anti–female genital mutilation laws and worked with the refugees, and something had to be done here in America.

Why couldn't we follow the example of not only the UK but also Denmark, Sweden, France, Canada, Switzerland, and Belgium, which had banned the practice? In France a Gambian mother was sentenced to five years in prison after paying lots of money to have her daughter mutilated.

Now, here in the United States, the issue was gaining ground, and the bill proposed in the Senate and the House would give the Department of Health and Human Services the power to create lists of mutilation survivors who had made their home in America. The lists would give an idea of how many people had brought the practice to the United States and intended to continue the legacy of pain.

Congresswoman Schroeder said, "We should try to empower those brave women in those cultures who are fighting to turn around this long ancient tradition."

⊹

When I got home after the show, the phone rang. It was Mother.

She began by saying the family had safely arrived in Canada, and everyone was doing well. Indeed, sister Shams and Raha had passed through Buffalo, New York, as I had thought, and they had lived with nuns.

"Oh, thank God," I exclaimed.

"I know you were on the television show," she said.

I asked for forgiveness and said my intention was not to embarrass my family or culture with my movie or my activism. I then paused, closed my eyes, and said what had been on my mind. "Mother, I would like to send you a copy of my movie, *Fire Eyes*. It's important for you to hear the doctor—Dr. Parham—talk about the medical horrors. Please, Mother, at least save my nieces from this pain."

"You want to destroy our family name!" Mother replied, "You talk about our painful relationship, and you just want to be famous. Focus on something worthwhile! Why do you want to upset your family and all the Somalis with your ideas and talk?"

I knew Mother's opinion reflected that of many Somali refugees. I had been warned by the Somalis who had been instrumental in helping me make *Fire Eyes* that some refugees were
not only angry with me but organizing to block the tour of *Fire
Eyes* around the country. I didn't take it seriously. The death
threats and phone calls kept coming, but I was still standing.

⊹

Soon after my call with Mother, I flew to New York to screen
Fire Eyes, along with other African films, at Lincoln Center.
At the Walter Reade Theater, I was pleased to see a group of
Somali women and men sitting among the audience.

But after the film, the question-and-answer session was suddenly interrupted when the event organizer approached me on
the stage. She leaned in and spoke quietly so her words would
not get picked up by the microphone or overheard.

"We need to get you out of the theater," she said. "We've
received information that someone is going to attempt to shoot
you, and we have every reason to believe the threat is real."

Now I was paying attention. As soon as the event was completed, I was rushed from the building and put on a plane back
to Los Angeles. I realized I could no longer ignore the death
threats.

⊹

Back in L.A., my friend Mick, a French filmmaker, met me at
the airport.

"My boat is docked in Marina Del Ray," he said as we
walked to his car. "I want you to use it as a safe house."

I shook my head. "Thank you, Mick, I appreciate it, but I
want to get back to my apartment. Besides, I could never live
on a boat—I'm afraid of water. . . ."

Mick continued to express his concern, and I was persuaded
to let go of the apartment. He called a friend who lived in Point
Dume, Malibu, to explain the situation to her, then drove me to
the woman's house.

At the gate, all I could see was a jungle of trees; the house was not visible. Mick pulled the car to a stop, opened the gate, and said, "Here no one will find you."

I heard the ocean waves crashing against the rocks as I followed him into the house. It sat on a high cliff and had a massive garden of exotic flowers, which reminded me of Hawaii, where I'd once gone on vacation. I met the owner, who said she spent most of her time on an island off the coast of Maine. She offered me a tiny room, bathroom, and private entrance for a small amount of money.

The place was beautiful, and even though I would miss my apartment, I reluctantly agreed.

While others were generously helping me change my life in order to save it—disconnecting my apartment phone, aiding me in settling into the new sanctuary—I found myself struck by unprecedented depression. All I wanted to do was eat and smoke cigarettes while watching the dolphins dance over the water.

After being alone for a while, I asked my friends if they were willing to visit me often so that the dark thoughts wouldn't hurt me. A childhood friend and neighbor, Kafia, flew from Washington, DC, while others traveled from the Los Angeles area as often as they could. Feeling restricted, just as in my childhood I would sneak out. I would visit Randy, my roommate from Sundance who lived nearby, and have dinner with his family. After a time, when no one came to kill me, I ventured out to explore the Malibu area, one day ending up at the post office wanting to get a box.

I stood in the long line, and when the man in front of me finally walked up to the clerk, I heard him ask to rent a post office box.

The woman smiled, reviewed his driver's license, and asked, "How long do you want it?"

He said, "Six months."

"OK." She told him the price, and he paid.

I stepped up in front of the same clerk.

"I'd like to rent a box for a year," I said.

She stared at me for a moment, then looked at my driver's license. "You reside here in Malibu?"

"Yes, near the Cliffside Drive area—how much?"

"I need you to get me a letter from the people you're working for," she replied.

I felt a sudden pounding in my head. "Excuse me?" I tried to control my voice. "I work for myself, and I think you're asking for trouble."

"I just—"

"You're embarrassing her!" a woman behind me shouted at the clerk.

I could hear other people in line becoming angry and jumping to my support.

"Give her the box!"

They gave me confidence. "Either you rent the box to me like you did that man, or I'll create the biggest headache for you!"

The manager, hearing the commotion, rushed in and cleared up the matter. I rented the box for a year. But I was still furious and needed a moment to calm down and breathe deeply.

"I'm sorry—you'll find nothing but warm people in Malibu," a woman with a kind face said to me.

"I know—thank you."

"She deserves . . . ," she began, then interrupted herself. "What are you going to do?"

"I'll just take a walk on the beach to calm down."

"I would love to join you, but I have a meeting in Santa Monica."

She said a warm good-bye.

⸸

The days passed, and I began to adjust to my new life. I was kept busy with interviews, including one with Renee Tawa, a journalist from the *Los Angeles Times* who was writing on the practice of female genital mutilation, and the American Medical Association, which came to shoot a segment for their documentary on FGM. I also received an invitation to speak and screen *Fire Eyes* at the Fourth World Conference on Women in Beijing, China.

Around this time, I was granted asylum. I had applied for it months ago, when I realized that I would never return to live in Somalia. After the civil war and the killing of my uncles, aunt, and cousin, I did not have the heart to go back to live in Mogadishu. In addition, my activism—shouting from the rooftops to stop the cultural harm done to children—made it unsafe for me to continue to claim my Somali citizenship. America was now my beloved home. It gave me the voice to heal and the freedom to make changes for the greater good of all.

55

going for the gold

As I drove to the INS (Immigration and Naturalization Services) facility, where I was trying to straighten out my asylum paperwork, I was thinking about the injustice done to Fauziya Kassindja. She had narrowly escaped genital mutilation by fleeing her country of Togo for the United States. But once in America, she was imprisoned by the INS and would remain jailed for two years.

So I was surprised when one of the INS officers asked me if he could show *Fire Eyes* to the others. He explained that the practice of female genital mutilation was becoming an asylum issue in this country, and they knew little about it. I passed the tape to him and asked him to let me know if I could visit and answer any questions or concerns they might have about the issue.

After leaving the offices of the INS, I was sitting in my red Geo Tracker, grateful for the INS officer's reaction but disappointed that my travel documents still had not been finalized. When my phone rang and a woman introduced herself as Oprah's producer, I thought a friend was playing a prank.

But it truly was Oprah's producer, inviting me to be a guest on an upcoming show on FGM.

"Does Lisa still work there?" I asked. I said she would remember how I drove from Los Angeles and begged for help five years ago, back in 1990.

"You will be able to ask her that question in person when you come to Chicago," she said kindly.

But I had a schedule conflict. "I can't be a guest on the *Oprah* show," I said, "because I'll be in Beijing for the Women's Conference at that time." I was disappointed but had already made the commitment. However, my lawyer still needed to work on the problem with my travel documents, without which I could not leave the United States.

"I understand the importance of going to the conference," the producer said, "but the show is watched by millions. Your cause would benefit greatly from you sitting with Oprah and telling your own story as a survivor of female genital mutilation."

I promised I would call with my decision in a day.

While I was weighing my decision, my lawyer, Cynthia Frey, called. She said that, with the assistance of Senator Dianne Feinstein's office, my application to travel to China was placed in the hands of an INS expediting officer. The INS required a letter from the NGO Forum on Women, indicating that I would be speaking at the Beijing Conference on Women. My flight was scheduled to depart on August 29, and it was already July. Cynthia told me she had provided the official invitation and conference documents with my speaking schedule, but the INS rejected them. She had sent a letter to the activities director at the NGO Forum on Women in Beijing, and the matter would take more time to resolve.

The date of my flight was rapidly approaching, and my confidence in getting approval for my trip was wavering. At that moment I planned that I would send Arisika, the dancer in the opening scene of *Fire Eyes*, on my behalf and that the Somali Women's Delegation would speak after the screening of *Fire Eyes*.

But Cynthia remained hopeful that my travel document would be approved and I would depart on time. We received the official confirmation letter from the NGO Forum on Women, and the director wanted me to take the matter to the Chinese embassy. But this letter had been among the documents already provided to the INS, and clearly I was running out of time.

I decided to call Oprah's producer and let her know that I was willing to be a guest on the show. I suggested they invite other survivors and activists, because I thought Oprah should hear their stories, too. Later, I was informed that Mimi, an Ethiopian survivor-activist, and Tobia, a Sudanese doctor, would be sharing the stage with me. Arisika took the plane to Beijing to represent *Fire Eyes* while I traveled to Chicago, this time at Oprah's expense.

⊹

I was at Harpo Studios getting my hair and makeup done when Lisa came to greet me.

"I am so happy about your success with *Fire Eyes*," she said.

I smiled. "Do you remember meeting me a few years ago?"

She seemed to struggle with her memory until I described the whole event and her assistant who had taken me into the audience.

Lisa laughed, grabbed my hand, and said, "It was you?" Afterward, she helped me sign the show releases, then I was rushed to meet Oprah.

My feelings were strong, and I still felt Oprah was a sister and could have helped with *Fire Eyes* if the circumstances were better. After her monologue, Oprah walked up and sat with Mimi and me, facing the tense audience. Mimi described the day she was mutilated back in Ethiopia, and I said the whole experience made you feel as if you were a goat.

"You were thirteen," Oprah said.

"You feel like you're not human," I said.

"I watched your film. I often wonder—the little girls were all placed in one room. They were all just there on the floor, numb and in shock, a lot of them. And I wonder when they finally come to the question, 'What do you think of your mother?'" Oprah asked.

"It's difficult for me—you have to go into silence. Because that was the only protection you have, trying to understand what happened to you," I said.

"Why did it happen to you so late? Wasn't thirteen considered late?" Oprah asked.

I told Oprah that Father saw what happened to my older sisters and protected me, and how one day Mother said I was going to get a gift and that I should come with her.

"So, they lied to you," Oprah said.

"I thought we were going to the store to buy something . . . ," I said.

"That's when she took you to the doctor," Oprah said.

I told Oprah that you can never hate your mother because, if you have hate in your heart, you cannot heal yourself and make a change to become a better person.

"So, you go to the doctor—by thirteen you knew what happens to girls. You knew, but at six Mimi didn't," said Oprah.

"Right—but no one would touch me because I wasn't clean," I said.

"How does everybody know?" Oprah asked.

"The celebration. . . ."

"What I don't understand," Oprah said, "I don't understand why the women don't just rise up and say you can't do this to our daughters. We are not going to allow this to happen—that I don't understand!"

"Then you're going to have to say my mother is a liar," I responded. "My grandmother was a liar. My great grandmother was a liar, and the whole culture, they all are liars—which is true, but you have to condemn in the culture what is bad."

"I don't understand why women who come from that tradition to this country—and have children—many times still feel they have to continue that in America," Oprah said.

"Some of the refugees I worked with said that by watching the American women in movies and how women 'rape' men, they feel their daughters will do the same," I said. These women believe that uncut women cannot control themselves, so seduction equates with rape. "To them you're a body without a head."

The show ended with warmth, and Oprah wrapped her arms around us, asking how we felt about the show. We happily agreed that it was very informative and powerful.

The show had been so huge that I began to receive offers to become a spokesperson for organizations challenging the tradition and working to end the practice of female genital mutilation. My entire adult life I had been a spokesperson on behalf of the African women who were genitally mutilated, and my only concern was that I not feel locked in with those who might not approve of the way I do things. However, I went ahead and sat in a meeting and listened to what these organizations were planning to do to end the practice.

To my surprise, most of them began speaking over my head, dismissing me when I objected to some terms and said I could not use the word *mutilation*. They were afraid that African women would be alienated by the truth of the word. I realized these women felt they had the right and the resources to make me their puppet without respecting or understanding what I went through. My face, the horrendous pain and suffering I went through, would be used for their own gain and purpose.

Midway through the meeting, I rose from my seat and walked out with my head held high. As I walked down the hallway, I started singing a Ray Charles song, "Hit the road, Jack ..."

I own my story, my body, and my voice, and no one can stop my mission to end the practice.

Soon after, I was speaking everywhere, ignoring death threats and vicious criticism. Courage was my weapon. I would not permit those behind the massive fear in my life to stop my message and bury *Fire Eyes*. My journey had been arduous and painful, but I had come too far to let my own fear, or my countrymen's and countrywomen's fear of change, stop me.

I decided to showcase *Fire Eyes* around the country by renting slots in theaters. I met one of the owners of the Laemmle Theaters in Los Angeles, who gave me a discount, and I was given a slot to screen the film at the Laemmle Sunset Five Theater in Hollywood.

The Washington, DC, screening shocked me because the whole African community came, mostly to support *Fire Eyes*. But the Somalis strolled in with force, accusing me of being in this for fame and money, nothing else. My advice to them was to stop pulling my hair and start protecting their daughters. I could not protect myself from the virulent anger some expressed over the issue. But that day in the theater I was struck with another realization: to win an argument with the herdsmen, I just needed to stop talking and stop reacting to their hostility.

That was when I noticed Deeqa, the Somali woman who helped me in Geneva, sitting in the audience. She got up and walked over, leading her daughters. Sobbing, she wrapped her arms around me. She introduced me to her two adult daughters, who expressed their gratitude and said not all Somalis feel hate toward me.

"I am so proud of the gift you are giving to the younger generations," Deeqa said.

Their words filled me with emotion, strengthening my resolve to stand strong in the face of my culture's criticism of me. My life was coming full circle, my work and the support of women like Deeqa healing my deep, private wound.

The *Fire Eyes* film tour ended on a powerful note. I then began a university tour around the country, which was meant to last a few months but lasted for years.

❖

Upon my return to Los Angeles, I received a letter from Burkina Faso's National Organizing Committee, inviting me to the Panafrican Film Festival of Ouagadougou. Known as FESPACO, the festival is an African award ceremony and film festival as popular among Africans as the Oscars is among Westerners. Since beginning in the late sixties to achieve the development of a genuine film industry in Africa, FESPACO has become highly respected internationally. The theme for 1995 was "Cinema and History."

I still had not received my travel documentation. A year earlier, I had showcased *Fire Eyes* as a work-in-progress at Los Angeles's Pan African Film Festival, which was headed by Babu, an African American living in both Los Angeles and Africa who had become a friend. He agreed to take *Fire Eyes* to Ouagadougou and represent me.

The film would, of course, be controversial, and I had to cut a scene of a woman getting corrective surgery, with Dr. Parham showing the Q-tip to separate the sealed vaginal tissue. I later heard that during the showing some African women rose and began slapping men sitting in the audience. They were just that angry.

⁜

In early 1996, a call came asking me speak before the Nevada's Health and Human Services Committee. The committee also wanted to view *Fire Eyes*. Waris Dirie, a model from Somalia who was a spokesperson against FGM, called and said she could not speak at the senate with me, but she asked me to show clips of her videotape. I told her others were sending tapes as well, and I would do my best to show them all.

In Carson City, I sat in front of the committee and began, "The children coming to this country need protection. . . ."

I was joined by representatives from Planned Parenthood, Soroptomist International, the Nevada Women's Lobby, the Nevada Nurses Association, and others. Committee members listened as we urged them to pass Senate Bill 192 to make the practice of female genital mutilation a felony. The bill would also make it harder for parents to take their child out of Nevada to another country to have FGM performed. I knew parents with means were taking their daughters to Kenya, Somalia, or even Egypt for mutilation. I also suggested we educate the teachers to watch for girls' behavioral changes after school breaks. Certainly the young child will withdraw right after the mutilation, and symptoms of complications, such as infections, might occur.

"It happens everywhere," I told the committee. "I know of children who were brought to this country when they were two and, when they turned nine, were taken back to Kenya or Somalia to have it done. We're not here to condemn the parents but to condemn the act. It's a human rights issue. Let's protect and give choices to the children."

While the committee members talked seriously among themselves about amendments to make the bill broader in scope, we activists felt hopeful that Bill 192 would pass. But you never know, and while choking back tears, I described the act of mutilation, then asked them to watch *Fire Eyes*. The committee members sat silently and stared without expression as the young girl was held down in preparation. But when she screamed with pain, some members turned away and stared at the wall.

The law criminalizing FGM in the United States passed in the fall of 1996.

56

father's shrouding

While speaking at the John Jay College of Criminal Justice in New York, I was presented a Winnie Mandela Award for uplifting African women. I was so excited that I couldn't wait for the screening to end so that I could call Mother and tell her the good news. I slipped out to call during the closing scenes.

Mother listened calmly, then said, "You could win all the awards and become famous, but you will always be nothing to me!"

Shock struck me in the depths of my soul, and the core of my being shattered. Something shut off within; I was numb, not hearing any other word that came from Mother's mouth.

I don't remember being brought up to the stage for questions and answers with the students. Facing the packed amphitheater, I felt myself shrink to the size of a helpless child. I needed a hug, a human touch, that would remind me of my strength and how I used to say to myself, *I am worthy and I am lovable.* That was when I heard the loud ringing in my right ear, and Mother's words became fast hot bullets. I had to distance myself from her.

A year had passed since I had called or spoken with Mother or anyone in my family, and this was the right time to cut our relationship. The last time I saw Father was when I took him back to Mogadishu after his Paris hospitalization. Mother and I last saw each other in Washington, DC, when she came to visit. I called to tell Father that I wished to never to see them again.

Sister Amal answered the phone. "Father is in the hospital, dying of lung cancer," she said. He had quit smoking twenty years earlier.

My stomach fell, and instantly my plans changed. "I am coming to see him," I said. But then remembered that I couldn't leave the country. My asylum had been granted, but my travel document had not yet shown up. My determination to sever ties switched to guilt for wanting to renounce my family and staying away for a year.

I pushed forward and made arrangements to go to Canada before Father's death. Father's doctor sent a letter to help Cynthia, my lawyer, attempt to expedite the process by filing an application for advance parole. Cynthia called and said that I did not meet the requirement for advance parole and couldn't travel to Canada.

Devastated, all I could do was to stay on the phone with Father and cry until I had no more tears. When he couldn't talk, sister Amal would get on the phone and try to calm me down. She said Father talked a lot about my childhood and how he laughed when remembering my investigative style around the neighborhood.

One day when I called, Father said, "I know why you can't travel to Canada to see me."

"Why?" I asked.

"God doesn't want you to see me suffer like this—with tubes stuck into me. I want you to remember me when my body was healthy and strong—keep that image."

"How can I ease your pain?"

"Forgive us all and remember that we're your family."

"Forgive me, Father, for being afraid of my own family."

"I watched your film and I'm very proud. Forgive your mother and be close to your family."

"I promise, Father—I'm coming very soon to see you."

I was in Big Bear, California, doing research for a script, when a sharp pain struck me in the stomach. Somehow the pain made me believe that Father had died. I rushed out of my meeting and checked my answering machine back in Los Angeles. Cold chills ran down my spine when I heard the somber voice of sister Shams.

I called my parents' home and discovered that Father's body was being prepared for the shrouding ceremony. According to Islamic law, he had to be buried within twenty-four hours of his death.

My travel documents showed up just at that time, and I rushed to the airport. Asis was waiting for me in Toronto.

"Father is already buried," he told me as if we hadn't talked the day before.

Guilt washed over me. Why had I not taken care of my papers years before? I could not stop crying, and Asis suggested that we sit for a while.

"You can't be too emotional when we get to our house—you can't upset Mother," he said.

All I could do was flash back to the day when I was twelve and Mother walked into my bedroom and informed me that the angel Azreal had taken Grandmother's body away and I should not cry because my tears would only burn her body.

Mother was standing in the hallway when Asis and I walked into the house. I struggled to hold back the hot tears, but I didn't have to because Mother let me fall into her arms. I wept, and Mother kept rocking me like a tiny baby. She took my hand and led me inside the house where the family was gathered. Everyone seemed to be adjusting to Father's passing, or maybe they were relieved that he was no longer in pain. Their mood was upbeat, the celebration was low-key, but they were planning a big feast for the next day.

Mother said I had been gone so long that I had forgotten how death was celebrated in honor of those who passed away. We sat around Mother as she walked down memory lane, recalling Father's charm. She said she had lost not only a husband but her best friend of the past fifty-four years. She ended the conversation by saying, "*Inna lillahi wa inna ilaihi raji'oon,*" which means, "As you come from God, you shall return to him."

Today was Father's third day of passing, and the family was preparing the big feast for the prayer meeting called *fatihah*. With the exception of Mother, who was in the *iddah* (mourning) period, the family, relatives, and community decided to visit Father's gravesite and recite the prayer.

I was no expert on Islam, but I believed Mother should not put herself in the *iddah* period, which would last four months and ten days. During this time, Mother was not allowed to beautify herself with jewelry, wear fancy clothes, or perfume her body.

I said, "Forgive me if I offend anyone, but my mother will not remarry and thus does not need *iddah*, a waiting period to see whether Father's stand-in will show up at her doorstep." I was in Mother's room explaining that leaving the house would qualify as an emergency because Father would want her to visit the gravesite.

There was a knock on the door, and it was Asis asking to speak to me.

"Are you the one who bought the yellow roses?" he asked me.

I nodded. "No one knew Father's favorite flowers, but since he liked bananas, I thought yellow roses might just be what he would choose."

"Where do you intend to put them?"

"On Father's gravesite."

"People will think you have clearly become polytheist!"

Mother stepped up behind me. "What is going on?"

"I bought Father yellow roses. . . ."

"Mother, do something, please."

"I should hose your brain and recite *al-hashir*!"

Stunned, I could not understand why I would be exiled for wanting to beautify Father's gravesite.

"I'm coming with you," Mother declared.

"Mother!" Asis exclaimed.

I smiled at her. "That's a wonderful idea."

On the way to Father's gravesite, Mother turned to me. "You should be thankful that this time no Somali is hunting you down for making *Fire Eyes*." She talked about how the Somali community visited Father at the hospital and how much they respected him. With all of my education, Mother said she couldn't understand why I had to continue talking about women's private parts.

Now, again, I heard the ringing in my right ear where Mother's words had penetrated. "You'll always be nothing to me!" Because of the death in our family, I told myself the honorable thing to do was to keep my mouth shut and stare out the car window.

But Mother kept on, refusing to stop digging her finger in the old wound, talking about what a lost child and worthless daughter I had become.

I had to say something. "You know how to stick the needle into my wound."

"Hand me the flowers," she demanded.

I knew she would throw the flowers away, so I clutched them to me, and before I left I placed them on Father's gravesite.

⁂

Mother insisted that during my visit to Canada I spend time with Aunt Ubax. But I discovered sister Shams's husband had proved to be a worthless man, and Shams needed to throw him out. So instead of visiting Aunt Ubax, I would sit in Shams's apartment and watch her put her children to bed. She would face the wall rather than me and let the tears run down her cheeks.

"Do you want me to send someone to Minnesota and break his legs?" I asked.

Horrified, Shams stared, then got up from the bed and stood in front of me.

"He's worthless, just like Asra's polygamist husband," I said, reminding her how Asra's husband married his second wife after Asra had lost her family by eloping with him. I was certain Shams's husband was fooling around and soon would bring home another wife.

"My husband went to look for work in Minnesota," said Shams.

"Of course, and by now he's an expert on how to oil-change his organs!" I exclaimed.

"I don't understand."

"Go and watch how the cars are oil-changed, and then decide what you want from your husband."

Everything seemed to be going fine until Mother said I was banned from any of the family affairs and especially from getting involved in my siblings' relationships. Once again, I found myself at odds with my family. Her mandate had come about because I could not understand the new trend among herdsmen, like brother Malik, of leaving their wives and children in Canada and traveling to another country for years. And I spoke out about it.

The women would stay home and raise the children alone, and now and then their husbands would show up for a quick oil change. Before the herdsman reached his soft nest in America or the Emirates, off on another job, he would find out that his wife was struck by another morning sickness.

In my opinion, this should be a crime, and these men should be held accountable for their unthinkable actions. In all truth, the world opened its doors to the refugees, and the Canadians welcomed the Somalis as if they were royalty. I witnessed how well the Somalis were living in Canada, with their colorful community buildings, furniture, buying expensive stuff that I, as an activist, could not afford. The Somali Arabs were very smart, opening their bakery businesses and stores, but still, sad but true, many young men and women chose to use the government's welfare system unfairly and chew qat all day, seven days a week.

Malik was well educated, and I could not understand why he decided to cross the American border to become a taxi driver in Washington, DC. He could have done that in Toronto and stayed with his wife and children. Although his wife said she trusted my big brother and those years apart didn't bother her at all, I had called him up and suggested that he either divorce his wife or let her find a replacement.

Before I was thrown out of my sister-in-law's apartment for interfering, I promised to stay out of her family affairs but asked Malik's wife not to mutilate her two daughters. She promised and said when they reached the ages of thirteen and sixteen they would call and thank me for my work against the practice of female genital mutilation. They did, and it was empowering news to hear.

57

bhadrakali

By 1998, I found myself hanging over a cliff, not knowing how to save myself from myself. While I had been with my family in Canada, I had not fully expressed the pain I was carrying. I showed signs, but I could not express my deep anger at losing Father without a chance to say what I needed to say to him. His death opened up the old wounds, and once again I was removed from the family circle. The pain was unbearable, and the silence was like shards of ice covering my whole being.

Back in the house where I was staying in Brentwood, loaned to me by a friend, I attempted to put words to my emotions and write a screenplay about my life. But I could not look in the mirror and face my own demons and correct my mistakes. The time had come to find another kind soul like Nigel, but when the doctor suggested that I take Valium or Prozac, I never went back again. I felt like those alcoholics who don't know their limits but benefit from being locked in an ashram somewhere in India.

What was available to me was a huge, empty house with colorful gardens and large refrigerators that held forbidden food. I locked myself in the house and fell madly in love with foods like dairy, French toast, and Chinese fried delicatessen items. Those became the medicine to sooth my depression and give me a reason to live. Yet I felt awake, present, and in control because I would not eat any meat, even seafood, or drink hard liquor to numb the pain inside.

Nonetheless, silently, I tortured myself until my body broke down and I wound up in the hospital from complications arising from an unhealthy and unfamiliar diet, facing a doctor. My unbelievable weight gain, from 115 to 175 pounds, somehow did not alarm me, but when I saw my friends sit in front of me and cry, their distress cut like a knife. They took turns showing up at my door and bringing bags filled with healthy greens. They cooked and ate with me, but when they left, I turned to my forbidden food and found a reason to smile.

One day, after a night of eating, I flashed back to my childhood, remembering how the Chinese doctor took away the pain by sticking needles into my body. I stood up, opened the refrigerators, removed all the forbidden food, and went out to find Chinese doctors. I was confident they could heal my addiction to food.

I was put on an intense body- and mind-cleansing regimen with natural herbs and acupuncture. I mingled with American Indian healers who worked gently for a while, then put my body through a sweat-lodge ceremony. They guided me through the trancelike state that relieved my anxiety and insomnia.

Slowly, I regained my health and my mind. I not only was ready to face the emotions that would arise in writing the screenplay of my life; I also realized the process of reviewing and presenting my experiences would be therapeutic, ultimately making me a stronger woman.

⁂

Seven months after my first trip to the Chinese doctors, with my autobiographical screenplay complete, the time had come for me to travel to Africa: *Fire Eyes* was going to be screened at the Zanzibar Film Festival. I would take full advantage of the trip by stopping along the way to work on making the film of my life story become a reality.

On the way from California to Africa, first I stopped in France to visit my college in Grenoble and film locations around the campus. I then traveled to Tirol, Austria, to scout a location. The Tirol Film Commission had read my screenplay and suggested the city could double for Grenoble and Geneva. The commission was willing to put up the location money if I came up with the rest of the film budget.

Shooting in Tirol seemed logical and would be cheaper than traveling to France and Switzerland. In search of funding, I traveled to London, but when nothing moved in my favor, I boarded the plane with the other filmmakers heading to Zanzibar for the festival. As the plane took off, I looked out the window, barely able to contain my excitement at the thought that in a few hours I would be putting my face to the ground and kissing the land of Africa.

⚜

Waves of joy washed through my belly. I was so excited that I couldn't stand still while the other passengers were getting off the plane.

Finally, I stepped out the door. The soft wind hit me, carrying the scent of African trees, bringing back the memories of my childhood. I took a deep breath and descended the steps. When my feet touched the African ground for the first time in fourteen years, since taking Father back to Mogadishu, I removed my shoes, set down my purse, knelt, and kissed the ground. I didn't care what others thought.

I looked up and saw a crowd gathering in the terminal, and I assumed they were families and friends waving and watching their loved ones arrive. I rose from my kneeling position and followed my fellow filmmakers and the other passengers into the crowded check-in area. People were everywhere, and airport officials were checking people's belongings. When it was my turn, I stepped forward and handed my US travel documents to the officer. He looked at them for a moment, then looked up at me and suddenly pushed me to the side. He signaled another officer and handed my documents to him. The second officer stared at them, then gazed directly in my eyes.

"You are not welcome here," he said.

Panic mixed with anger rose inside me. "What do you mean?" I demanded.

"You don't have the proper documents."

"I believe I have the best document," I said, keeping my voice steady. "I am a filmmaker invited by your festival. . . ." I turned my head just as the crowd that had been in the terminal pushed into the check-in area. I turned back to the second officer. "What are they shouting about?"

He smiled. "They say you are not welcome here!"

I heard him laugh aloud as I was escorted into a room where my luggage was being opened and checked over and over again.

My fellow filmmakers were puzzled, as I was. I could not understand what was going on.

"You can call the head of the festival and verify my story," I said to the officers.

That's when the festival representatives arrived to pick up the filmmakers. After talking to the officers, the festival representatives told me the plane was being held and I was being shipped back to London. They did not know what to do, as the officers claimed I did not have the proper documents or visa.

Eventually, the officers admitted the authorities knew about *Fire Eyes* playing in the festival and were convinced my presence would create trouble. They were aware that violence had broken out when *Fire Eyes* played in Ouagadougou.

I asked in frustration, "Do I need a special visa to assure everyone I won't disappear after the festival and remain in the country?"

Two men from the festival made calls to help settle this matter as quickly as possible while the plane in which I had arrived continued to be held.

But nothing was working in my favor. As if I were a criminal, an officer ordered me to follow an armed guard back to the plane and never return to Tanzania again.

"How can this be?" I cried. "These documents got me into Canada, Austria, France, and England! No one said I didn't have the proper papers." Dizzy with confusion and anger, I said good-bye to my fellow filmmakers and the festival representatives as I followed the officer back to the plane.

As we walked, I could still hear the shouts of the crowd. I asked, "What are they saying now?"

"They are telling you to get out of our country."

I felt a stab of emotional pain and reminded myself that Africa gave me birth, and, just as with Mother, we had difficult relationship issues. Europe raised me, and America made me the woman I had become. I would always be a child of Africa, but I belonged to the world.

I broke down crying, not because Africa had rejected me but because I felt like an exiled criminal. In the entryway to the plane, I saw the flight attendant waiting. I saw the curious faces peering down at me from the plane's windows, wondering what crime I had committed. They had been forced to sit in the plane, waiting for the person being deported from Zanzibar.

Devastated, I prayed silently and called for God's help to ease the pain I was feeling. As I approached the steps, I was stunned to see the image of Bhadrakali, a Hindu goddess, hovering over the plane.

I turned to the officer. "Do you see her?"

"Move up!" he shouted.

But I was stuck; I couldn't move my legs. I saw Bhadrakali's calm transform into a fierce and disturbing side of Kali. Her nearness frightened me more than her glaring red eyes and skull necklace. A friend of mine was Kali's devoted student, and she spoke often about how Kali is a destructive force, always ready to slash your ego with her sharp sword. But today, Kali's appearance told me everything would be renewed; I would be blessed with fierce strength.

I was taken to my seat and closely monitored by flight attendants who brought food and drinks. While staring at my full plate, I saw an image of a snake with a white head stamped on my neck. I took this as a sign of protection from Lord Shiva. When I got back to California, I would get a tattoo of that image.

58

lifework

O nce I was back home, I had little time to focus on the negative. The phone rang, and it was the playwright and poet
Eve Ensler, calling from New York after hearing about *Fire
Eyes*. She was in the process of putting together a play about
women called the *Vagina Monologues*. The show would benefit
the organizations working to end violence against women.

Eve wanted me to write a monologue about the practice of
female genital mutilation and to perform it. I wrote the monologue about my own experience with the ritual and faxed it
to Eve. Immediately after reading it, she called and was very
emotional. She said she was flying to Los Angeles to meet me
in person and talk about the upcoming *Vagina Monologues* performance in New York, on V-Day.

Eve, her stage manager, and I met at the Rose Café in Venice
Beach. The meeting was successful, and I decided that Eve's was
an important mission and that she truly wanted to empower
women around the world.

In the meantime, I was hanging out with amazing women,
and our dinner gatherings centered on improving conditions for
women and being there for one another. One of those women
was Diane Lane, whom I had met during the Women's Day

award ceremony at the Directors Guild of America. We both won awards that day.

Actress Shirley Knight also became my friend. Shirley and I performed the first *Vagina Monologues* benefit performance at the Hammerstein Ballroom in New York. It was an amazing experience, and I felt supported by the whole cast and crew. Soon after, V-Day became a very strong movement, and each year in the month of February we would perform the show and raise funds to end violence against women globally.

In 1998, I flew to New York to meet with Waris Dirie at her Brooklyn home and talk about our work to end FGM as well as my autobiographical film. I knew she would be great for the lead and asked her to audition when the time came. She and I focused on ways to use our personal stories for the greater good and our cause, and we promised to be there for each other and to continue with our mission.

Later that year, I was invited to speak and screen *Fire Eyes* at the United Nations fiftieth anniversary of the signing of the Universal Declaration of Human Rights in Geneva. A project was under way to honor the filmmakers whose work promoted change and gave voice to the wrongs that had been done to others. What I didn't know was that I would be one of those filmmakers chosen to receive a human rights silver statue.

The day after the ceremony, I was struggling against my fear of facing the intelligent crowd to speak out against the practice. Someone rushed in and gave the thumbs-up, indicating that I was cleared to speak at the subcommission session. I took a deep breath and walked into the room where Wilda Spalding, founder the Human Rights Consortium, was preparing to moderate the session. Walking up to the stage, I could feel hot tears fill my eyes and tingling running through my body. I couldn't understand what I was afraid of, since many fellow African delegates expressed the urgency to end the practice of female genital mutilation. At that time, twenty-eight countries continued to perform the ritual of genital mutilation. This was a huge step forward; when I had left Somalia in 1978 the practice was common in fifty-four countries. I knew ending the practice entirely would take time. (Today, twenty-eight countries persist with the tradition.)

I realized my fear and anxiety were caused by the heavy schedule and my need to find a spare moment to walk up to the Office of the World Health Organization and sit with Efua Darkenoo, a founder of the Foundation for Women's Health, Research and Development. But it seemed I would not have a moment to squeeze in anything other than the schedule I had been given.

But I did, indeed, accomplish my goal of meeting Efua. As I spoke with her about our shared mission of giving voice to those who have none, I was not only humbled and empowered but overwhelmed by my blessings. I had once lived in fear in this very town, trapped in an abusive arranged marriage, hiding in my bedroom and planning my escape. Returning to Geneva as a world citizen to speak and win an award was triumph, and meeting with Efua was wonderful evidence of how far I had traveled.

After accepting an invitation from Harvard's Swanee Hunt to speak and show *Fire Eyes* at the John F. Kennedy School of Government, I returned to Los Angeles and received another call from Eve Ensler asking me to rejoin the ever-expanding cast of the *Vagina Monologues*. This time we were going to perform the show at the Old Vic in London. By now, I was getting comfortable performing my piece and mingling with the star actors.

At rehearsal, I tried to skip the script reading. Instead, I sat with an actress who seemed too frightened to stand on the stage to perform, trying to encourage her. This actress had done great films for years but had never performed in front of a live audience. While Eve and her assistant were looking for me, I was sitting in a dark corner telling the famous actress that the audiences are like our best friends and family who want us to hit the mark with confidence.

When I was discovered and brought up to the stage to face Eve, I turned and saw Cate Blanchett encouraging me. Intellectually, I knew I should rehearse the piece because it brought so much pain and I didn't want to break down during the performance. But emotionally, my role remained difficult.

Afterward, Cate and I rushed up to my dressing room and talked, which allowed me to forget the pain inside. I craved a cigarette, but when I finally got a chance to light one, my dressing room partner forced me to put it out.

When the whole cast met for a postshow reception, I couldn't eat anything, but I was eager for them to bring out the cake made to look like a vagina. But when the time came, that, too, was hard to eat. The cast gathered around the beautiful cake and admired it before digging their fingers inside and eating it. Because the cake represented the vagina, we were not allowed to use knives and forks.

The following year, Eve called to say we were performing for V-Day in Los Angeles at the Wiltern Theatre. My friend Diane Lane showed up for support and, once again, Shirley Knight performed the show with me. After I left the stage, Harvey Keitel came backstage and said how moved he was by the performance and suggested that I should stick with theater.

My last performance with the cast of the *Vagina Monologues* was at Madison Square Garden in New York in 2001. Eve asked me to go over the monologues for the other two African women who would be sharing the stage with me. One was a young girl, Beatrice, who had escaped the mutilation in Kenya and found refuge with the help of Eve, then came to the United States to perform the show. The other woman was Agnes, a fierce Kenyan activist against FGM. This show and the V-Day organizers helped Agnes to build the first safe house in Africa to receive the young girls and women escaping mutilation.

This show was so huge that Oprah joined us, and Jane Fonda stood on the stage and donated one million dollars to the V-Day Foundation to stop violence against women. During our backstage break, we gathered in the green room, stood in a circle, and held hands in prayer. Oprah was standing in front of me, and I tried my best not to stare.

Afterward, Oprah walked up to me, shook hands, and said, "I remember you."

"Thank you for sending the letter after the show," I said. I hadn't thought she would remember me, and I was so pleased.

Our talk was short because we were moved to our positions to get ready for the show. I joined my fellow activists and survivors and went over our monologues. When our time came, I talked to Beatrice, telling her to follow her emotions and to stop if it became overwhelming. As we were rushed up to the stage, I didn't have time to inform Eve about what I had told Beatrice.

That night, we had eighteen thousand cheering in the crowd, but when the three of us walked onto the stage, the audience became totally silent. The audience knew what was coming, and hands rose to cover faces. They realized we would be telling our own stories.

The cameras' flashing lights blinded me as I began the monologue. Beatrice choked back tears and found it impossible to continue. I walked away from the microphone and went to hold her hand.

"We are with you," I said. "Don't be frightened."

While she walked to the microphone, Beatrice was powerfully reciting her monologue, and I could feel the audience's emotional reaction. As I came down from the stage, I saw Oprah waiting for me with open arms. Holding back the tears, she wrapped me with her warmth and said, "I love you."

"Thank you—I love you, too," I responded, moved.

Oprah was getting ready to do her monologue, "Burka," so I held myself back from continuing to talk about my mission to end FGM. I hurried to find Agnes and Beatrice and was relieved to see them laughing with the cast and staff. When we heard Oprah's thundering voice, we rushed out to watch her performance. A woman wearing a burka slowly walked onto the stage while Oprah spoke. I cannot adequately describe the power and magic of that night.

⁂

Back home in Los Angeles, I was awakened in the middle of the night by my ringing phone. It was a distraught mother named Ming, calling from Mali. Her daughter, Kadi, was married to an American man, and they were living in Tennessee.

"Please help me," Ming said, choking back a sob. "First, my daughter called to tell me she had married an American, and I was shocked. She had gone to America for school. Then she told me she was having problems with her husband. But they are so far away. . . . I don't know what to do! Kadi told me to go to you for help. Please . . ."

"I will do what I can," I promised. "I will call you back after speaking with your daughter and her husband."

When I called the couple, I knew something was deeply wrong when Kadi spoke to me in French and had me translate her words for her husband. They had married too young, she said, and she had hidden her genital mutilation experience from him. Shocked, he could not understand what had happened to his bride, and she would not open up and share her pain. He was not able to understand why intimacy with his wife was difficult. He would get angry and fight with her, hurting her deeply with his words. Both knew they could not continue living this way.

I told him to go to my website, and once he did, he felt horrible for not understanding her private pain. He listened as I explained her reasons for not feeling comfortable in speaking about that pain.

"Had you seen signs while you were dating that might have indicated something was wrong?" I asked.

"Yes, I did." He paused, and I heard him taking a deep breath. "I assumed she was a proper girl. All I wanted was to marry her. But I am willing to do anything to help Kadi recover emotionally or even physically, if that's even possible."

I counseled them for a while, talking about how to connect deeply and comfortably and experience intimacy. I talked about the reversal surgery and said I might be able to find a doctor who could help them. I offered to travel to Nashville and look for a local doctor with whom they would be safe and feel comfortable. They said they couldn't afford to pay for treatment, but they knew the surgery was the only way to save their marriage. I promised not only to pay for the doctor visit but to find a hospital that would do the surgery for free.

Before grabbing my contact list from my desk, I remembered that I had spoken at Vanderbilt University in Nashville, and I recalled how advanced their hospital was. People at Vanderbilt would surely help me find a doctor who was willing to do the surgery.

But after many calls, and many disappointments, I still did not have a doctor for Kadi. With increasing anxiety, I called Alice Walker for advice. I explained the situation.

"Alice, what can I do? I need to help Kadi!"

She asked, "How are you?"

I shook my head. "I'm stressed! I need to help her—"

She interrupted my rush of words. "Can you sit and check in with yourself?"

"What?" I asked, at first confused. "But I'm fine! Kadi needs—"

"Soraya." Alice's voice remained calm. "You can't fill a bottomless pit."

"We have to! We can't stop until this torture is stopped!"

"Where are you living now?" Alice asked.

When I told her I was at my friend Telma's, she asked to speak with her, and I passed my roommate the phone.

In my practical mind, I knew Alice was right: I could not take care of every mutilation victim and save every woman from our culture. But in my heart, I knew I would never give up.

I eventually tracked down Dr. Nour, an obstetrician/gynecologist who founded the African Women's Health Clinic in Boston. Dr. Nour remembered talking with me during an FGM conference a few years before and, after hearing about the Malian patient, she offered to perform the reconstructive plastic surgery for free. However, the hospital needed me to pay ten thousand dollars, and once more I was at a dead end, unable to raise the amount.

But again, fortune smiled on me. I found a doctor right in Los Angeles willing to perform the corrective surgery pro bono at a hospital I could afford. Kadi flew to Los Angeles and met with the doctor, who explained how he would perform the surgery. It was then we realized she would have only a local anesthetic, as no anesthesiologist was willing to forgo the fee for general anesthesia. My stomach sank as I recalled the sound of the scissors, the horror and the fear that overwhelmed me when I had faced the men in white coats. The doctor was confused and concerned, but I understood why she was overwhelmed with fear and could not go through with the surgery. Although I was saddened and disappointed, I could not blame her when she gave up and returned to Tennessee.

But soon after, I received a call from another mother who had fought for her daughter—Fortunate, the mother of the young child in the Atlanta genital mutilation case. She thanked me again for speaking the truth and updated me about the death threats and how the Ethiopian community was raising funds to free her husband, Khalid Adem, from the Atlanta prison where he was serving ten years for mutilating his daughter with scissors. In protest of his sentence, two thousand Ethiopians marched in the streets of Addis Ababa shouting "Free Khalid."

I told her I was still getting threatening e-mails for not believing in Khalid's right to cut his daughter's genitals.

"What I know for sure," I told her, "is that we are right, morally and spiritually right. Your husband committed a crime, and he must pay."

I paused, feeling my own courage and hope rising once more, speaking to her, but also to myself.

"You and I have done the right thing," I said. "Focus on healing your daughter, and never again succumb to fear or despair."

epilogue

What would you do if you were forcibly subjected to the ritual of cutting? You would be left only to dream about what could have been before your life was stolen. When a basic part of me was cut away and stolen by a culture that deemed the theft a "gift," my spirit began to drift to a place far, far away. A place where it could not root itself, could not attach itself to those things the rest of the women around the world take for granted. Hearing the sound of the scissors cutting away the flesh between my legs made me feel the curse, the curse of being born into a female body. This curse burns the blood and rots the flesh. The curse signifies that a mistake was made when I was created as a woman—

The phone rang in the summer of 2008, and I put down my pen. It was a friend who suggested that I turn on the television show *60 Minutes*. The show's title, "War Against Women in the Congo," struck a chord and brought back painful memories.

In horror, I watched as women talked about surviving the unthinkable rape and the destruction of their lives. Suddenly, in my mind's eye, I saw the image of women, like lambs tied to the jungle trees, with firm hands grabbing their necks and dragging their bodies into the mud and the melting concrete. Powerless, we women have to watch in horror as our bodies

epilogue

are ripped open like curtains, raped, mutilated, stoned to death, sold into prostitution, or forced into unwanted marriages. Are we destined to be scared lambs with sutured lips and empty minds?

Watching the show was like experiencing death itself. I had to take a moment to go back into my body and feel what I was feeling. After a while, I called my friend Marilyn, who was copyediting my manuscript, and she suggested that I write uplifting things in my final chapter. She reminded me how I challenged my parents, siblings, relatives, society, and culture. No doubt, I challenged everyone, and I paid the price for it.

However, all the while, I knew I was right. And I never gave up. But still I struggled, asking myself how to summarize my experience and give a message of hope for the future and for the girls of the world.

I have been doing this work for thirty years, and the atmosphere today is much different than it was when I began. While I walked through the blazing fire and shouted from the rooftops to end the practice of female genital mutilation, a rainbow appeared, carrying a miracle.

My father told me he was proud of me after watching my *Fire Eyes* documentary! Of course, Mother couldn't watch, because she was the source of my suffering. Every time she looked at me, she remembered what she did to me. I didn't just take it; I used that terrible experience for good, to help others, the thing my mother was unable to do. She was caught in the culture and could not escape from it herself; now she is ashamed of what she did to me.

I love my mother and do not want to hate her. It's unfortunate that she can't bring herself to ask forgiveness, as I have asked for hers for challenging her, our culture, and her inability to grow beyond her own boundaries. It's understandable that she may never be able to do that.

Still, my father gave me the true gift; he told me how proud he was of me. And I don't think he wanted me to see him as a dying man. He wanted to protect me to the very end.

My work as a survivor of a cultural act of violence, pain, and betrayal, then, is to never forget what happens to women and girls. My duty is to voice the hidden struggle of women who have been tortured. There is no power greater than finding the strength to go into the world and do the work you have been put on earth to do. That is why writing this book was important for me.

Sharing my story allows me to show others that it is possible to heal. My story is about finding hope. It is about women reclaiming their humanity and dignity as a creation of God.

"Pain is the journey of life," my grandmother used to say. She believed that to know glory is to know and understand pain. She taught me that women need to experience pain in order "to make their spine firm and teach them how to carry the load."

I believe pain has nothing to do with the journey of life and is an evil that shatters one's soul. I have been there, and without the brave souls who helped me reclaim my humanity, dignity, and sexuality, I would not be here telling my story. They taught me how to forgive those cruel hands that left the scars in my mind and on my body. This act freed and empowered me and left me knowing I had to dedicate my life to fighting to end this practice.

The journey was hard and painful; I was an activist without roots or a country, disowned by my own family and culture. My intimate story is necessary for an understanding of this ritual. Terror, humiliation, and anxiety are constant reminders of the torture a girl or a woman has endured, making it hard for her to look at herself in the mirror. It takes great courage for her to look deep into her own soul.

My story is meant to break the chains that bind women. It is meant to inspire and show how one heart can hold the light and never let go, ultimately shining far and wide so that others can see. It is a story of strife and courage, and it is a story of the glorious forms of love that are the basis of it all. I've written this memoir both to free my soul and to pass that freedom on. It is my sincere effort at expanding the national and international dialogues that are needed to bring about this change. In the meantime, and until the mutilation of women and girls ends, I will keep saying, "No more! What you do is wrong, and we will not suffer silently! The world will know! We are women, and we will survive and overcome!"

My journey offers a look into the culture that condones this ritual, beginning with the horror of the "gift" and moving through my transformation and empowerment. My duty is to be clear about what I'm saying about myself. Did I forgive myself fully? Am I checking in and loving myself no matter what anyone else says?

Now, I believe I *have* the wisdom and knowledge and I *do* know. I am proud to have made a difference in the world. I rose from the depths to my destiny—from standing alone to standing in a world that embraces my voice and my vision.

There is hope.

acknowledgments

A special thank-you goes to brother Adaax, who became the head of the family and encouraged me to tell the truth and forgive. Thank you to my cousin Khadra Abshir, who still asks forgiveness for the pain her brother Yusuf caused me; to Maryan Jamac Miré, who believed in me when others didn't and insisted that I graphically tell my story; to Fawsiya "Fadwa" Kukaye, who still remembers our childhood mischief; and to brother Asis, who took the wrong path but never stopped loving God. Without Asis's help, I could not have met those wonderful herdsmen in Los Angeles.

Marilyn Milos not only copyedited the first manuscript but also became my adopted American mother. I owe so much to you, and each day my love for you deepens. I'm very grateful to Marcie Polier Swartz for her generous support and for bringing in Veronica Rosenblatt from the Will Rogers Motion Picture Pioneers Foundation. Thanks to Richard Utley at PRO-TEK for providing encouragement.

A special thanks to Eve Ensler for being a friend and taking this journey with me. I really appreciate your sending those wonderful notes. Thank you to my big-sister figure, Alice Walker, for being there when I needed help and for giving me advice on finding the right path to release the past. I will always love you. And thanks to Telma Hopkins, who welcomed me back to L.A. and kept me safe while I prepared to write this book.

Big thanks to those who listened to my story, read the manuscript, edited chapters, and sent their notes: Russell Green, Linda C. McCabe, Norma Johnson, Lorran Garrison, Queenae T. Mulvihill, Faith Trimel, Arezou and Louis Petrie, and Keynaan Mohamed, who became my big brother during our college days in Grenoble. Thank you for reading those college chapters and adding more insights. Thanks to Dr. Garane Garane, who played a loving role back in Grenoble, and Keith Laqua, who, after getting back from my screening at the Cannes Film Festival, pushed me to put down the camera and write the book. Thanks to Jama Ibrahim for doing the best research and correcting the political chapters. Many thanks to brother Adaax, half sister Safia Miré, and cousins Khalifa, Fatima Abshir, and Maryan Abshir for helping me with my research on Somalia's civil war.

I would like to thank those special souls who kept the journey safe: the talented team at Lawrence Hill Books, starting with my editor, Susan Bradanini Betz. Her insightful counsel has made me a proud writer. Thank you to Lisa Reardon, my developmental editor, who shepherded this book through production; to Mary Kravenas, for working through the marketing storm; to Kelly Wilson, for her wonderful notes; and to Cynthia Sherry and Jill Nofsinger. Thank you also to Lori Shepler, who took my beautiful author photos.

Thank you, Tobe Levin, for being so loving and for distributing flyers for this book at the United Nations in Geneva; Rhonda Finkel, for being a true friend and getting me out of the house when I needed it most; Bailey Barash, Don, and Max, for opening up your home in Atlanta to me; Justin Dunn; Maria Sanchez, Geanine Labrador, Abuelita, and Xavier, my other Columbian family; and Idriss Moui and his family for their love and support. As a former mental health worker, I want to thank my boss, Anthony Ford, for his care and guidance with clients.

My gratitude also goes to those who trained my body and balanced my mind: Christa Pryor, Rachel Ross, Monica Schuller, Diana Klein, Chappell Westlake, and all my friends at Yogaworks.

resources

Books

Dorkenoo, Efua. *Cutting the Rose: Female Genital Mutilation: The Practice and Its Prevention*. Austin, TX: Harry Ransom Humanities Research Center, 1996.

El Saadawi, Nawal. *The Hidden Face of Eve: Women in the Arab World*. London: Zed Books, 2007.

Gruenbaum, Ellen. *The Female Circumcision Controversy: An Anthropological Perspective*. Philadelphia: University of Pennsylvania Press, 2001.

Karanja, Daniel Njoroge. *Female Genital Mutilation in Africa: Gender, Religion and Pastoral Care*. Longwood, FL: Xulon Press, 2003.

Lightfoot-Klein, Hanny. *Prisoners of Ritual: An Odyssey into Female Genital Circumcision in Africa*. Binghamton, NY: Haworth Press, 1989.

Walker, Alice. *Possessing the Secret of Joy: A Novel*. New York: New Press, 2008. First published 1992 by Harcourt Brace Jovanovich.

Films

Miré, Soraya. *Fire Eyes*. 1994. Documentary.

Sembéne, Ousmane. *Moolaadé*. 2004. Drama.

Smith, Mary Olive. *A Walk to Beautiful*. 2008. Documentary.

Organizations

Note that an organization's contact information and/or website can change frequently. The contact information and URLs below were accurate as of press time.

The Female Genital Cutting Education and Networking Project
Website: http://www.fgmnetwork.org/index.php

International Campaign to Ban Female Genital Mutilation Worldwide
Website: http://www.banfgm.org/BanFGM!/Home.html

Solidarity for African Women's Rights
Website: http://www.soawr.org/en
E-mail: bkombo@equalitynow.org

Burkina Faso

Voix des Femmes
Website: http://courantsdefemmes.free.fr/Assoces/Burkina/VoixFemmes
/voix_femmes.html
E-mail: vofemme@yahoo.fr

Cote d'Ivoire

Organisation Nationale pour l'Enfant, la Femme et la Famille (ONEF)
E-mail: ongonef@yahoo.fr

Djibouti

Union Nationale des Femmes de Djibouti (UNFD)
Website: http://www.soawr.org/en/soawrmember/union_nationale_des
_femmes_de_djibouti_unfd/
E-mail: unfd@intnet.dj

Ethiopia

Inter-African Committee on Traditional Practices (IAC)
Website: http://www.iac-ciaf.net
E-mail: iac-htps@uneca.org

The Gambia

GAMCOTRAP
Website: http://www.gamcotrap.gm/content/index.php

Guinea

Cellule de Coordination sur les Pratiques Traditionnelles Affectant la Santé
des Femmes et des Enfants (CPTAFE)
Website: http://www.soawr.org/en/soawrmember/cellule_de_coordination
_sur_les_pratiques_traditionnelles_affectant_la_sant/
E-mail: morissanda@yahoo.fr

Kenya

Marakwet Girls and Women Project
Website: http://marakwetgirls.org/
E-mail: info@marakwetgirls.org

Womankind Kenya (WOKIKE)
Website: http://www.womankindkenya.org/
E-mail: staff@womankindkenya.org

Mali

Association Malienne pour le Suivi et l'Orientation des Pratiques
Traditionnelles (AMSOPT)
Website: http://courantsdefemmes.free.fr/Assoces/Mali/AMSOPT
/AMSOPT.html
E-mail: amsopt@datatech.toolnet.org

Sierra Leone

Amazonian Initiative Movement (AIM)
Website: http://www.aim-sierra-leone.de/, http://www.facebook.com/pages
/AIM-Sierra-Leone/116171761739755
E-mail: aimgn2001@yahoo.com

Somalia

Galkayo Education Center for Peace and Development (GECPD)
Website: http://www.tucacas.info/somalia/gecpd/gecpd.htm
E-mail: gecpd2004@yahoo.com

Switzerland

Inter-African Committee (IAC), liaison office
Website: http://www.iac-ciaf.net
E-mail: cominter@iprolink.ch

Tanzania

Legal and Human Rights Centre (LHRC)
Website: http://www.humanrights.or.tz
E-mail: lhrc@humanrights.or.tz

Network Against Female Genital Mutilation (NAFGEM)
Website: http://www.world-unite.de/en/volunteering/network-female
-genital-mutilation.html
E-mail: nafgemtanzania@yahoo.com

index